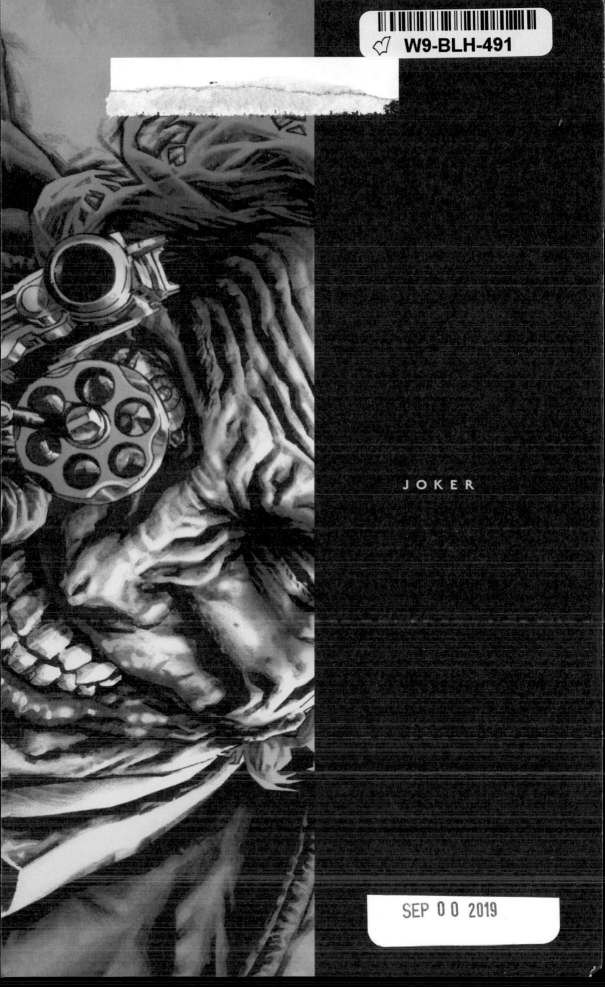

JOKER

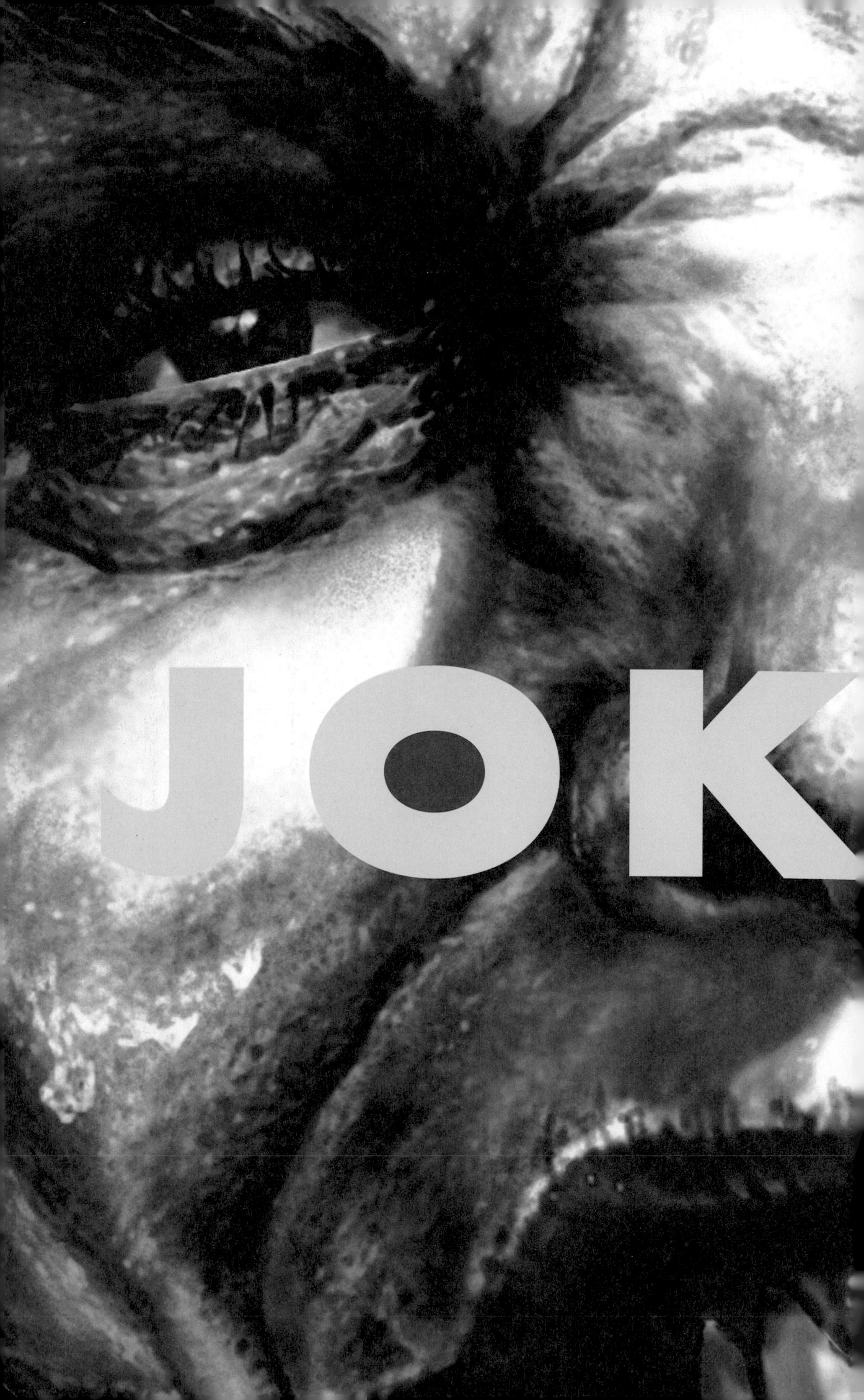
JOK

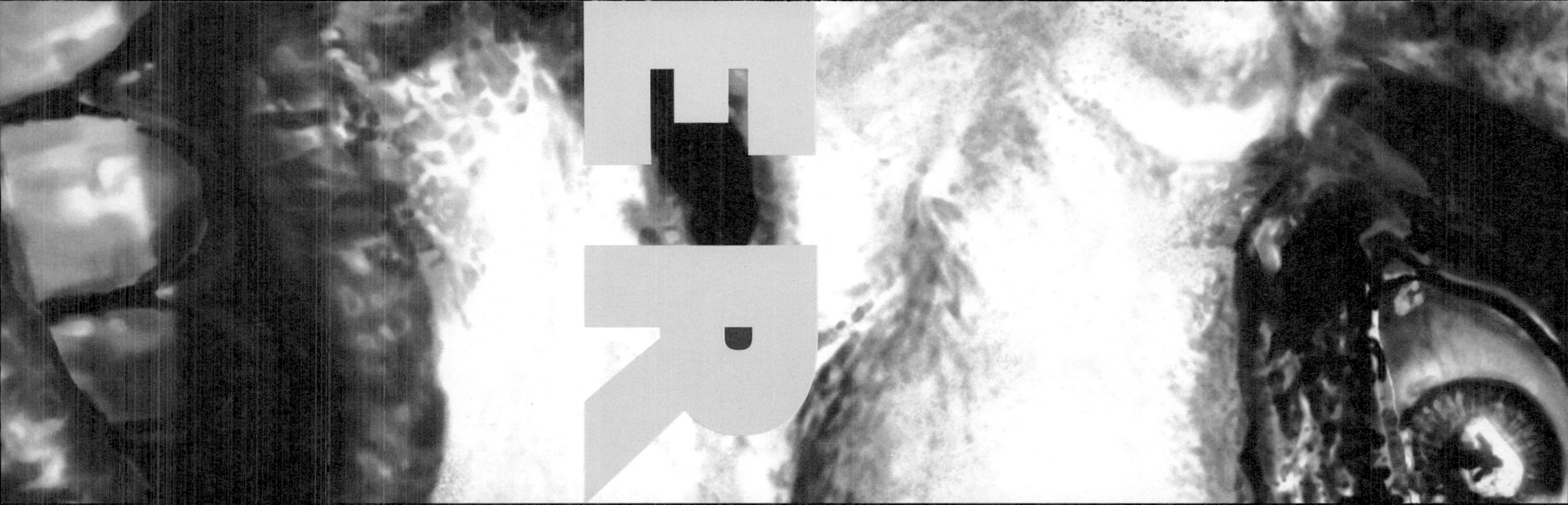
ER

BRIAN AZZARELLO WRITER

LEE BERMEJO PENCILLER

WILL DENNIS Editor – Original Series
JEB WOODARD Group Editor – Collected Editions
ALEX GALER Editor – Collected Edition
STEVE COOK Design Director – Books
LOUIS PRANDI Publication Design
DANIELLE DIGRADO Publication Prodution

BOB HARRAS Senior VP – Editor-in-Chief, DC Comics
PAT McCALLUM Executive Editor, DC Comics

DAN DiDIO Publisher
JIM LEE Publisher & Chief Creative Officer
BOBBIE CHASE VP – New Publishing Initiatives & Talent Development
DON FALLETTI VP – Manufacturing Operations & Workflow Management
LAWRENCE GANEM VP – Talent Services
ALISON GILL Senior VP – Manufacturing & Operations
HANK KANALZ Senior VP – Publishing Strategy & Support Services
DAN MIRON VP – Publishing Operations
NICK J. NAPOLITANO VP – Manufacturing Administration & Design
NANCY SPEARS VP – Sales
MICHELE R. WELLS VP & Executive Editor, Young Reader

JOKER

Published by DC Comics. Compilation originally published as ABSOLUTE JOKER Copyright © 2013
DC Comics. All Rights Reserved. Originally published in single magazine form in JOKER and ABSOLUTE
JOKER. Copyright © 2008, 2013 DC Comics. All Rights Reserved. All characters, their distinctive
likenesses and related elements featured in this publication are trademarks of DC Comics. The stories,
characters and incidents featured in this publication are entirely fictional. DC Comics does not read or
accept unsolicited submissions of ideas, stories or artwork. DC – a WarnerMedia Company.

DC Comics, 2900 West Alameda Ave., Burbank, CA 91505
Printed by LSC Communications, Owensville, MO, USA. 5/31/19. First Printing.
ISBN: 978-1-4012-9186-0

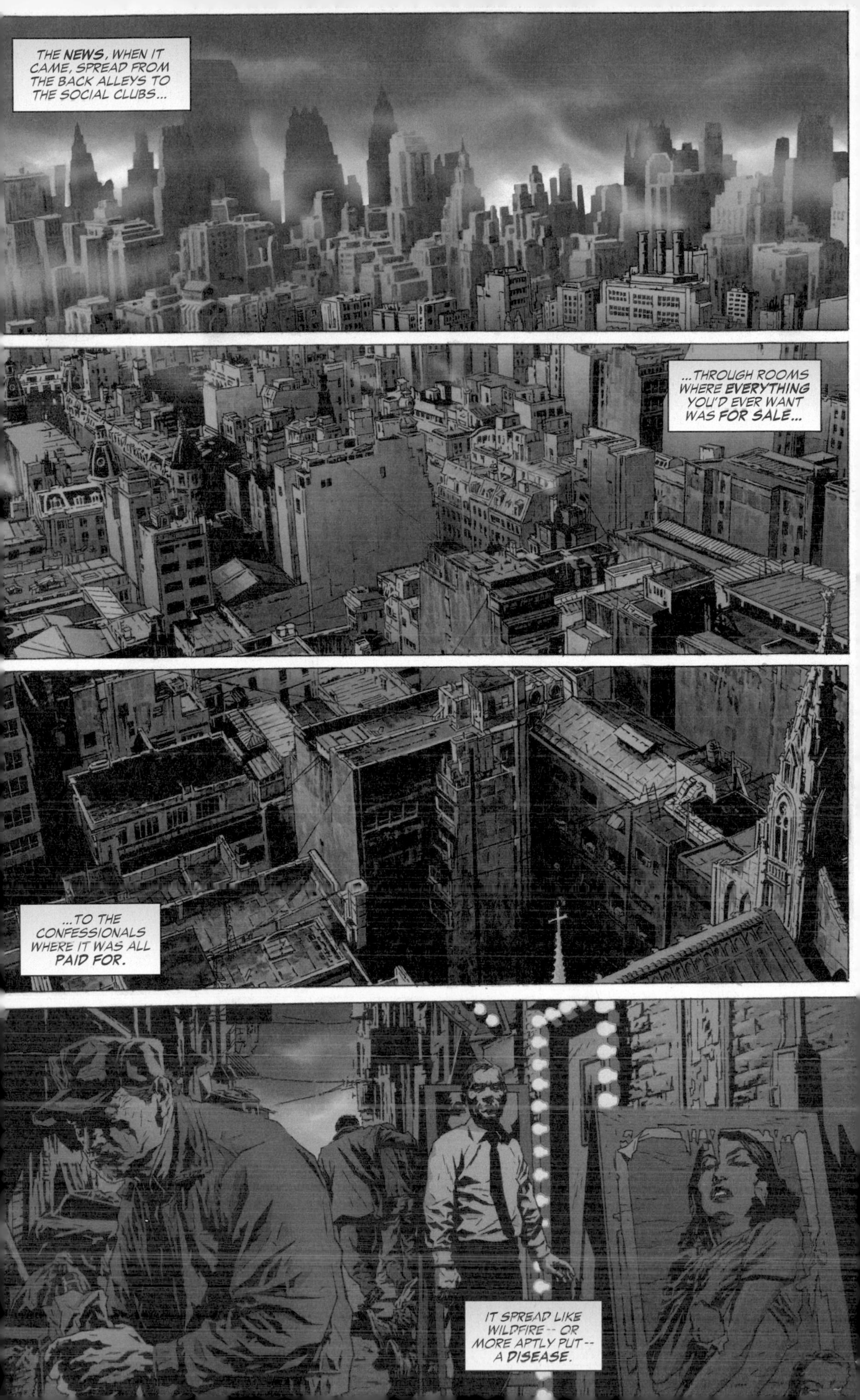
THE NEWS, WHEN IT CAME, SPREAD FROM THE BACK ALLEYS TO THE SOCIAL CLUBS...
...THROUGH ROOMS WHERE EVERYTHING YOU'D EVER WANT WAS FOR SALE...
...TO THE CONFESSIONALS WHERE IT WAS ALL PAID FOR.
IT SPREAD LIKE WILDFIRE -- OR MORE APTLY PUT -- A DISEASE.

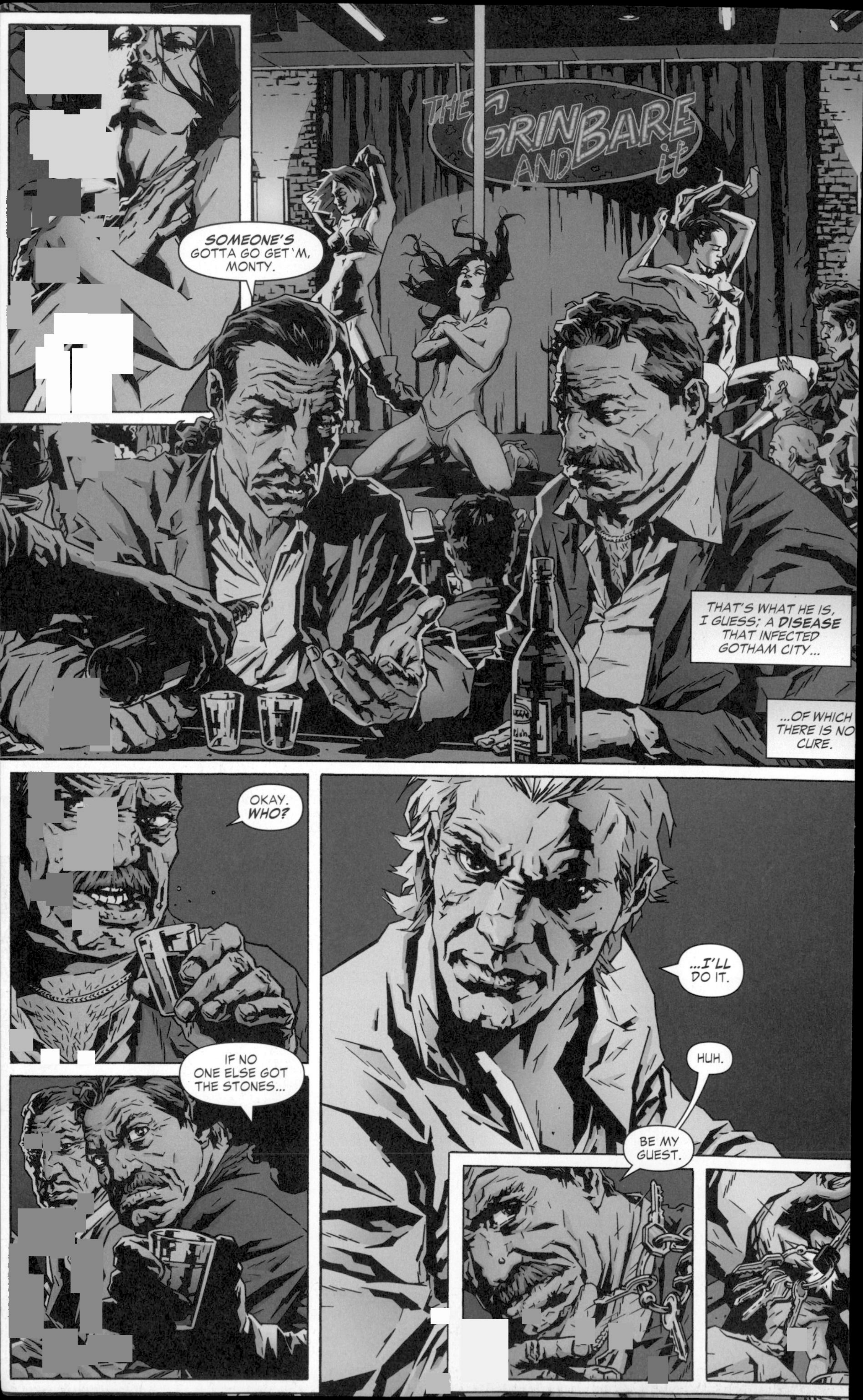
THE GRIN AND BARE it
SOMEONE'S GOTTA GO GET 'M, MONTY.
THAT'S WHAT HE IS, I GUESS; A DISEASE THAT INFECTED GOTHAM CITY...
...OF WHICH THERE IS NO CURE.
OKAY. WHO?
IF NO ONE ELSE GOT THE STONES...
...I'LL DO IT.
HUH.
BE MY GUEST.

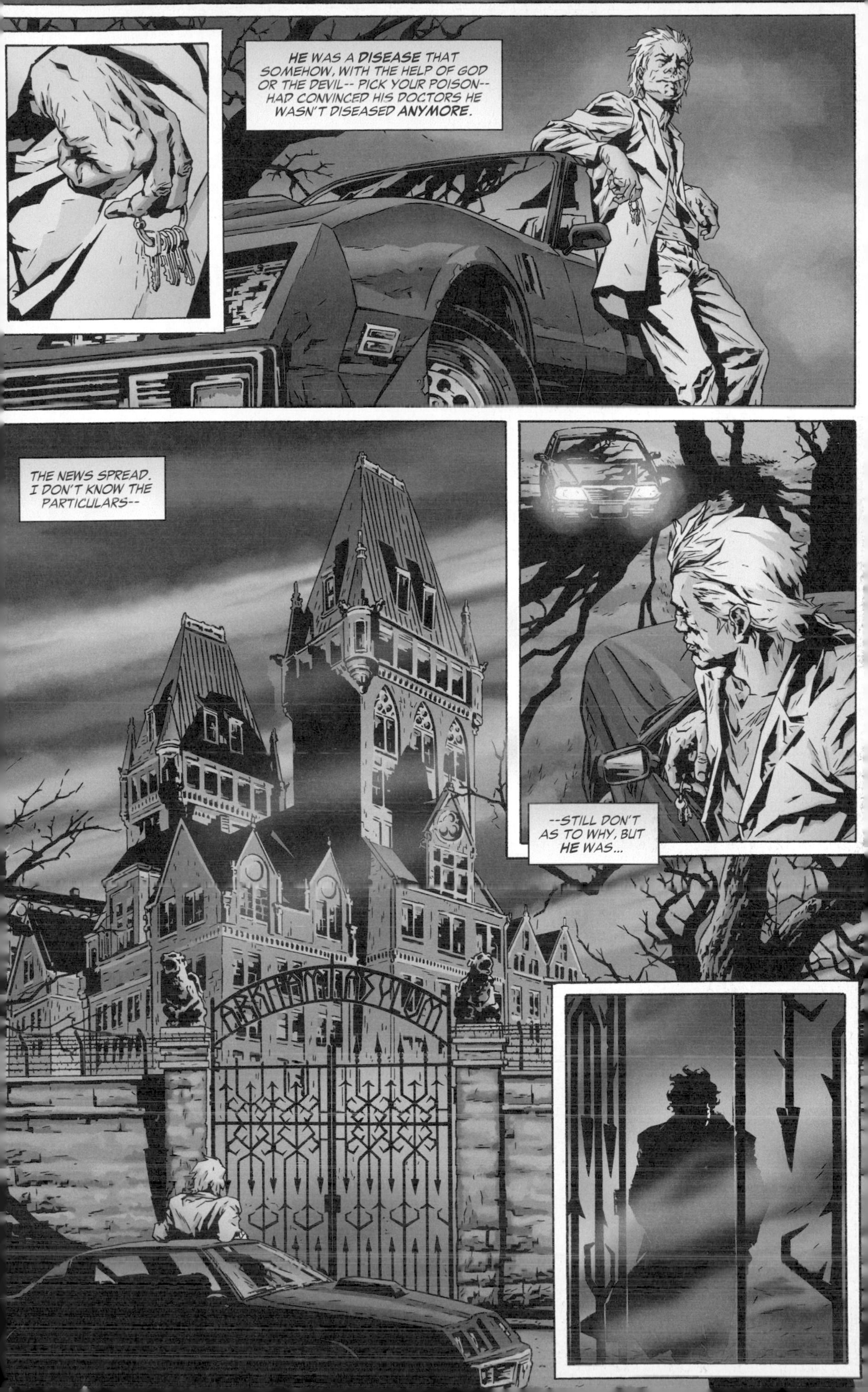
HE WAS A DISEASE THAT SOMEHOW, WITH THE HELP OF GOD OR THE DEVIL-- PICK YOUR POISON-- HAD CONVINCED HIS DOCTORS HE WASN'T DISEASED ANYMORE.
THE NEWS SPREAD. I DON'T KNOW THE PARTICULARS--
ARKHAM ASYLUM
--STILL DON'T AS TO WHY, BUT HE WAS...

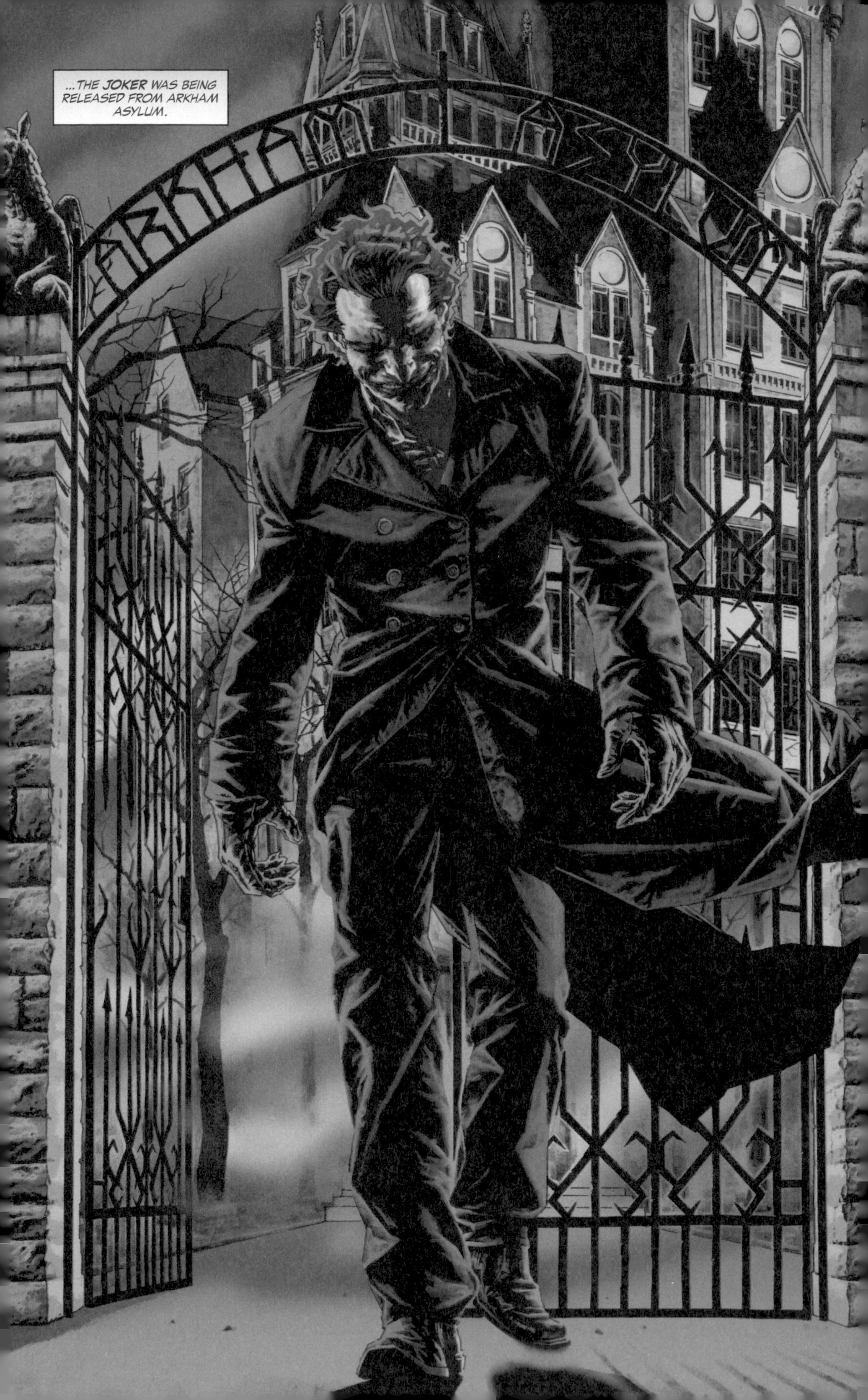
...THE JOKER WAS BEING RELEASED FROM ARKHAM ASYLUM.

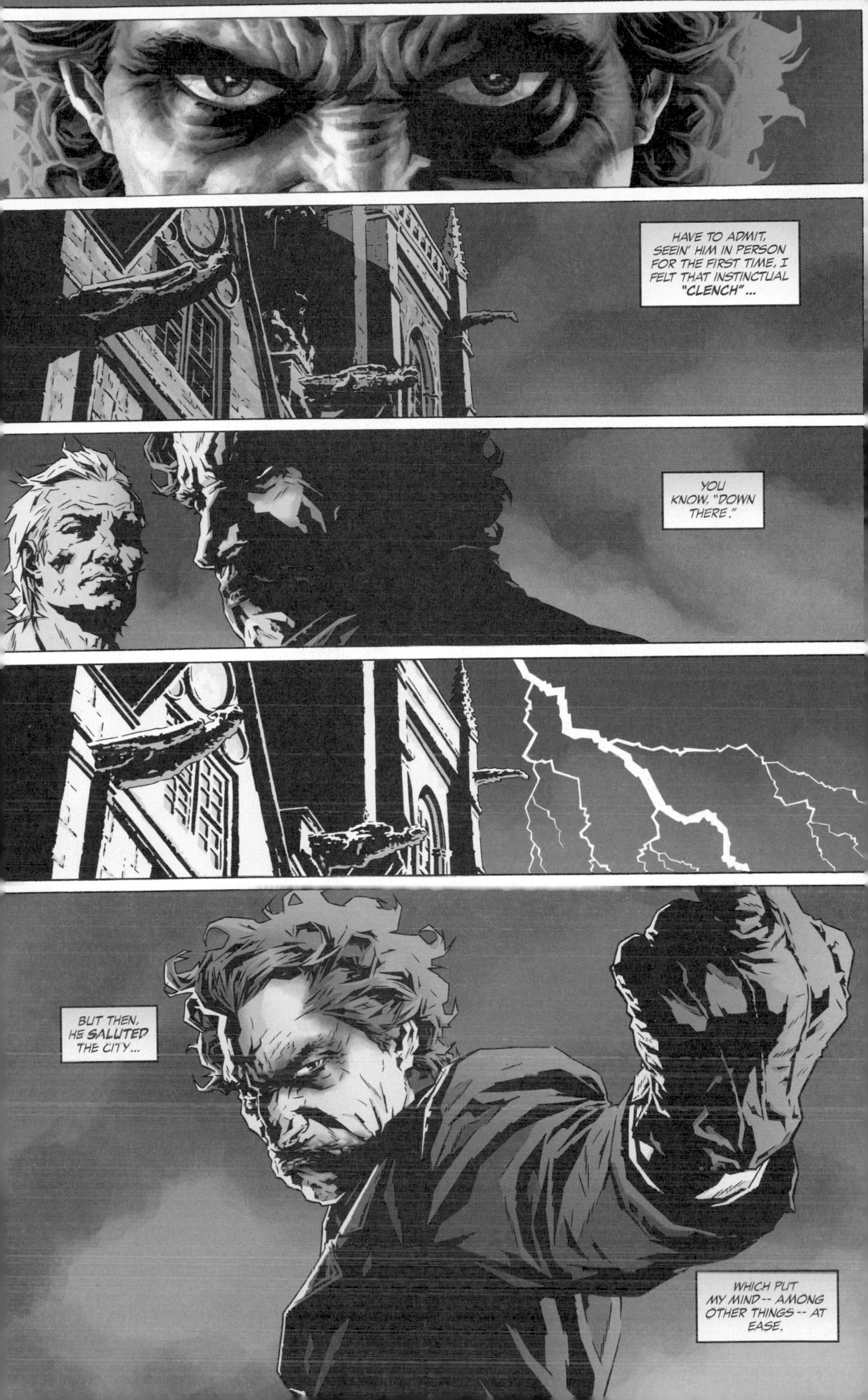
HAVE TO ADMIT, SEEIN' HIM IN PERSON FOR THE FIRST TIME, I FELT THAT INSTINCTUAL "CLENCH"...
YOU KNOW. "DOWN THERE."
BUT THEN, HE SALUTED THE CITY...
WHICH PUT MY MIND-- AMONG OTHER THINGS-- AT EASE.

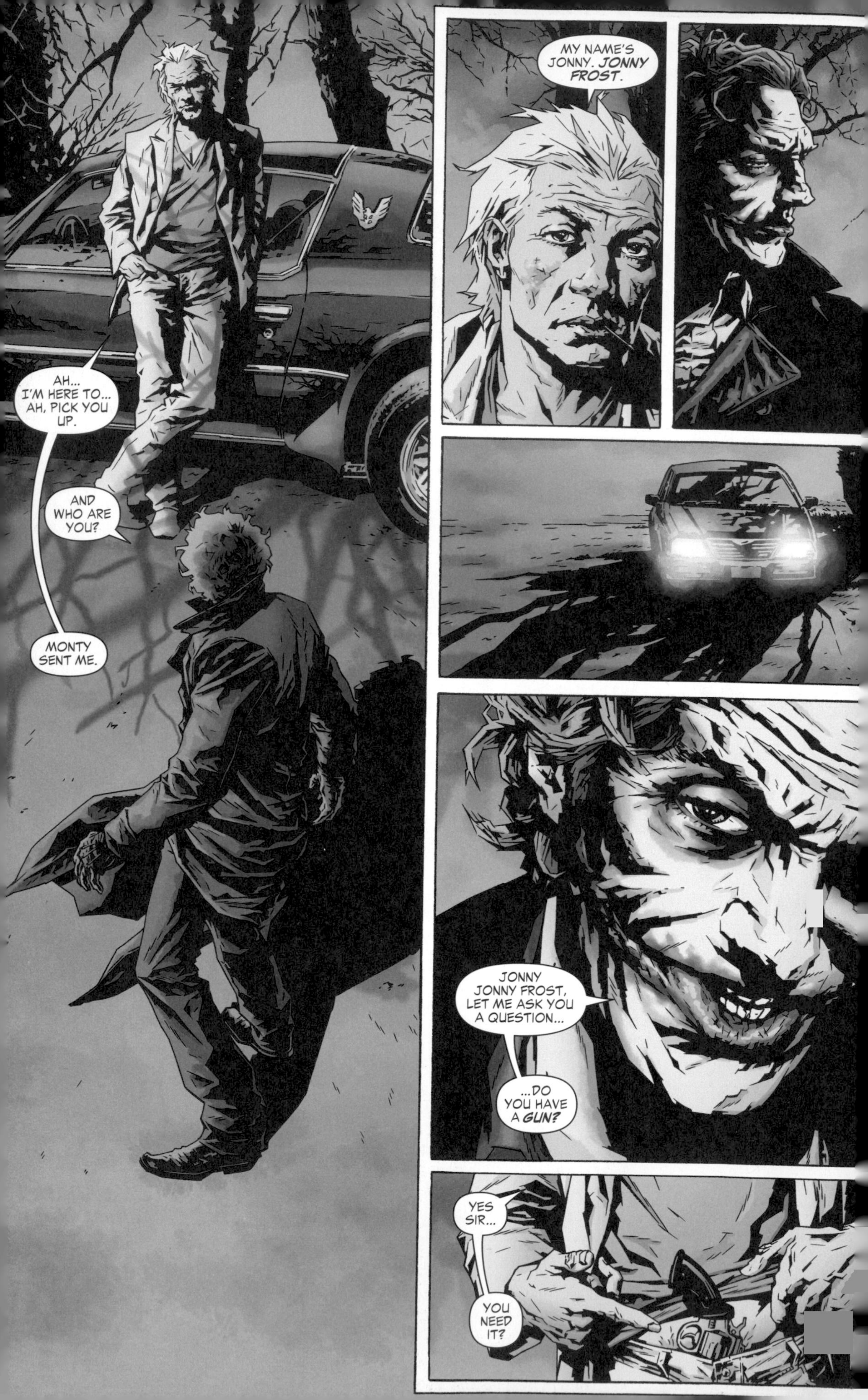
AH... I'M HERE TO... AH, PICK YOU UP.
AND WHO ARE YOU?
MONTY SENT ME.
MY NAME'S JONNY. JONNY FROST.
JONNY JONNY FROST, LET ME ASK YOU A QUESTION...
...DO YOU HAVE A GUN?
YES SIR...
YOU NEED IT?

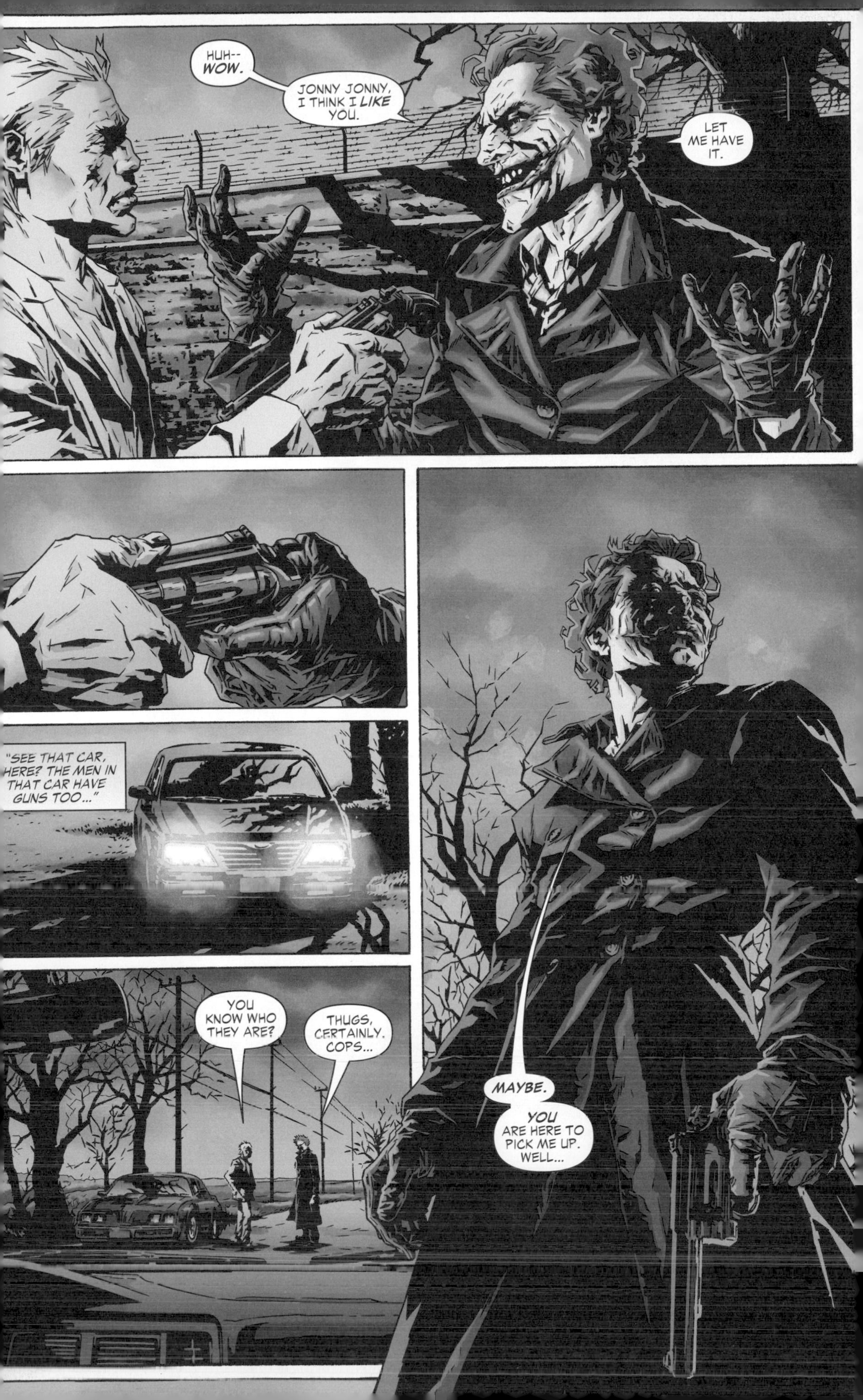
HUH--
WOW.
JONNY JONNY, I THINK I LIKE YOU.
LET ME HAVE IT.
"SEE THAT CAR, HERE? THE MEN IN THAT CAR HAVE GUNS TOO..."
YOU KNOW WHO THEY ARE?
THUGS, CERTAINLY. COPS...
MAYBE.
YOU ARE HERE TO PICK ME UP. WELL...

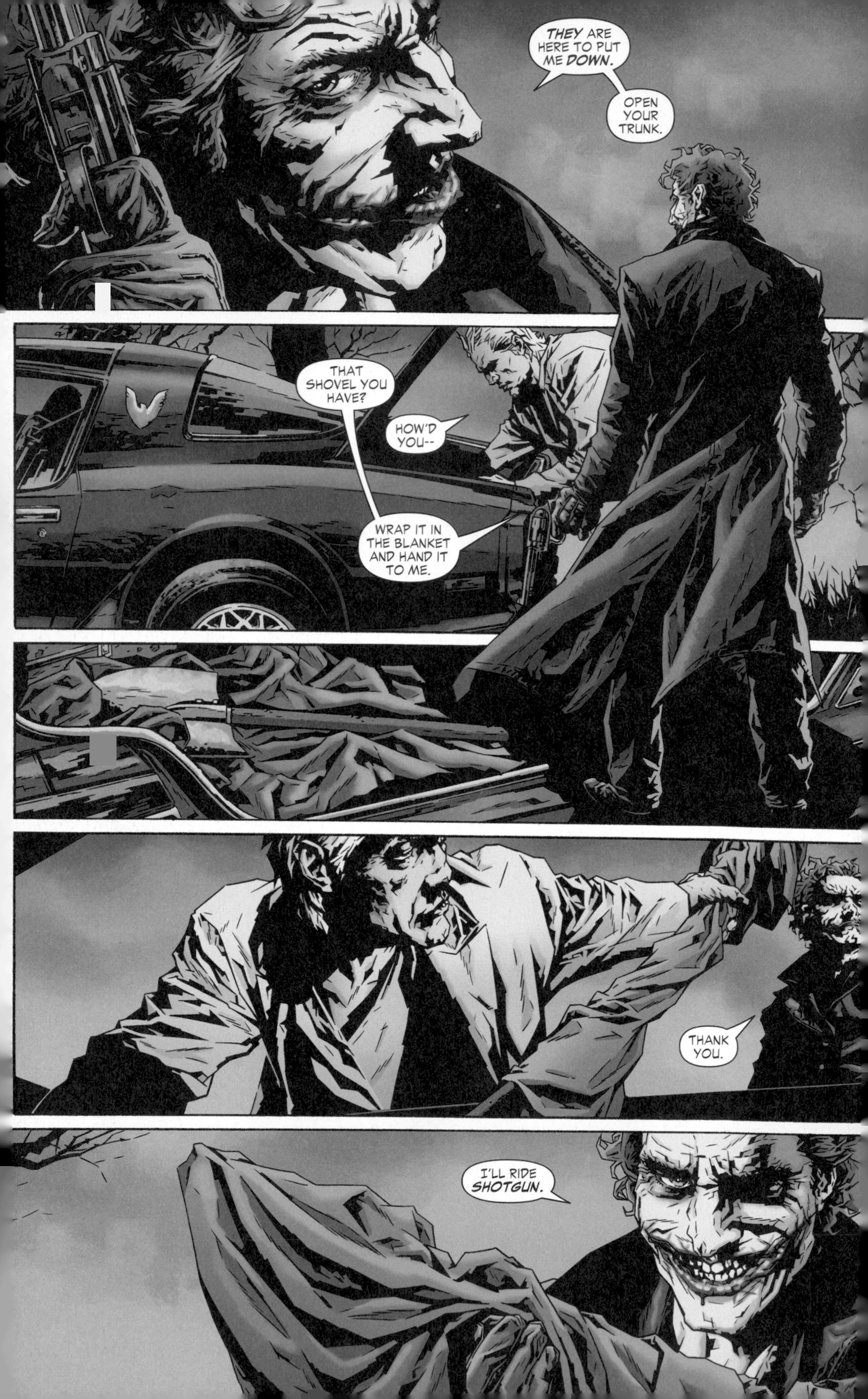
THEY ARE HERE TO PUT ME DOWN.
OPEN YOUR TRUNK.
THAT SHOVEL YOU HAVE?
HOW'D YOU--
WRAP IT IN THE BLANKET AND HAND IT TO ME.
THANK YOU.
I'LL RIDE SHOTGUN.

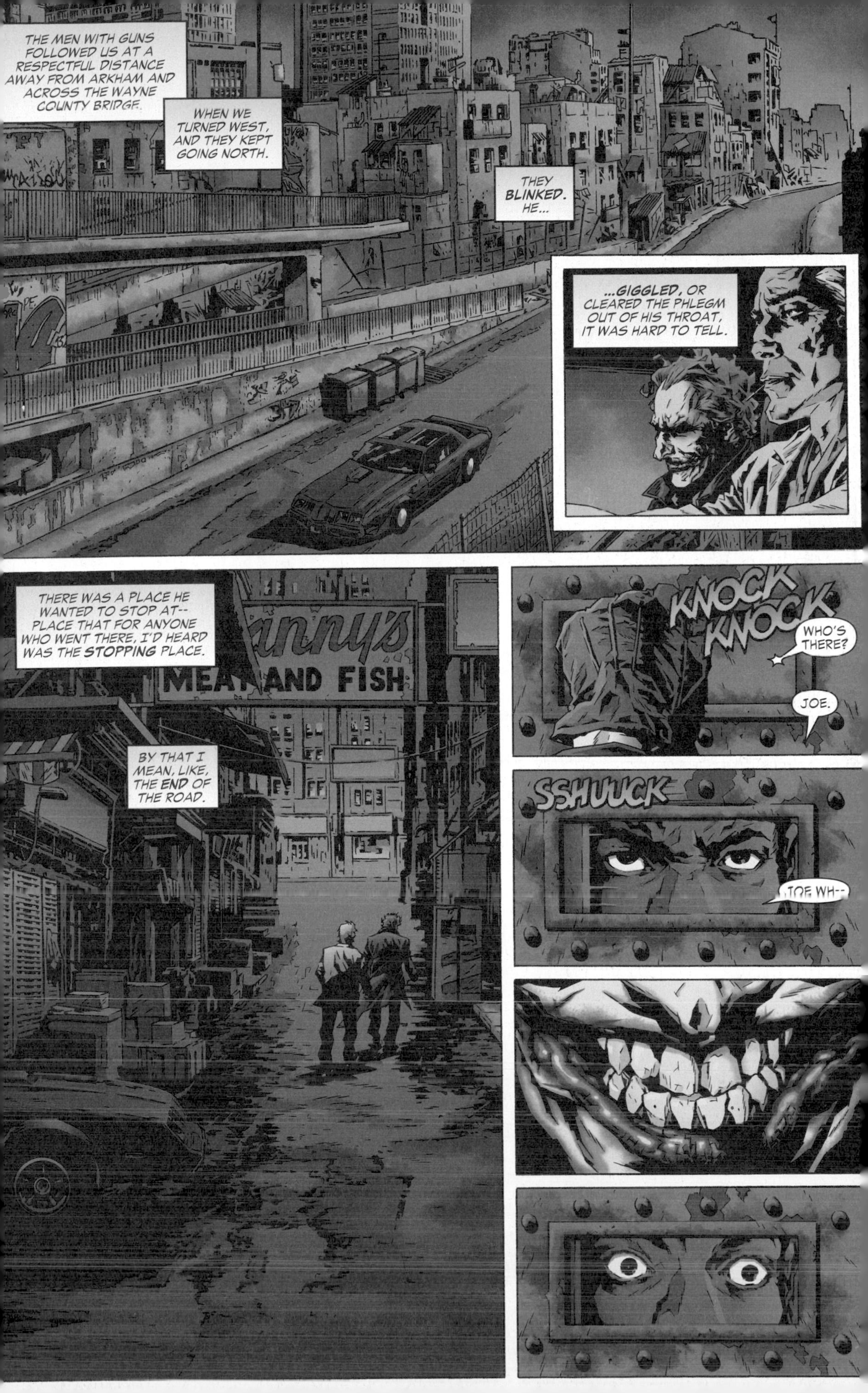
THE MEN WITH GUNS FOLLOWED US AT A RESPECTFUL DISTANCE AWAY FROM ARKHAM AND ACROSS THE WAYNE COUNTY BRIDGE.
WHEN WE TURNED WEST, AND THEY KEPT GOING NORTH.
THEY **BLINKED**. HE...
...**GIGGLED**, OR CLEARED THE PHLEGM OUT OF HIS THROAT, IT WAS HARD TO TELL.
THERE WAS A PLACE HE WANTED TO STOP AT-- PLACE THAT FOR ANYONE WHO WENT THERE, I'D HEARD WAS THE **STOPPING** PLACE.
MEAT AND FISH
BY THAT I MEAN, LIKE, THE **END** OF THE ROAD.
KNOCK KNOCK
WHO'S THERE?
JOE.
SSHUUCK
JOE WH--

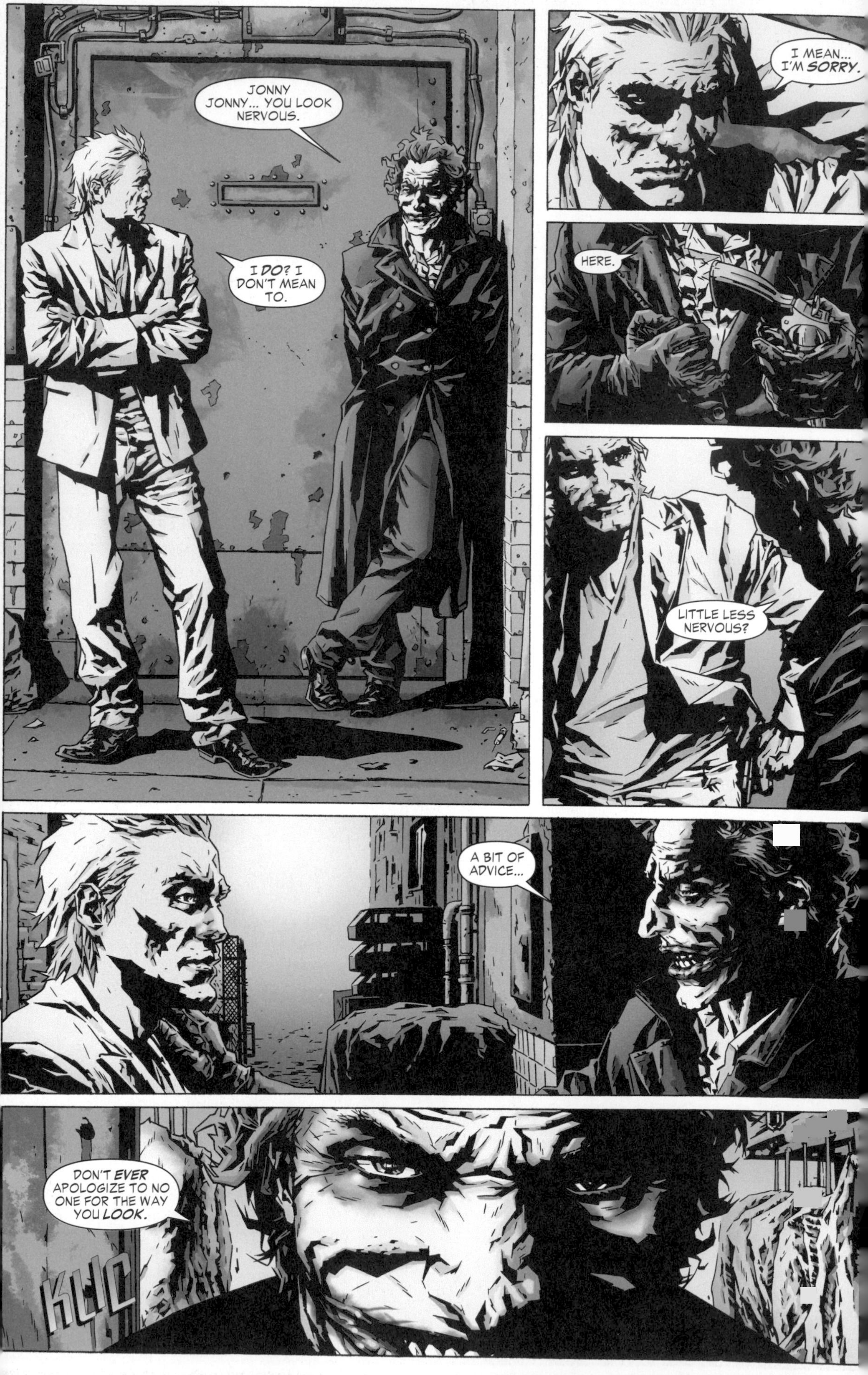
JONNY JONNY... YOU LOOK NERVOUS.
I DO? I DON'T MEAN TO.
I MEAN... I'M SORRY.
HERE.
LITTLE LESS NERVOUS?
A BIT OF ADVICE...
DON'T EVER APOLOGIZE TO NO ONE FOR THE WAY YOU LOOK.
KLIC

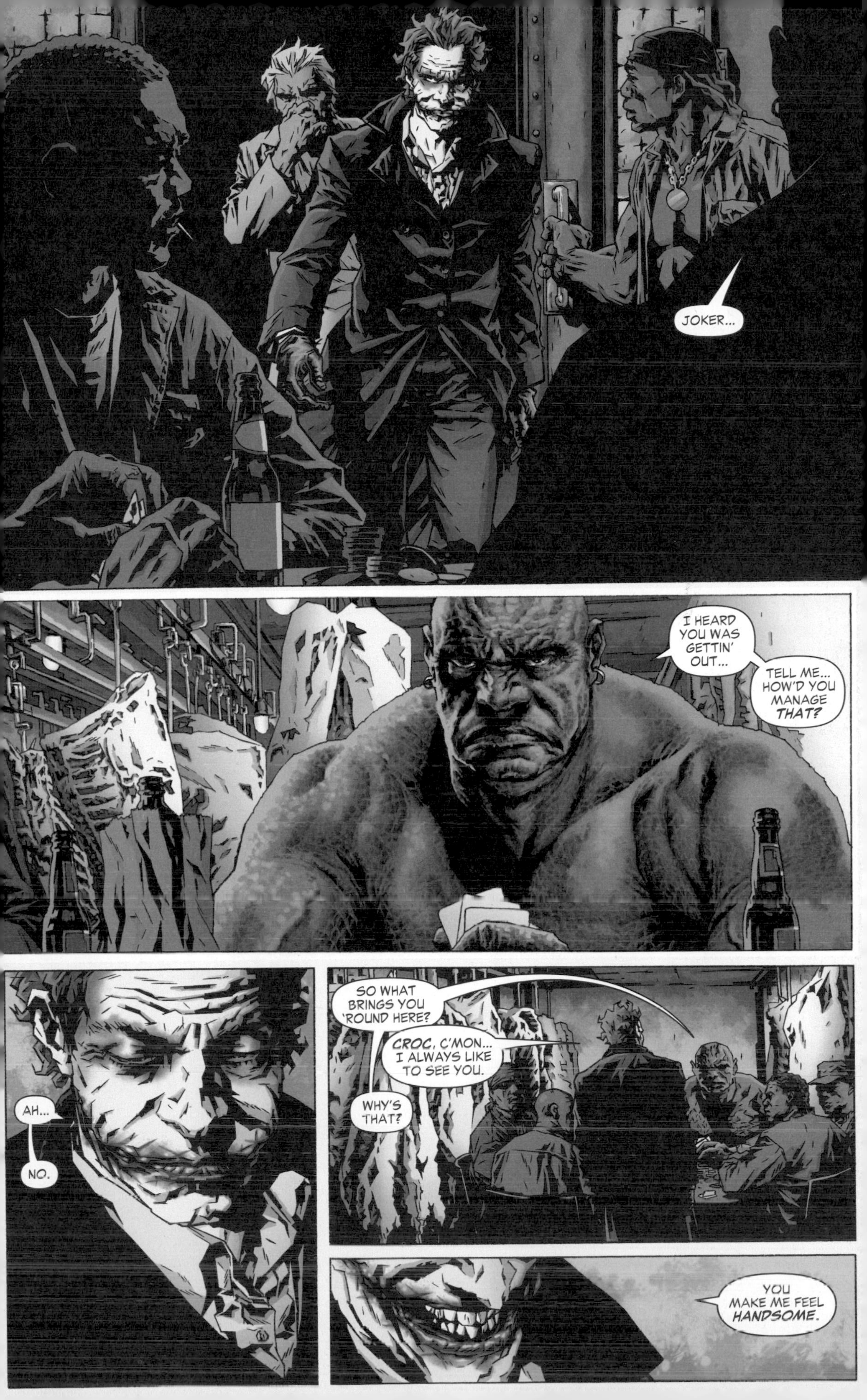
JOKER...
I HEARD YOU WAS GETTIN' OUT...
TELL ME... HOW'D YOU MANAGE *THAT?*
AH...
NO.
SO WHAT BRINGS YOU 'ROUND HERE?
CROC, C'MON... I ALWAYS LIKE TO SEE YOU.
WHY'S THAT?
YOU MAKE ME FEEL *HANDSOME*.

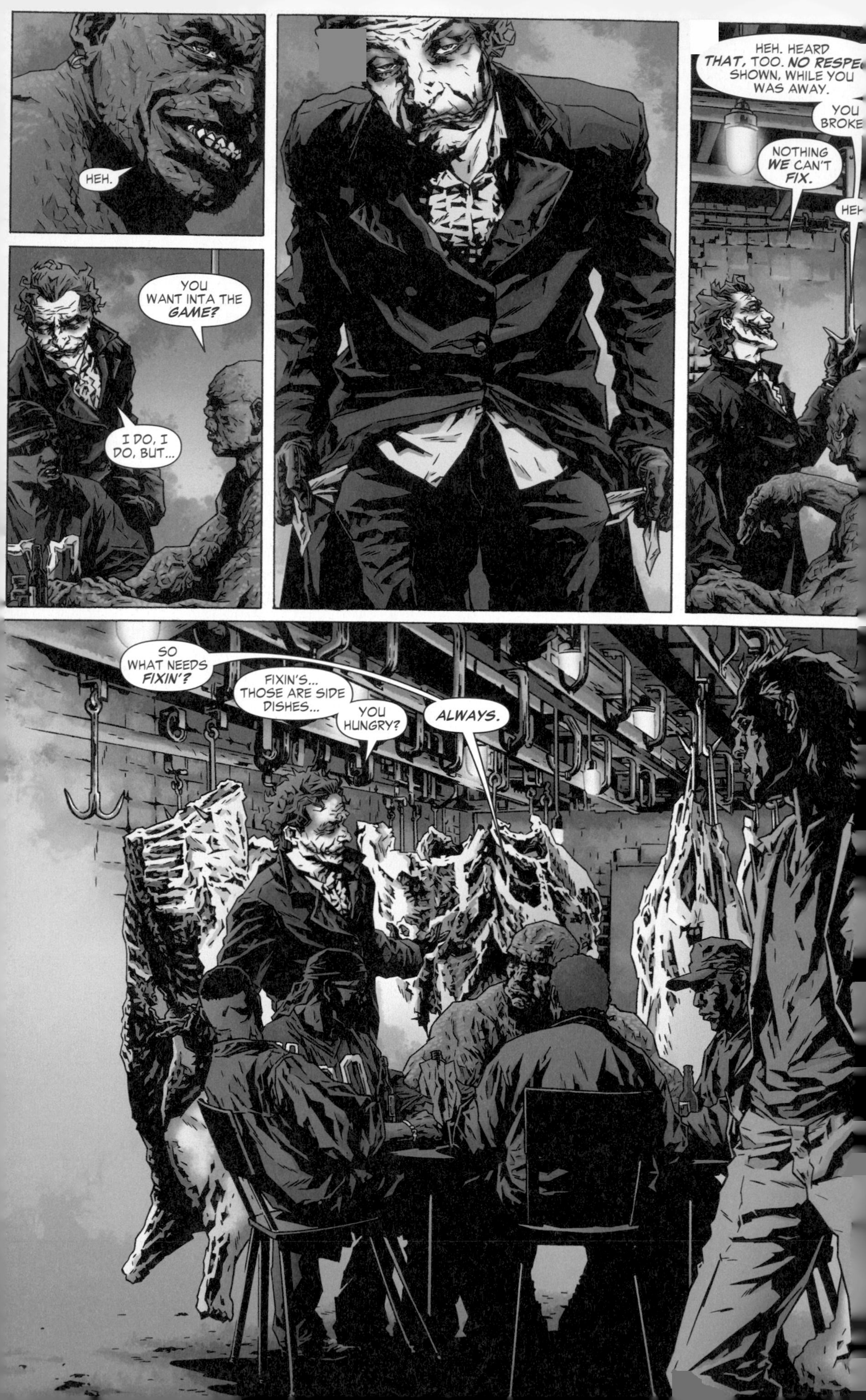
HEH.
YOU WANT INTA THE GAME?
I DO, I DO, BUT...
HEH. HEARD THAT, TOO. NO RESPE SHOWN, WHILE YOU WAS AWAY.
YOU BROKE
NOTHING WE CAN'T FIX.
HE
SO WHAT NEEDS FIXIN'?
FIXIN'S... THOSE ARE SIDE DISHES...
YOU HUNGRY?
ALWAYS.

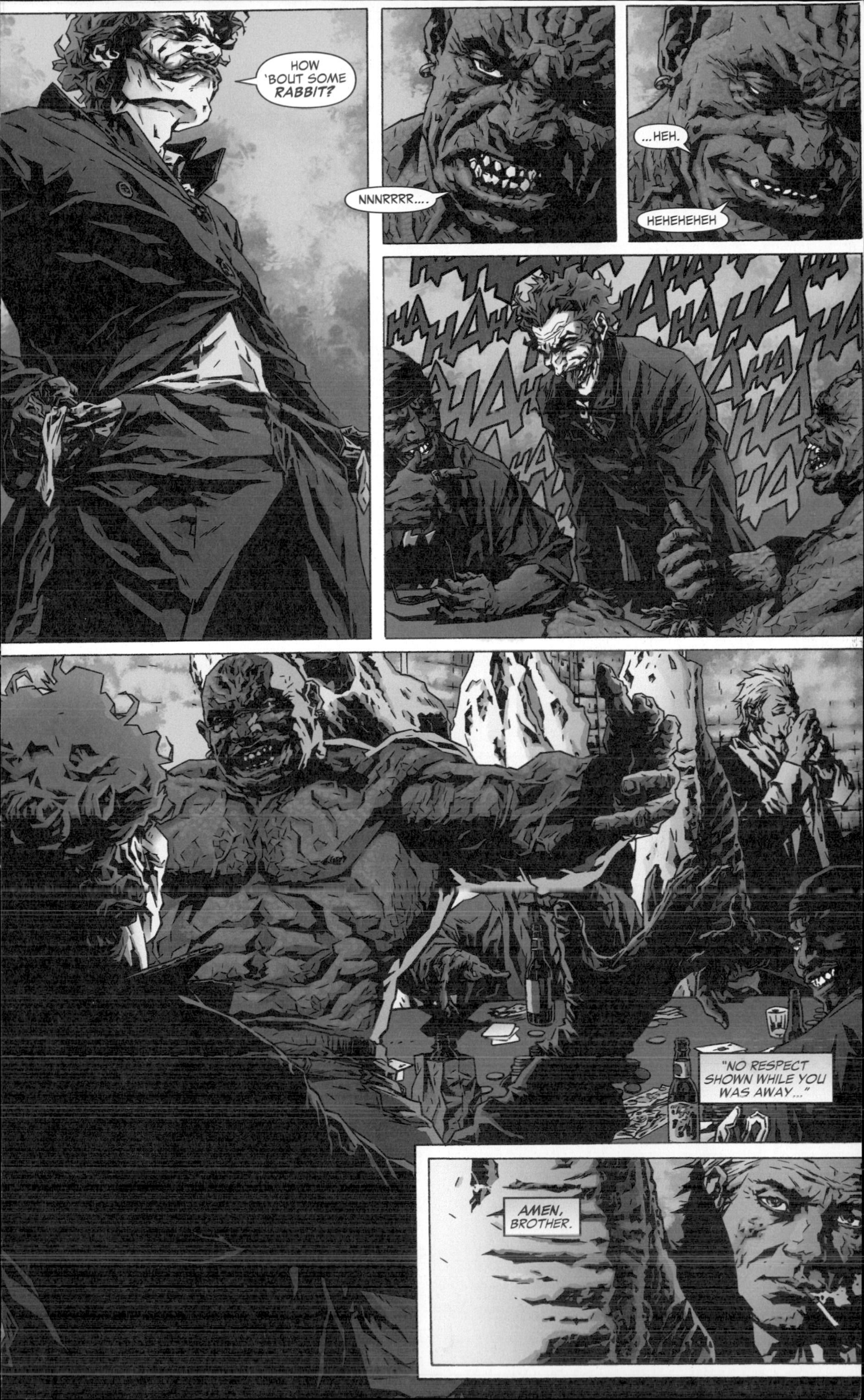
HOW 'BOUT SOME RABBIT?
NNNRRRR....
...HEH.
HEHEHEHEH
"NO RESPECT SHOWN WHILE YOU WAS AWAY..."
AMEN, BROTHER.

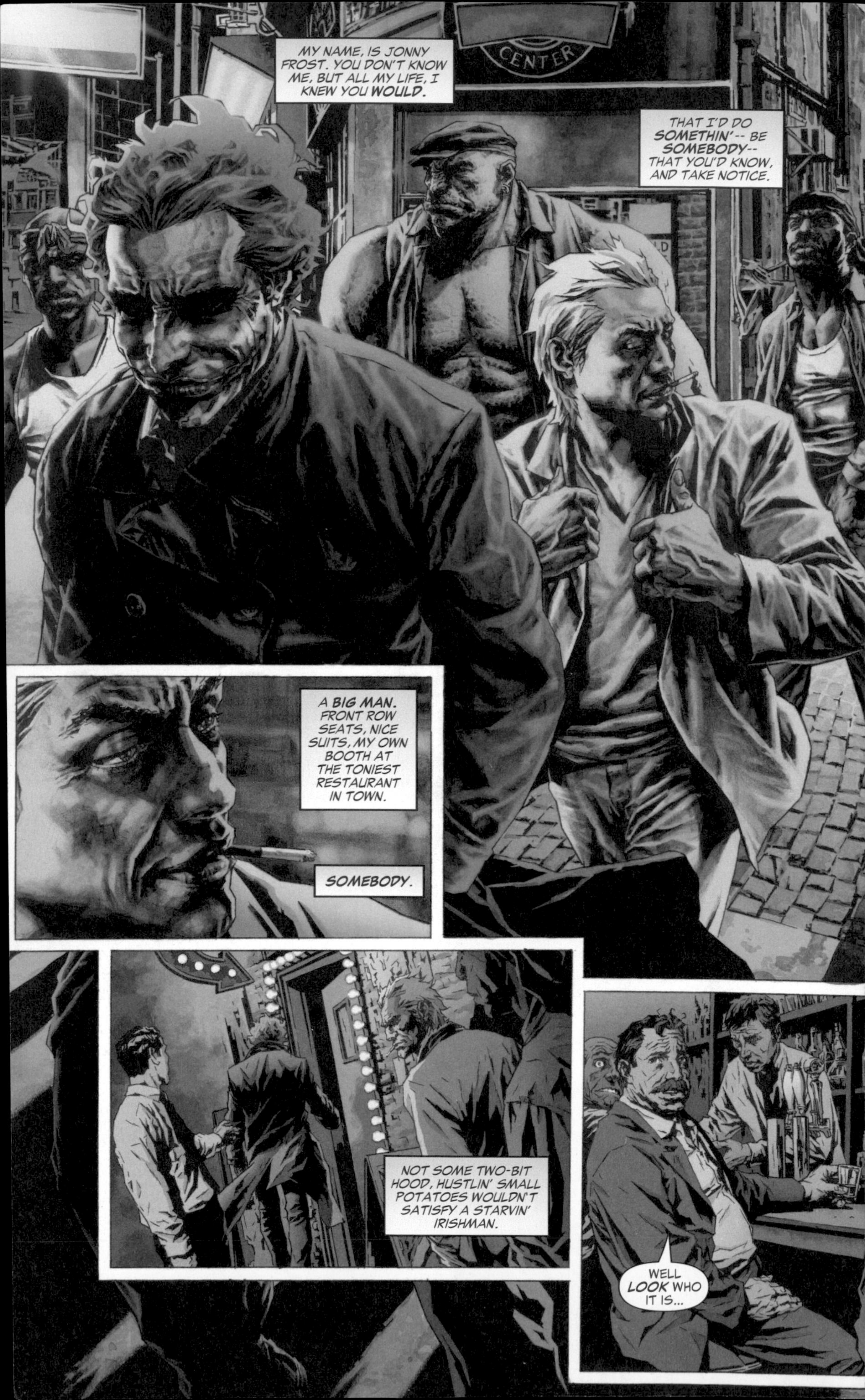
MY NAME, IS JONNY FROST. YOU DON'T KNOW ME, BUT ALL MY LIFE, I KNEW YOU WOULD.
THAT I'D DO SOMETHIN' -- BE SOMEBODY-- THAT YOU'D KNOW, AND TAKE NOTICE.
A BIG MAN. FRONT ROW SEATS, NICE SUITS, MY OWN BOOTH AT THE TONIEST RESTAURANT IN TOWN.
SOMEBODY.
NOT SOME TWO-BIT HOOD, HUSTLIN' SMALL POTATOES WOULDN'T SATISFY A STARVIN' IRISHMAN.
WELL LOOK WHO IT IS...

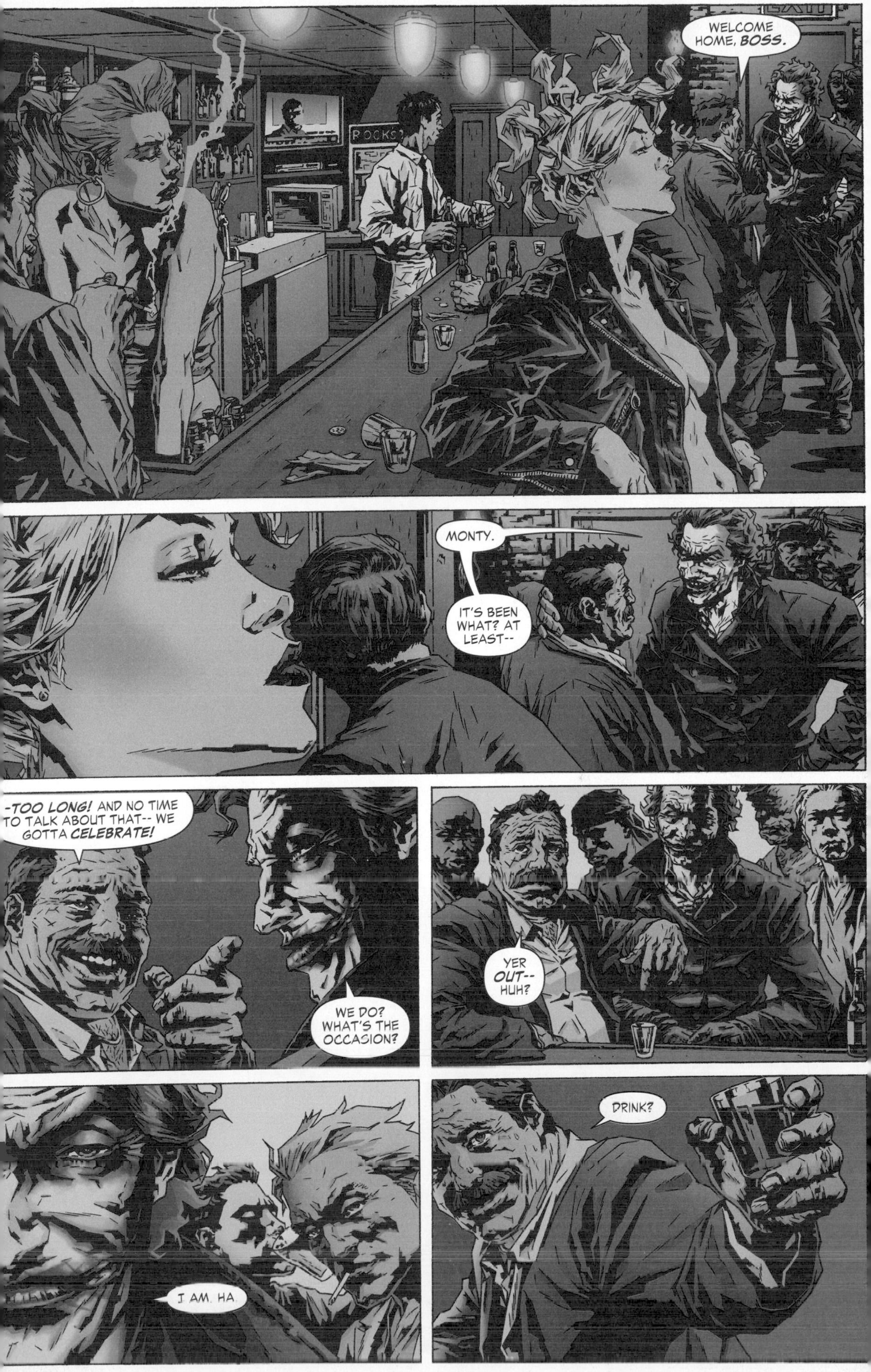
ROCKS
WELCOME HOME, **BOSS.**
MONTY.
IT'S BEEN WHAT? AT LEAST--
-**TOO LONG!** AND NO TIME TO TALK ABOUT THAT-- WE GOTTA **CELEBRATE!**
WE DO? WHAT'S THE OCCASION?
YER **OUT**-- HUH?
I AM. HA.
DRINK?

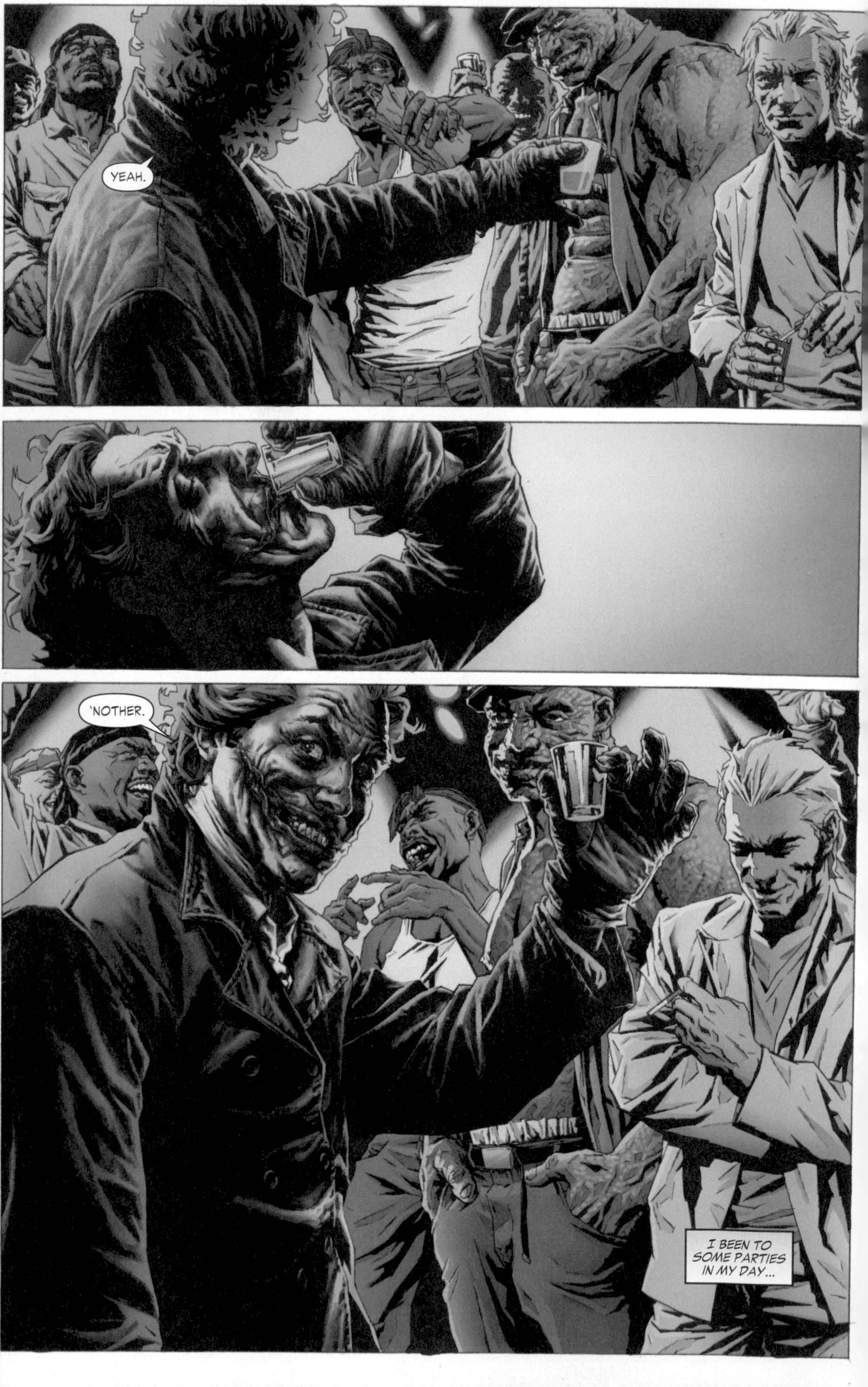
YEAH.
'NOTHER.
I BEEN TO SOME PARTIES IN MY DAY...

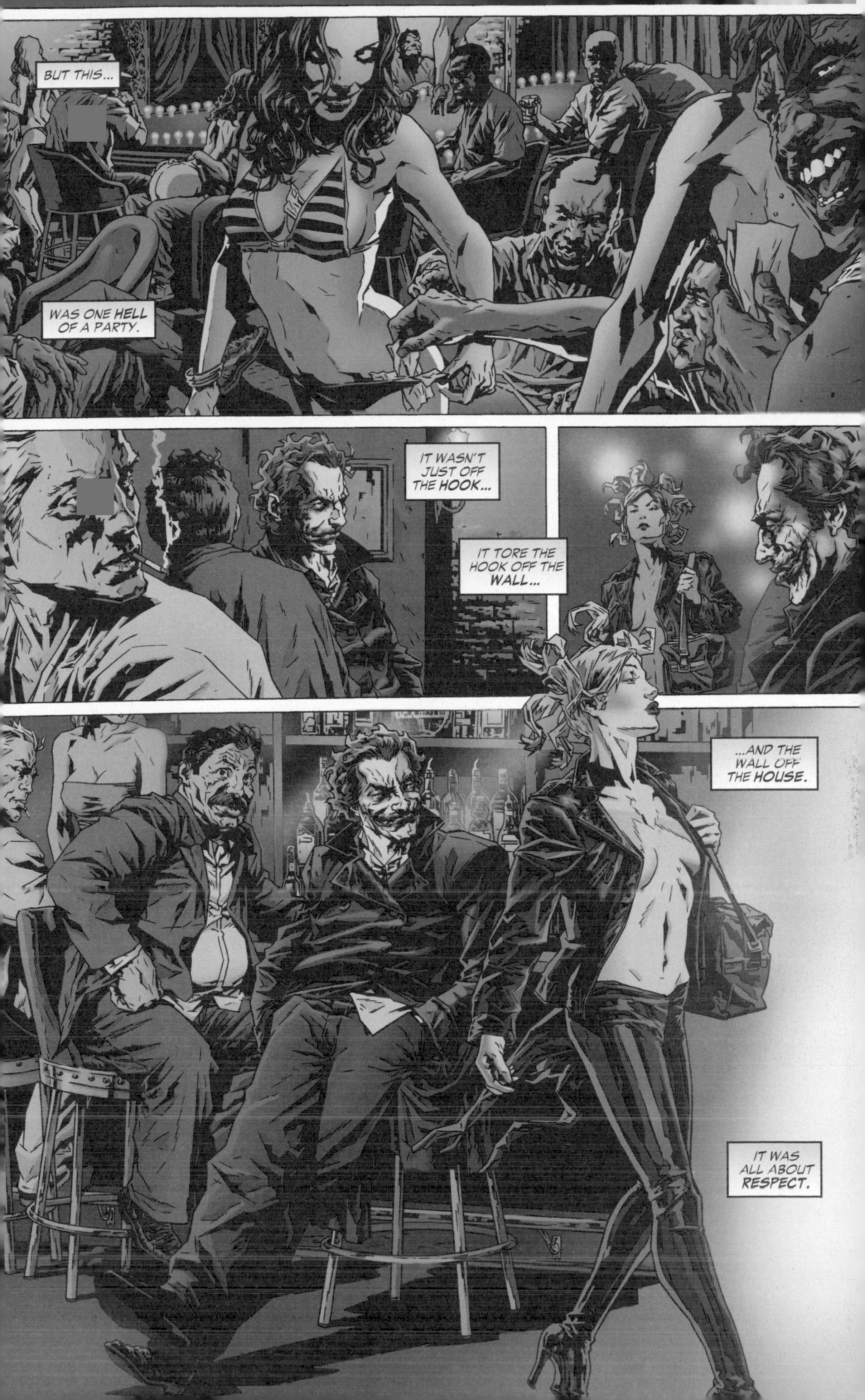
BUT THIS...
WAS ONE HELL OF A PARTY.
IT WASN'T JUST OFF THE HOOK...
IT TORE THE HOOK OFF THE WALL...
...AND THE WALL OFF THE HOUSE.
IT WAS ALL ABOUT RESPECT.

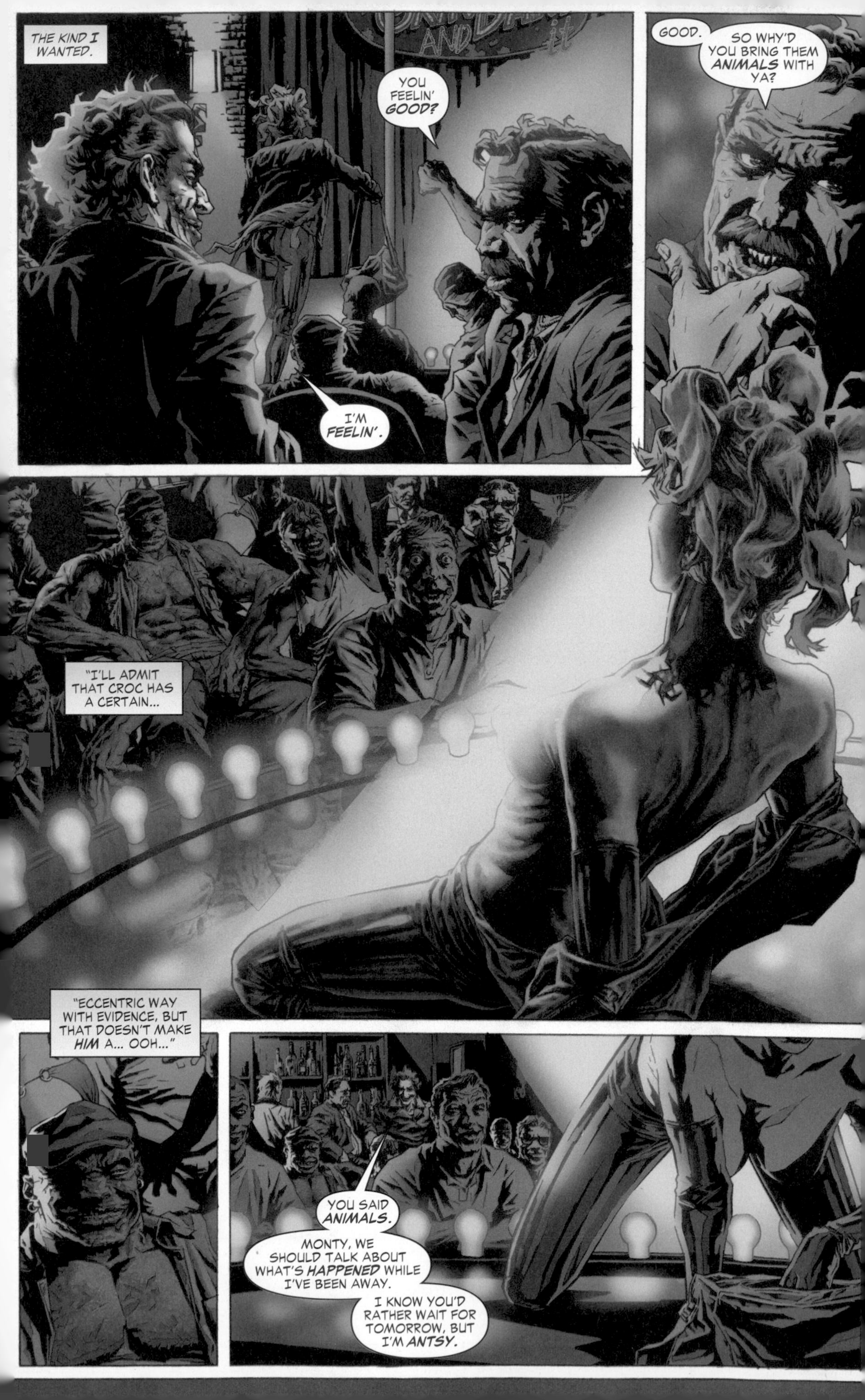
THE KIND *I* WANTED.
YOU FEELIN' *GOOD?*
I'M *FEELIN'.*
GOOD.
SO WHY'D YOU BRING THEM *ANIMALS* WITH YA?
"I'LL ADMIT THAT CROC HAS A CERTAIN...
"ECCENTRIC WAY WITH EVIDENCE, BUT THAT DOESN'T MAKE *HIM* A... OOH..."
YOU SAID *ANIMALS.*
MONTY, WE SHOULD TALK ABOUT WHAT'S *HAPPENED* WHILE I'VE BEEN AWAY.
I KNOW YOU'D RATHER WAIT FOR TOMORROW, BUT I'M *ANTSY.*

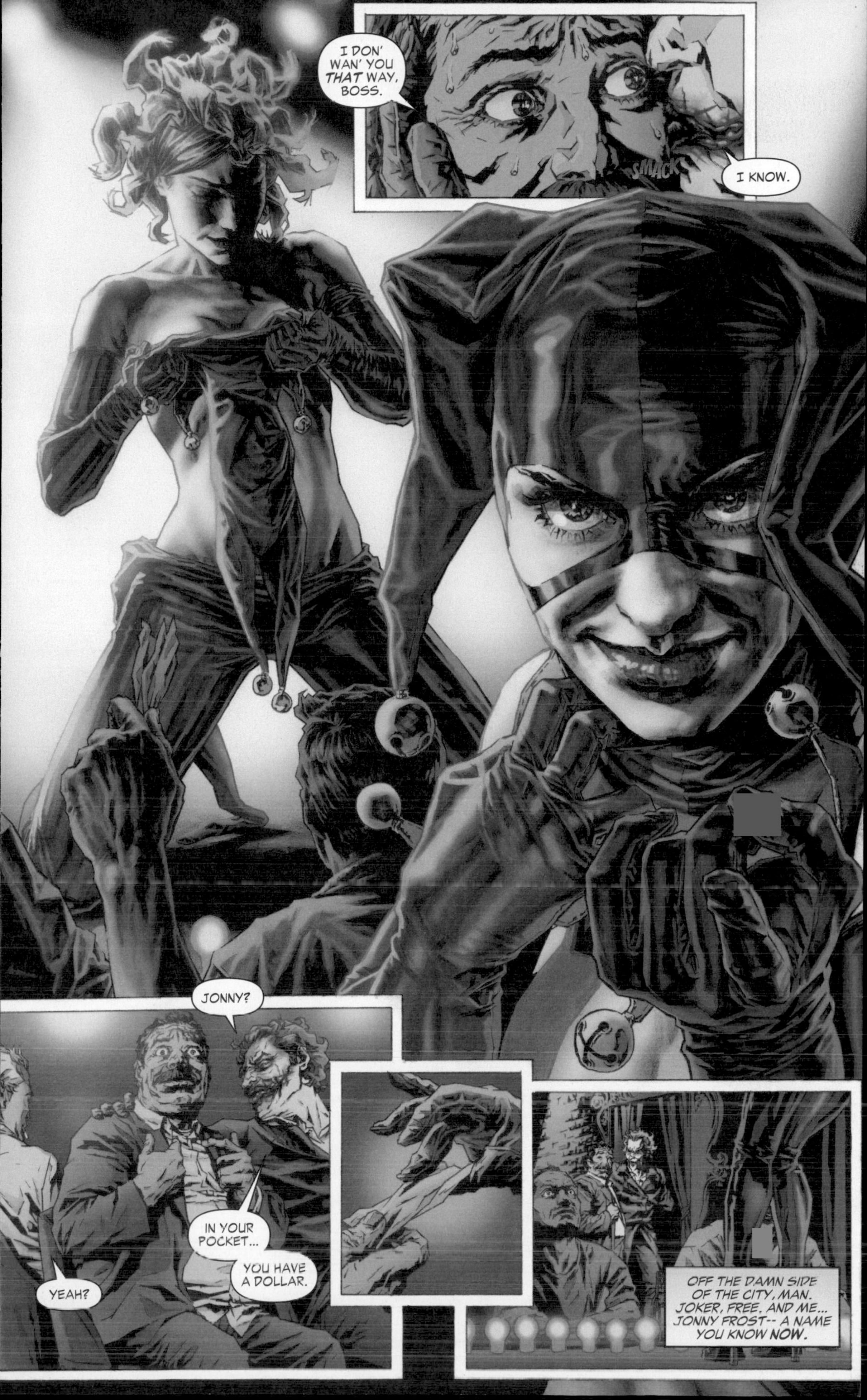

I DON' WAN' YOU *THAT* WAY, BOSS.
SMACK
I KNOW.
JONNY?
YEAH?
IN YOUR POCKET...
YOU HAVE A DOLLAR.
*OFF THE DAMN SIDE OF THE CITY, MAN. JOKER, FREE. AND ME... JONNY FROST-- A NAME YOU KNOW **NOW**.*

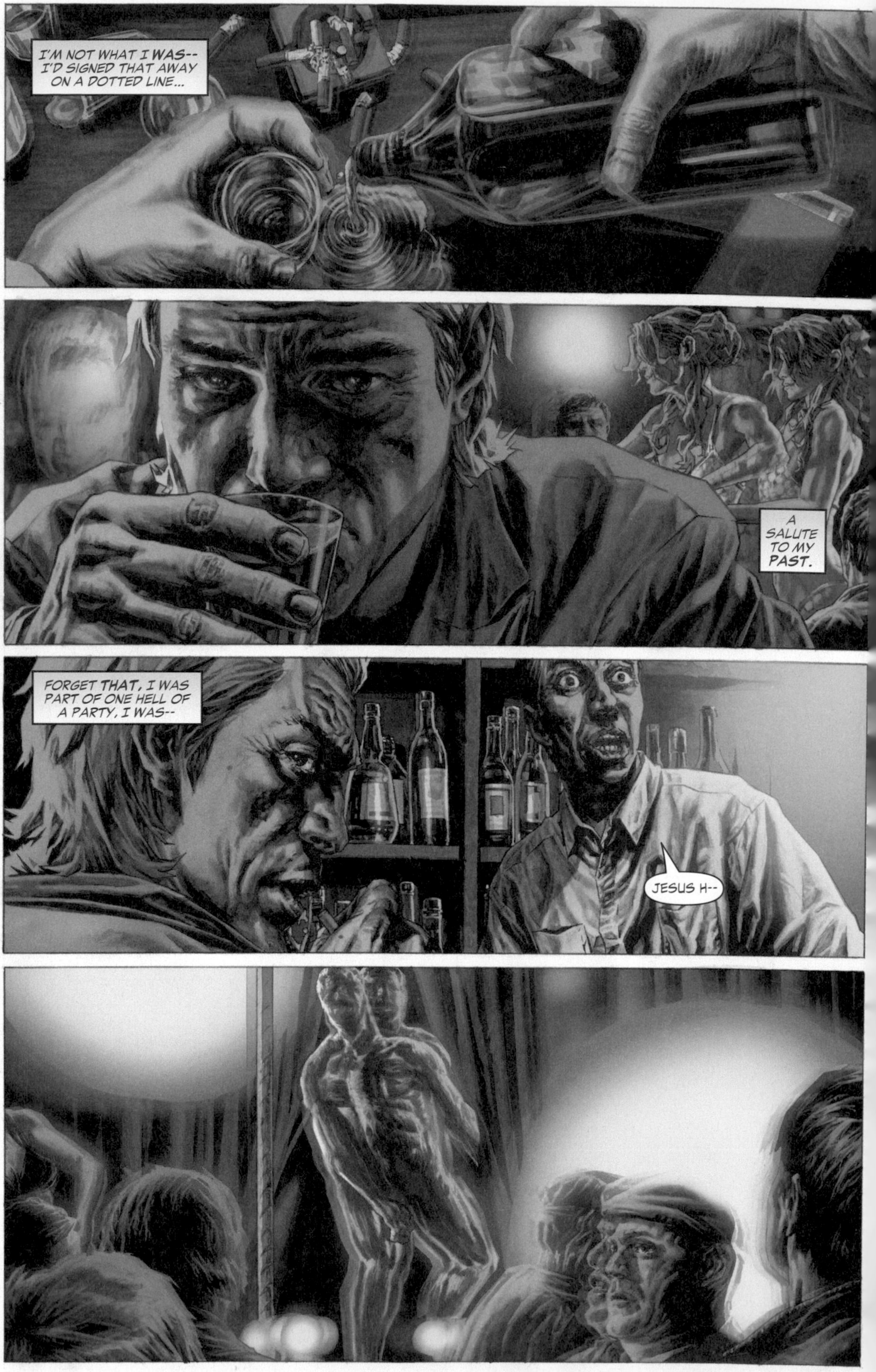
I'M NOT WHAT I WAS-- I'D SIGNED THAT AWAY ON A DOTTED LINE...
A SALUTE TO MY PAST.
FORGET THAT, I WAS PART OF ONE HELL OF A PARTY, I WAS--
JESUS H--

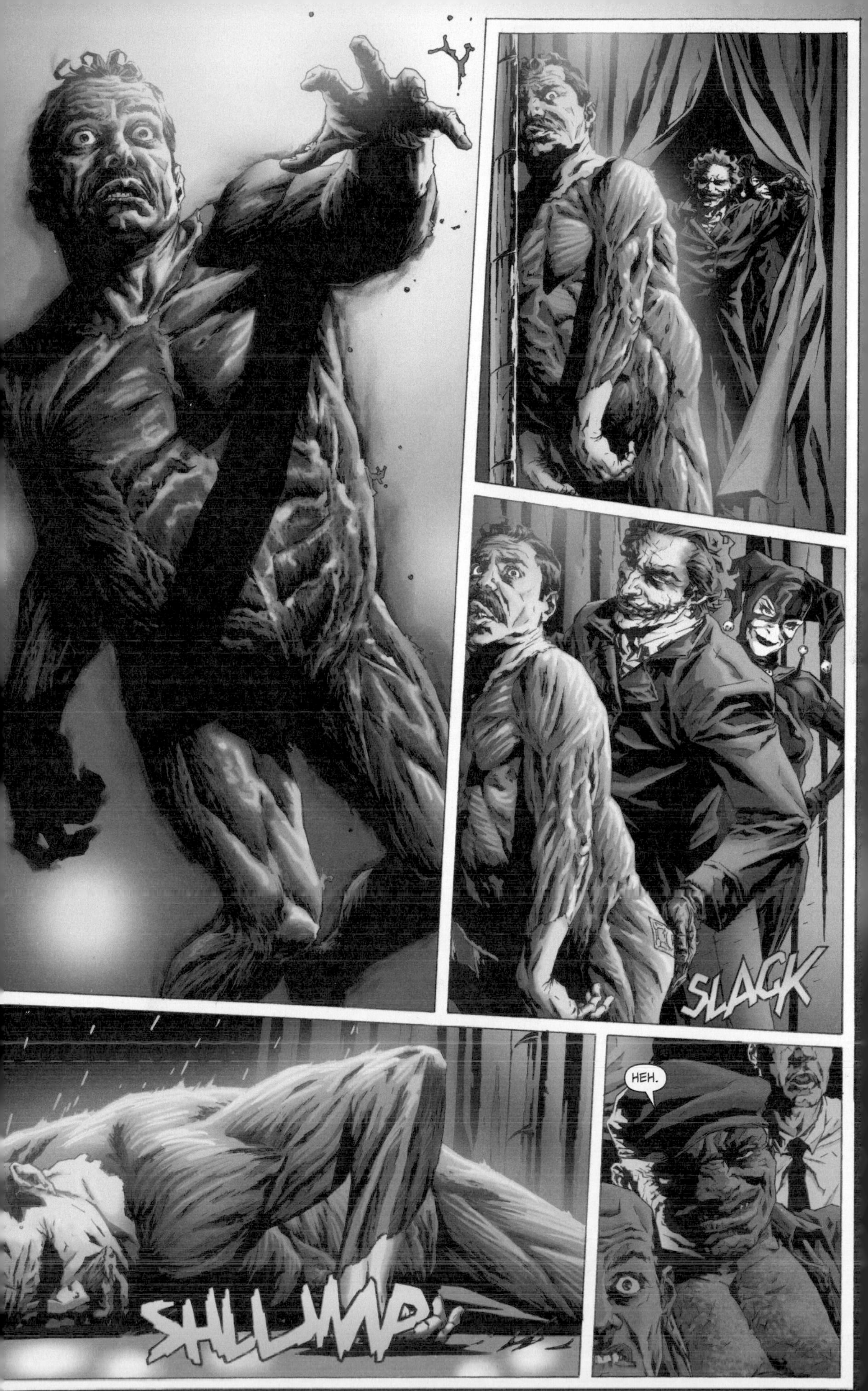
SLACK
SHLUMP!
HEH.

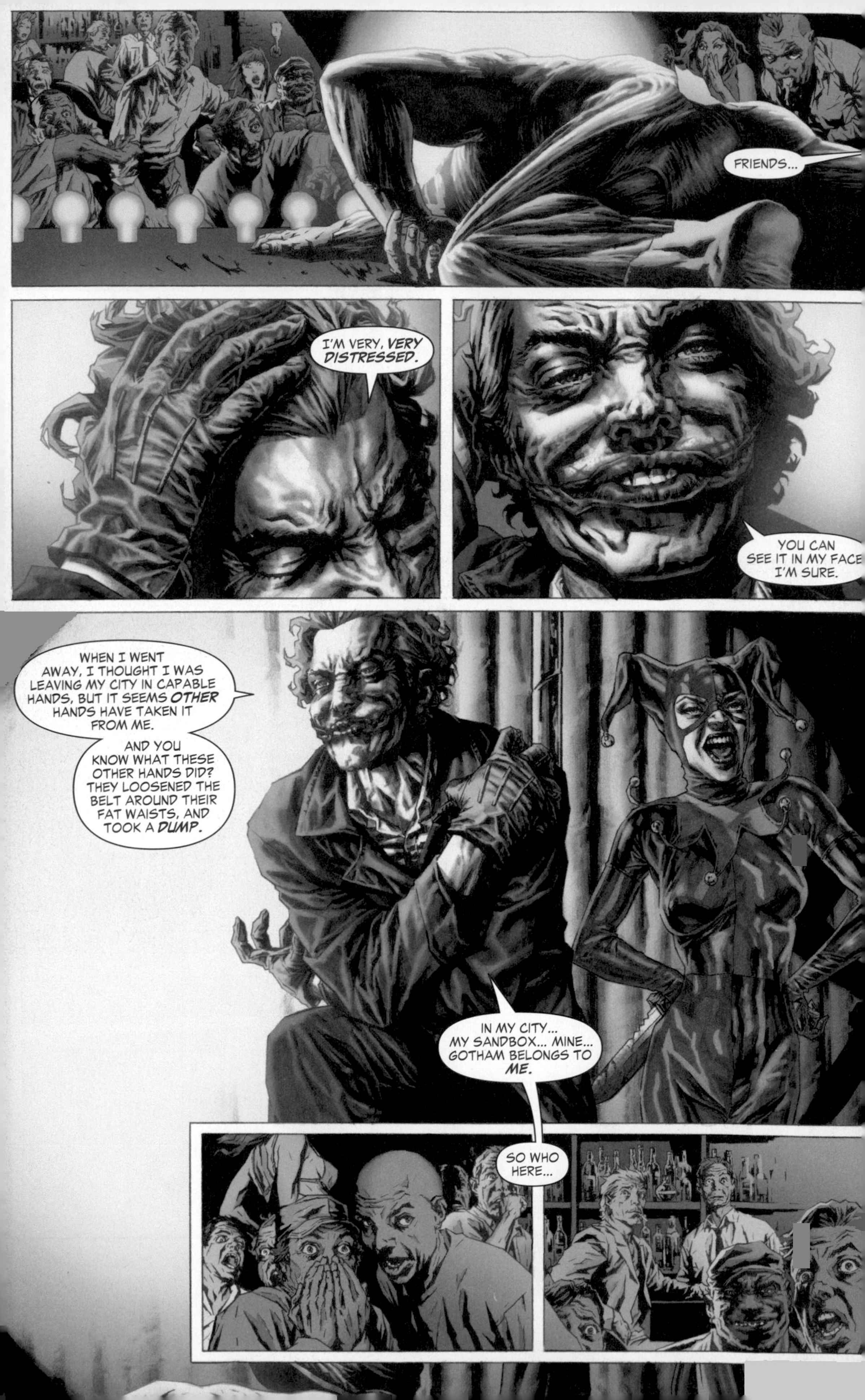
FRIENDS...
I'M VERY, VERY DISTRESSED.
YOU CAN SEE IT IN MY FACE I'M SURE.
WHEN I WENT AWAY, I THOUGHT I WAS LEAVING MY CITY IN CAPABLE HANDS, BUT IT SEEMS OTHER HANDS HAVE TAKEN IT FROM ME.
AND YOU KNOW WHAT THESE OTHER HANDS DID? THEY LOOSENED THE BELT AROUND THEIR FAT WAISTS, AND TOOK A DUMP.
IN MY CITY... MY SANDBOX... MINE... GOTHAM BELONGS TO ME.
SO WHO HERE...

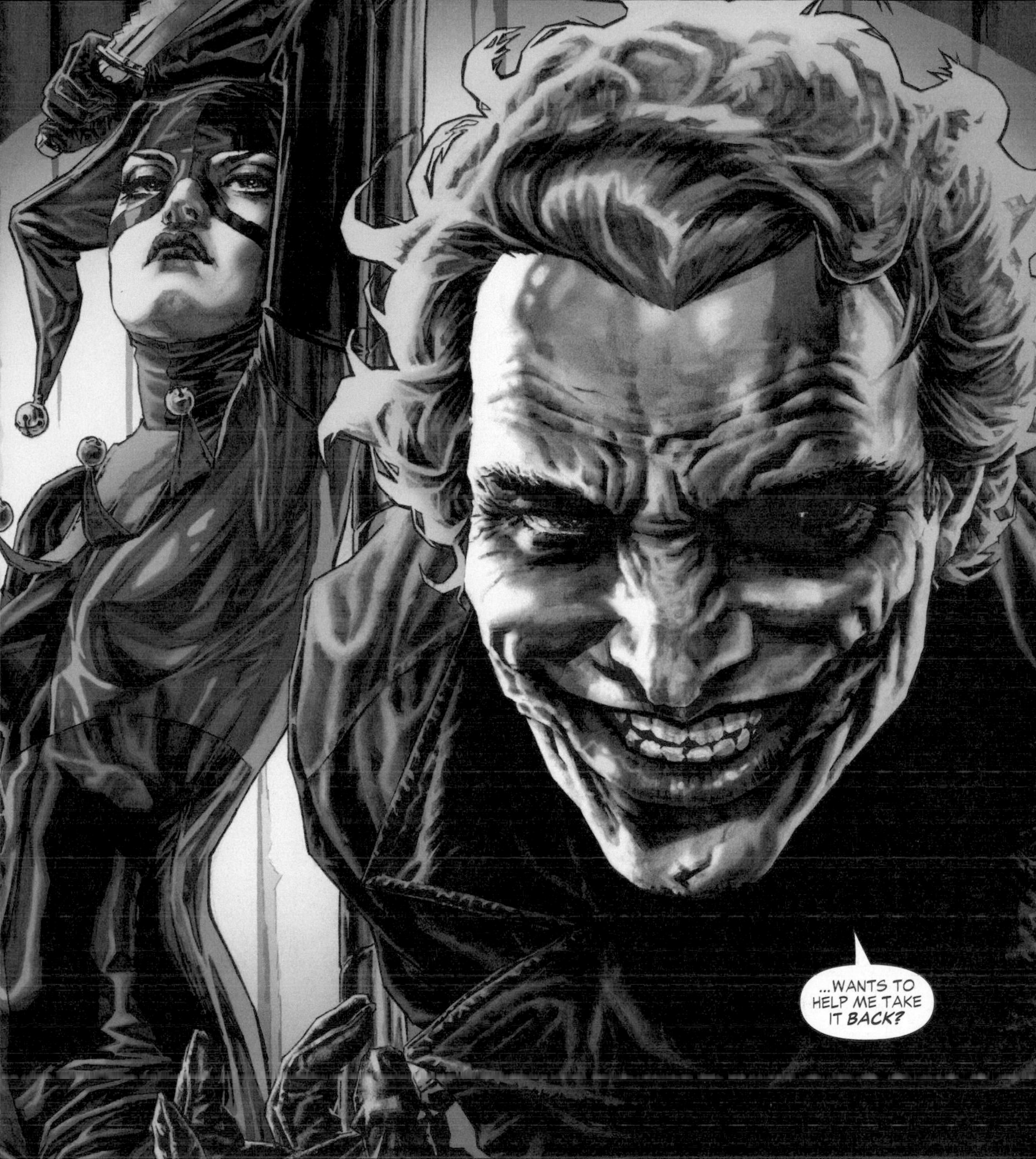
...WANTS TO HELP ME TAKE IT BACK?

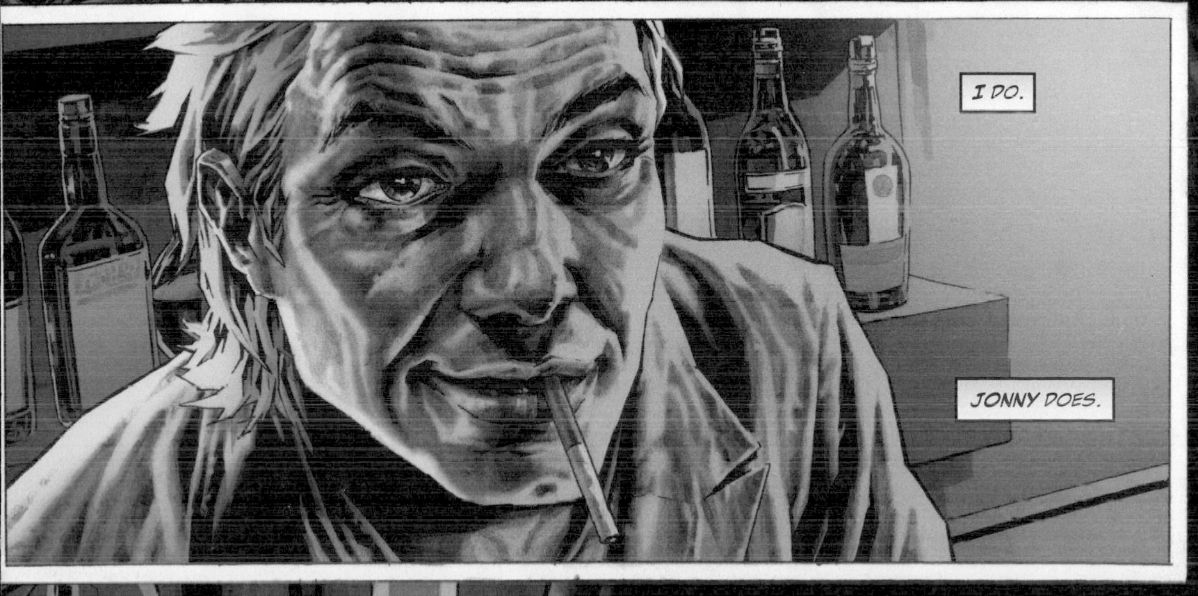
I DO.
JONNY DOES.

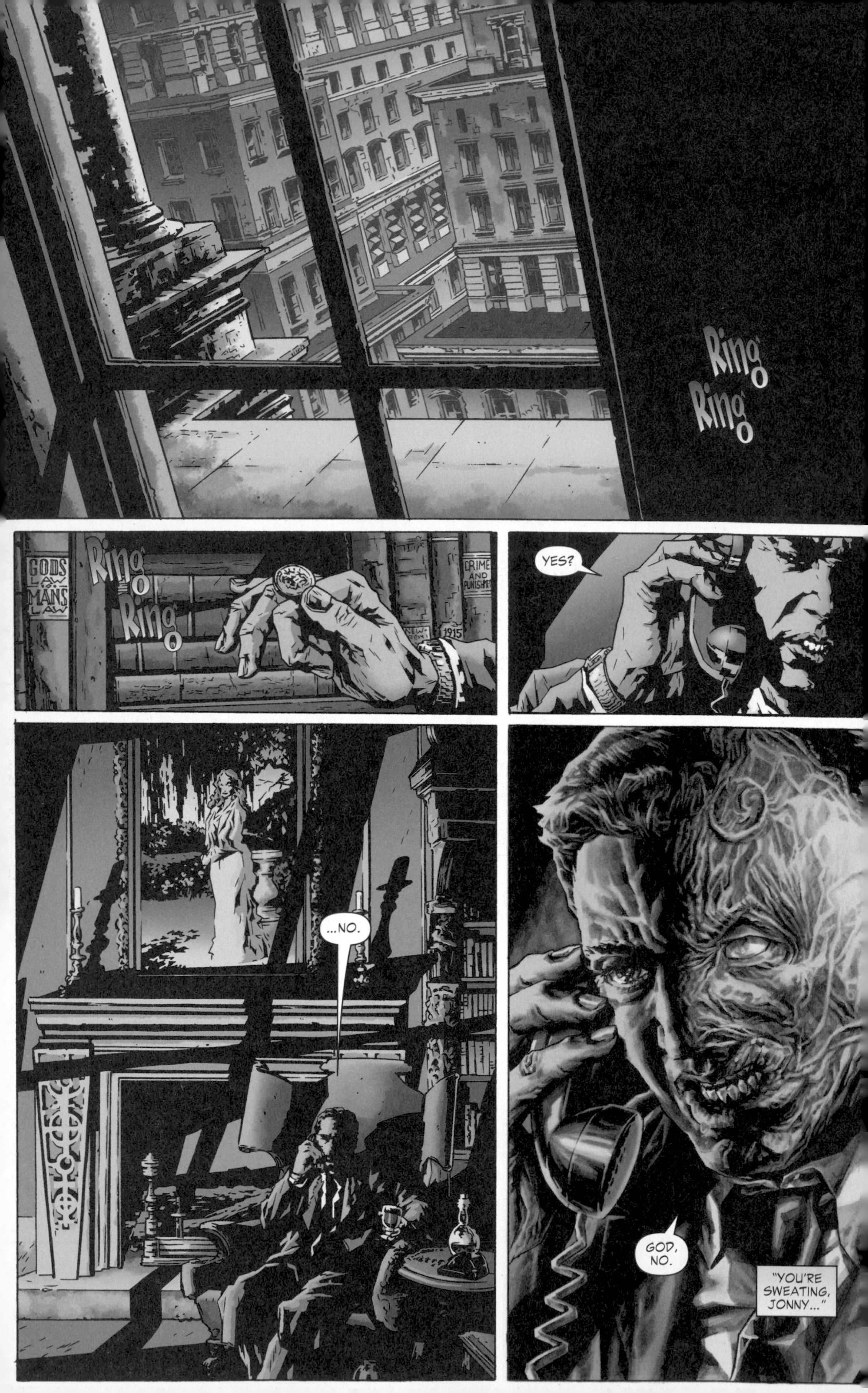

Ring
Ring
Ring
Ring
GODS LAW MANS LAW
CRIME AND PUNISHMENT
1915
YES?
...NO.
GOD, NO.
"YOU'RE SWEATING, JONNY..."

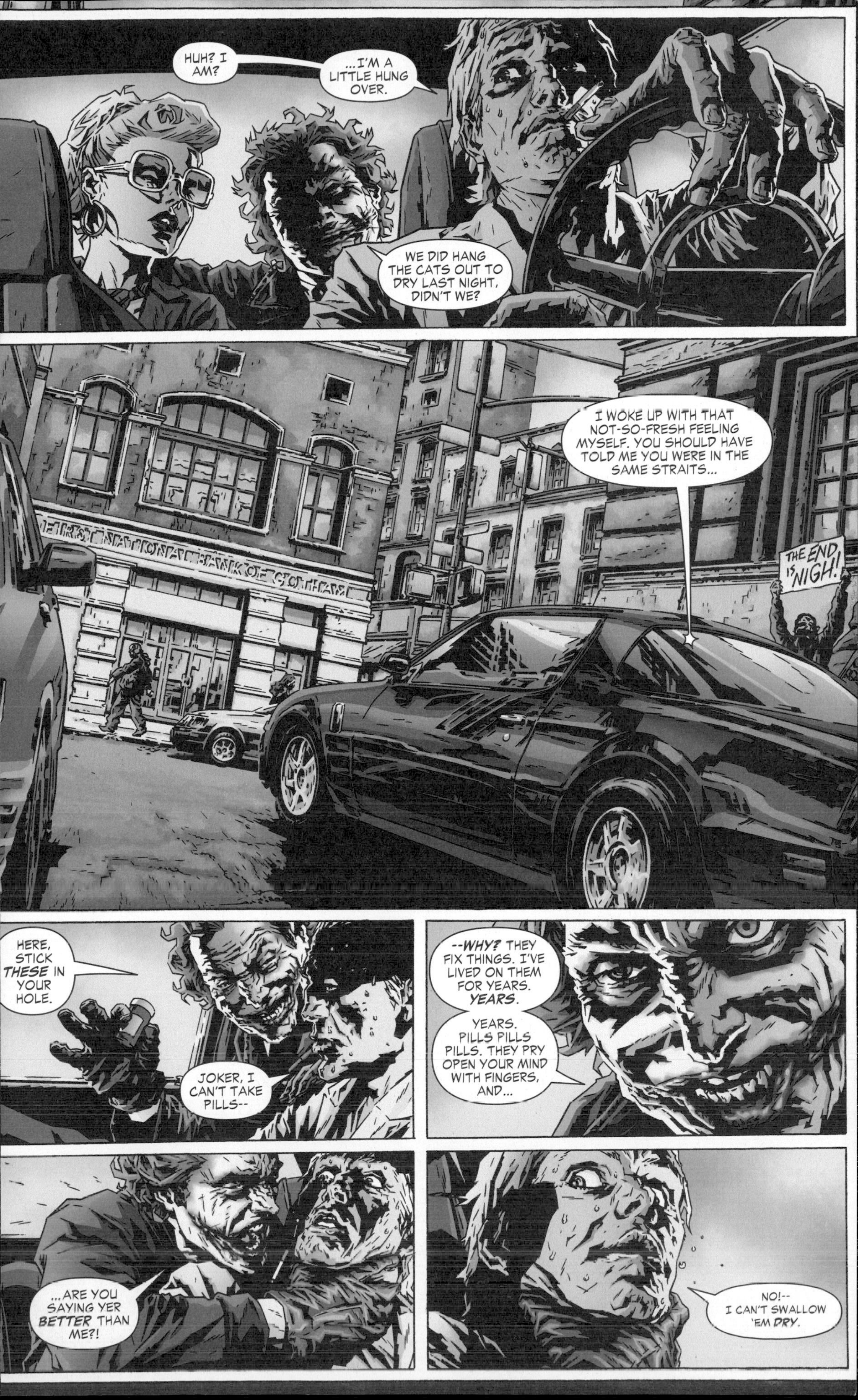

HUH? I AM?
...I'M A LITTLE HUNG OVER.
WE DID HANG THE CATS OUT TO DRY LAST NIGHT, DIDN'T WE?
I WOKE UP WITH THAT NOT-SO-FRESH FEELING MYSELF. YOU SHOULD HAVE TOLD ME YOU WERE IN THE SAME STRAITS...
FIRST NATIONAL BANK OF GOTHAM
THE END IS NIGH!
HERE, STICK *THESE* IN YOUR HOLE.
JOKER, I CAN'T TAKE PILLS--
--*WHY?* THEY FIX THINGS. I'VE LIVED ON THEM FOR YEARS. *YEARS*.
YEARS. PILLS PILLS PILLS. THEY PRY OPEN YOUR MIND WITH FINGERS, AND...
...ARE YOU SAYING YER *BETTER* THAN ME?!
NO!-- I CAN'T SWALLOW 'EM *DRY*.

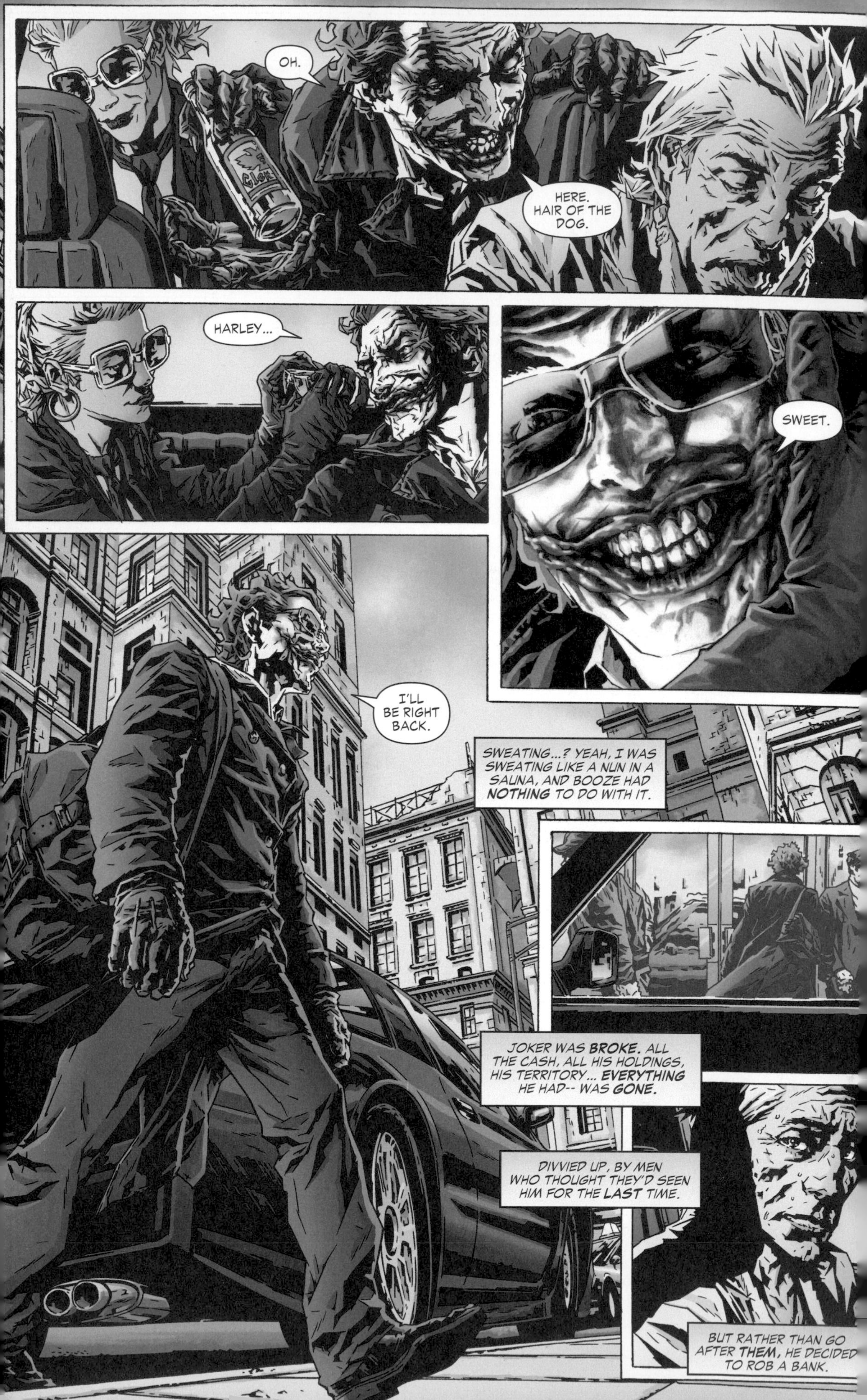
OH.
HERE. HAIR OF THE DOG.
HARLEY...
SWEET.
I'LL BE RIGHT BACK.
SWEATING...? YEAH, I WAS SWEATING LIKE A NUN IN A SAUNA, AND BOOZE HAD NOTHING TO DO WITH IT.
JOKER WAS BROKE. ALL THE CASH, ALL HIS HOLDINGS, HIS TERRITORY... EVERYTHING HE HAD-- WAS GONE.
DIVVIED UP, BY MEN WHO THOUGHT THEY'D SEEN HIM FOR THE LAST TIME.
BUT RATHER THAN GO AFTER THEM, HE DECIDED TO ROB A BANK.

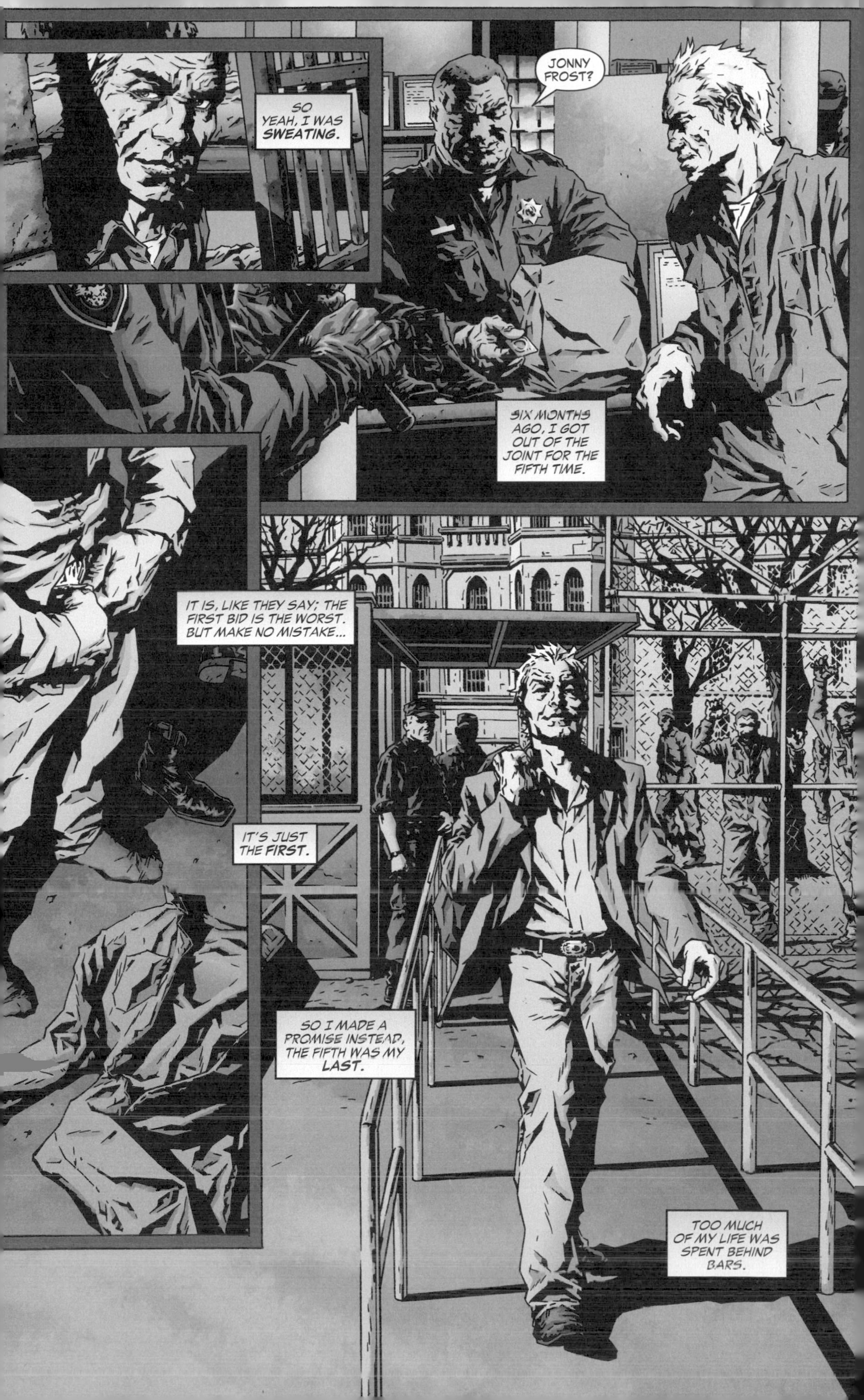
SO YEAH, I WAS SWEATING.
JONNY FROST?
SIX MONTHS AGO, I GOT OUT OF THE JOINT FOR THE FIFTH TIME.
IT IS, LIKE THEY SAY: THE FIRST BID IS THE WORST. BUT MAKE NO MISTAKE...
IT'S JUST THE FIRST.
SO I MADE A PROMISE INSTEAD, THE FIFTH WAS MY LAST.
TOO MUCH OF MY LIFE WAS SPENT BEHIND BARS.

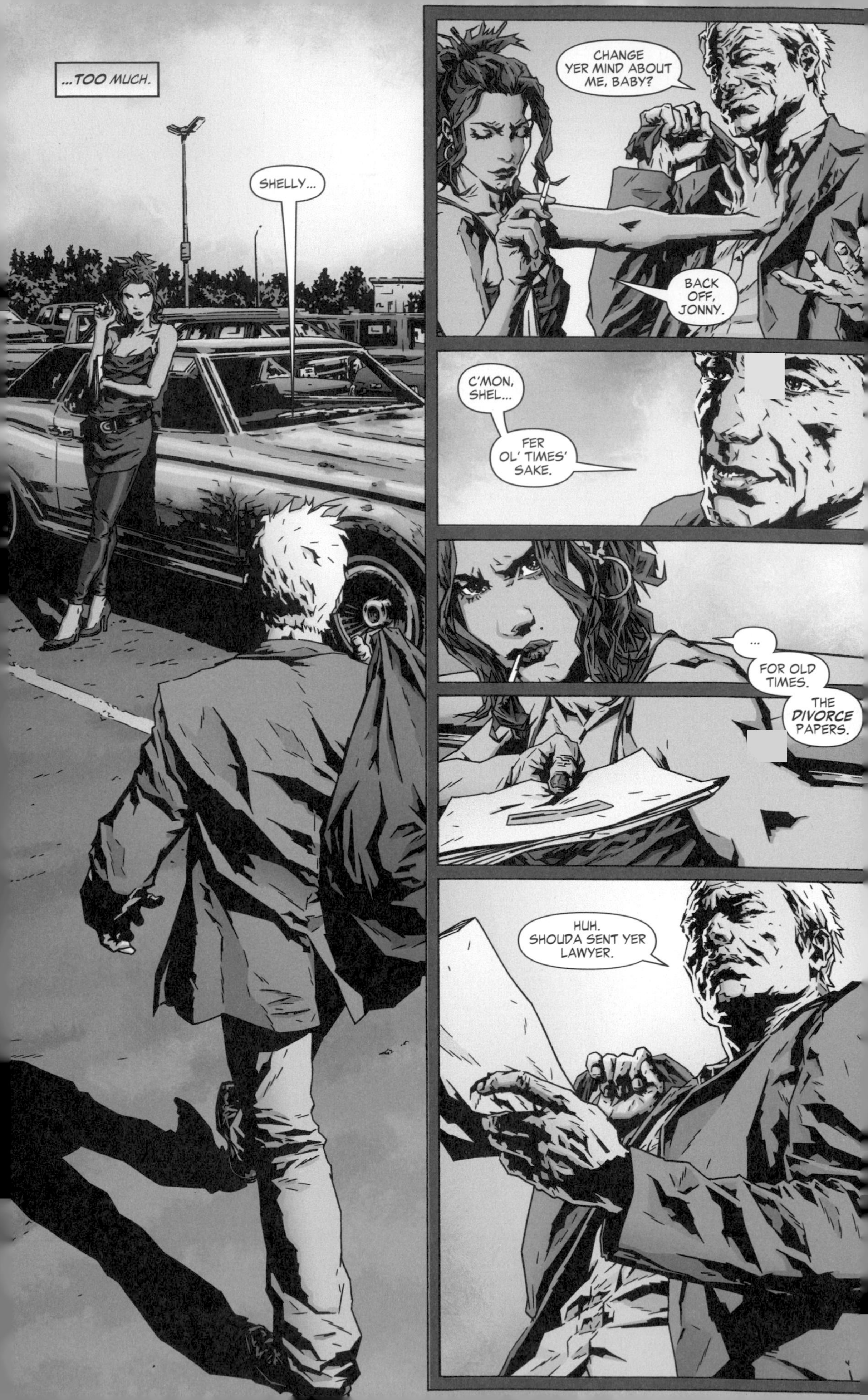
...TOO MUCH.
SHELLY...
CHANGE YER MIND ABOUT ME, BABY?
BACK OFF, JONNY.
C'MON, SHEL...
FER OL' TIMES' SAKE.
...
FOR OLD TIMES.
THE DIVORCE PAPERS.
HUH. SHOUDA SENT YER LAWYER.

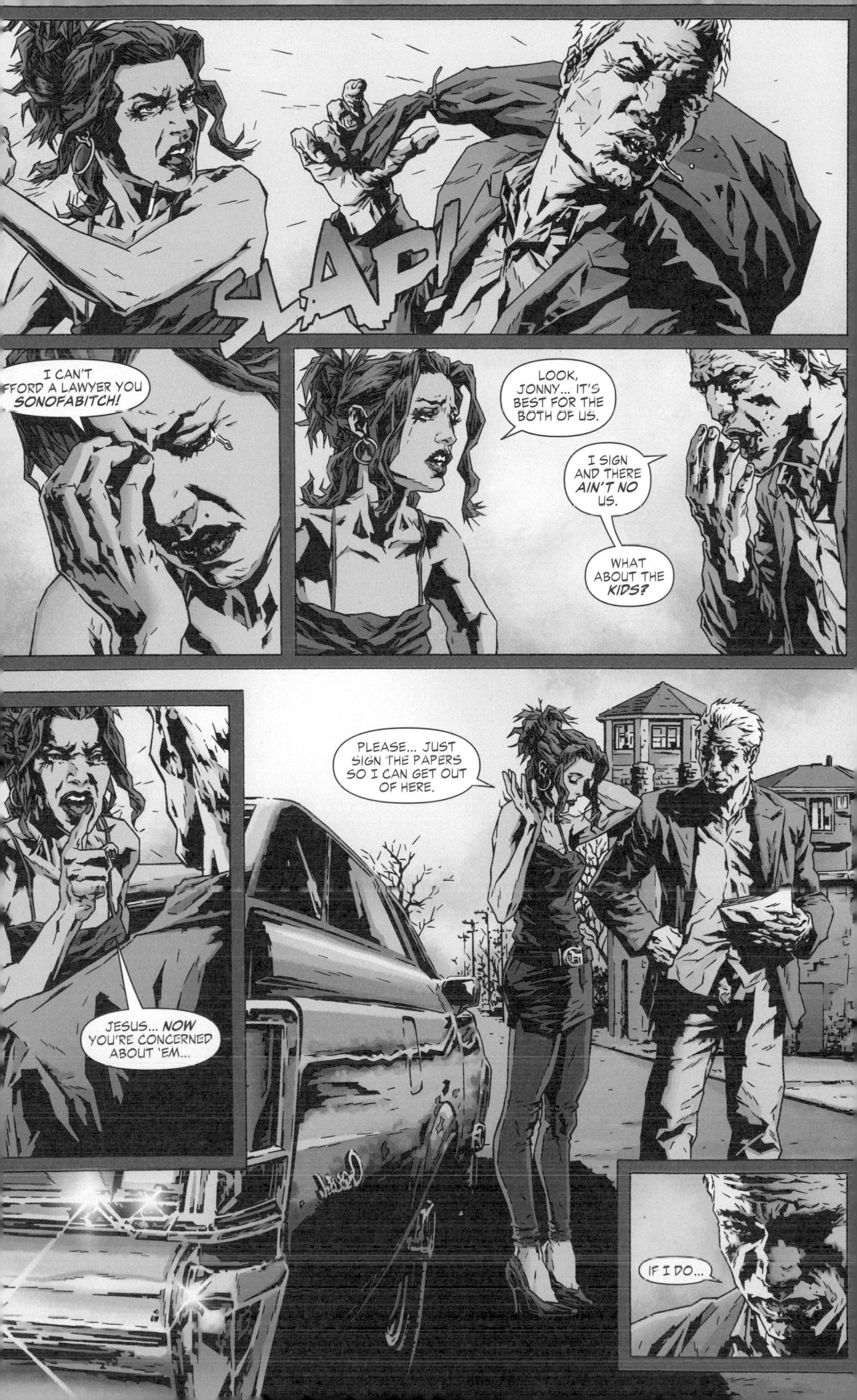
SLAP!
I CAN'T
FFORD A LAWYER YOU SONOFABITCH!
LOOK, JONNY... IT'S BEST FOR THE BOTH OF US.
I SIGN AND THERE AIN'T NO US.
WHAT ABOUT THE KIDS?
PLEASE... JUST SIGN THE PAPERS SO I CAN GET OUT OF HERE.
JESUS... NOW YOU'RE CONCERNED ABOUT 'EM...
IF I DO...

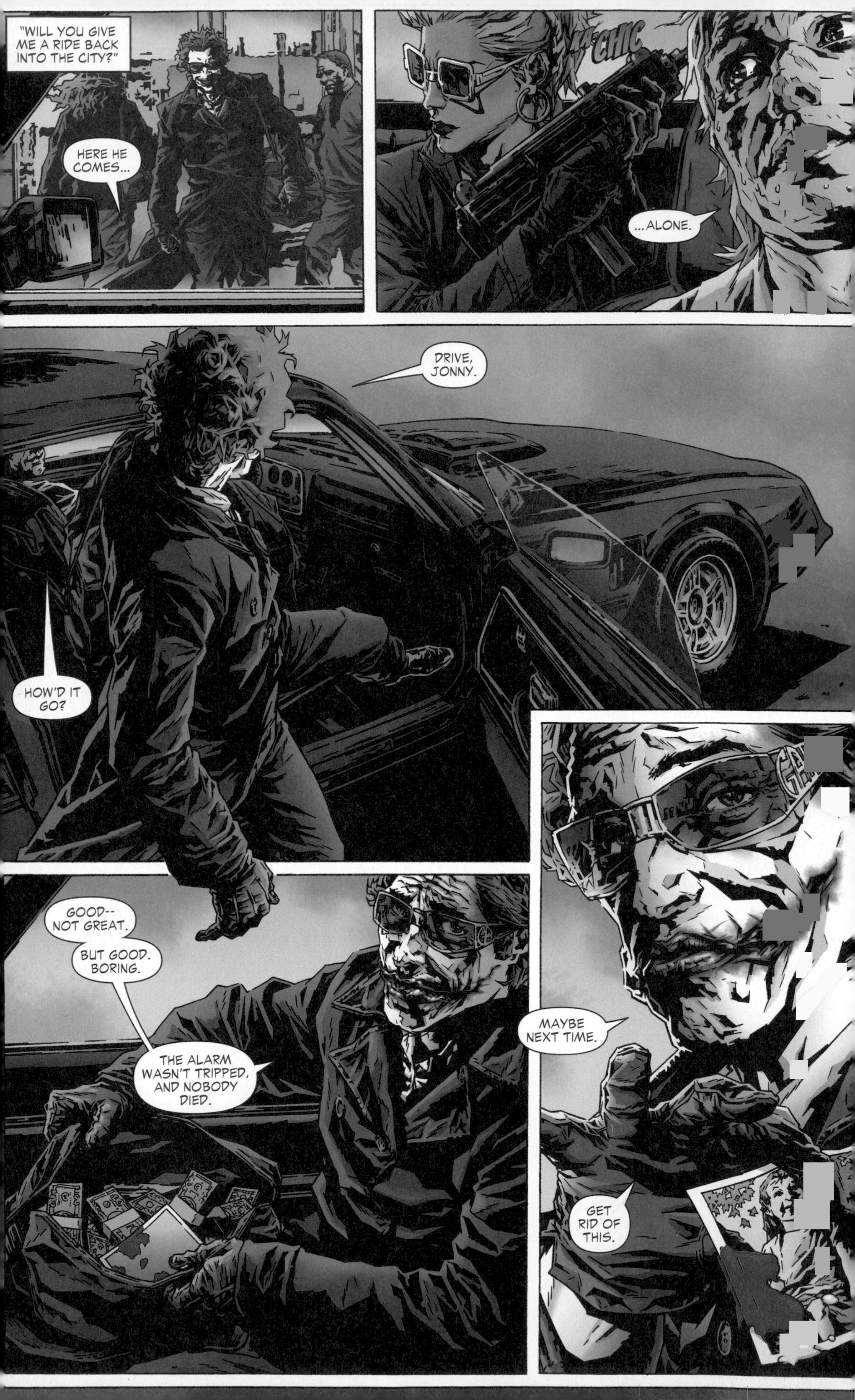
"WILL YOU GIVE ME A RIDE BACK INTO THE CITY?"
HERE HE COMES...
KA-CHIC
...ALONE.
DRIVE, JONNY.
HOW'D IT GO?
GOOD-- NOT GREAT.
BUT GOOD. BORING.
THE ALARM WASN'T TRIPPED, AND NOBODY DIED.
MAYBE NEXT TIME.
GET RID OF THIS.

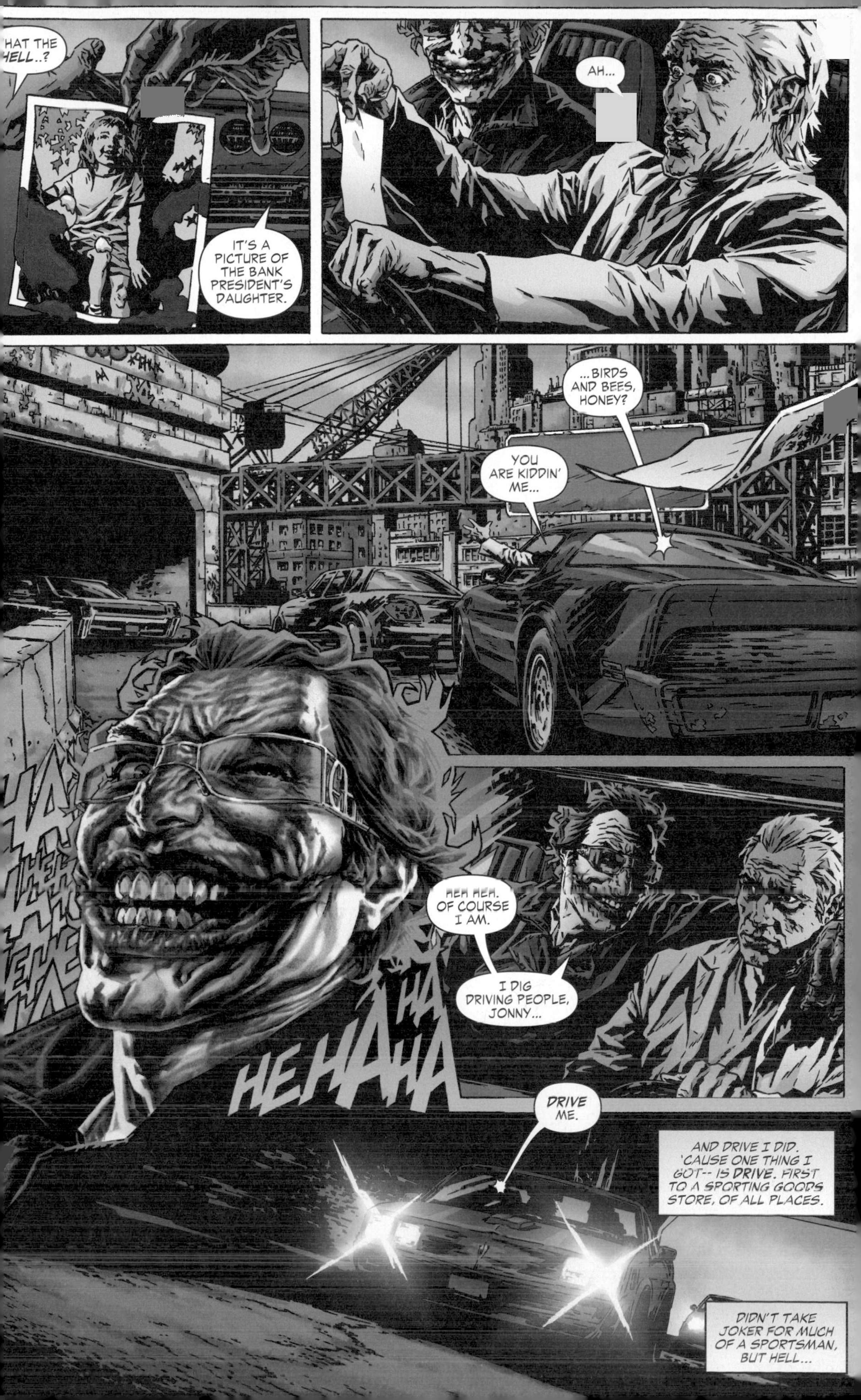
HAT THE HELL..?
IT'S A PICTURE OF THE BANK PRESIDENT'S DAUGHTER.
AH...
...BIRDS AND BEES, HONEY?
YOU ARE KIDDIN' ME...
HEH HEH. OF COURSE I AM.
I DIG DRIVING PEOPLE, JONNY...
HA
HEHAHA
DRIVE ME.
AND DRIVE I DID. 'CAUSE ONE THING I GOT-- IS DRIVE. FIRST TO A SPORTING GOODS STORE, OF ALL PLACES.
DIDN'T TAKE JOKER FOR MUCH OF A SPORTSMAN, BUT HELL...

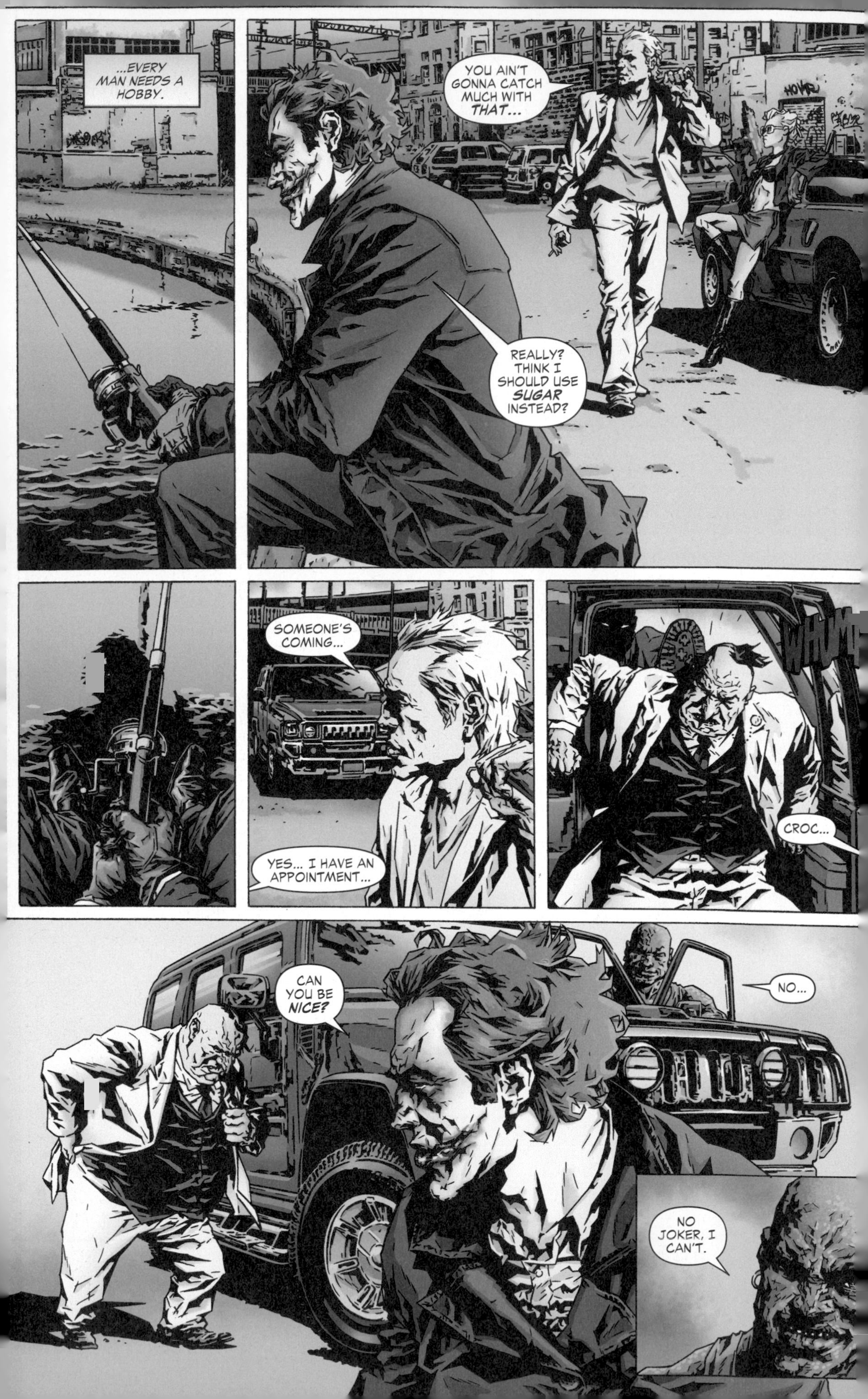
...EVERY MAN NEEDS A HOBBY.
YOU AIN'T GONNA CATCH MUCH WITH THAT...
REALLY? THINK I SHOULD USE SUGAR INSTEAD?
SOMEONE'S COMING...
YES... I HAVE AN APPOINTMENT...
WHUMP
CROC...
CAN YOU BE NICE?
NO...
NO JOKER, I CAN'T.

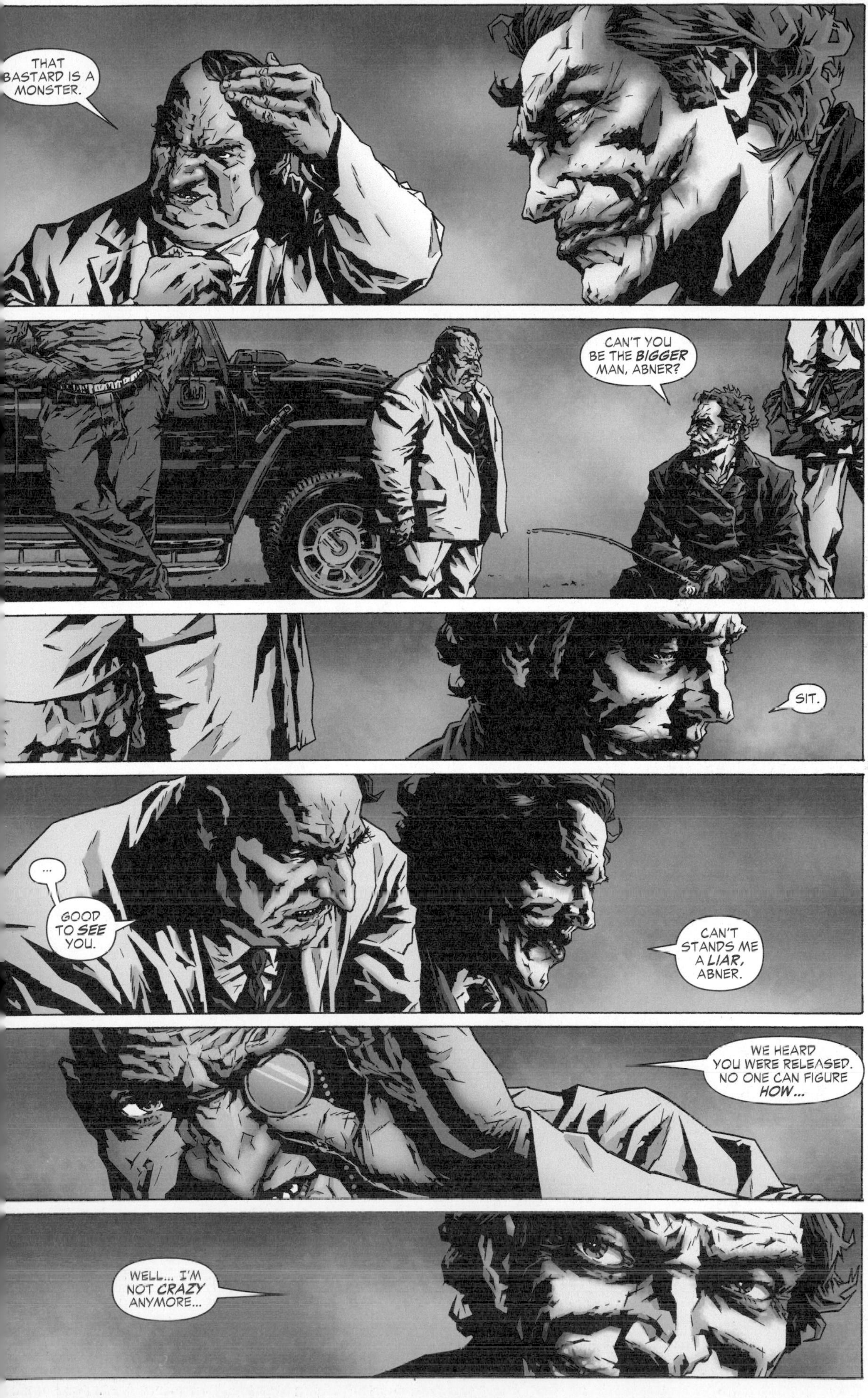
THAT BASTARD IS A MONSTER.
CAN'T YOU BE THE BIGGER MAN, ABNER?
SIT.
...
GOOD TO SEE YOU.
CAN'T STANDS ME A LIAR, ABNER.
WE HEARD YOU WERE RELEASED. NO ONE CAN FIGURE HOW...
WELL... I'M NOT CRAZY ANYMORE...

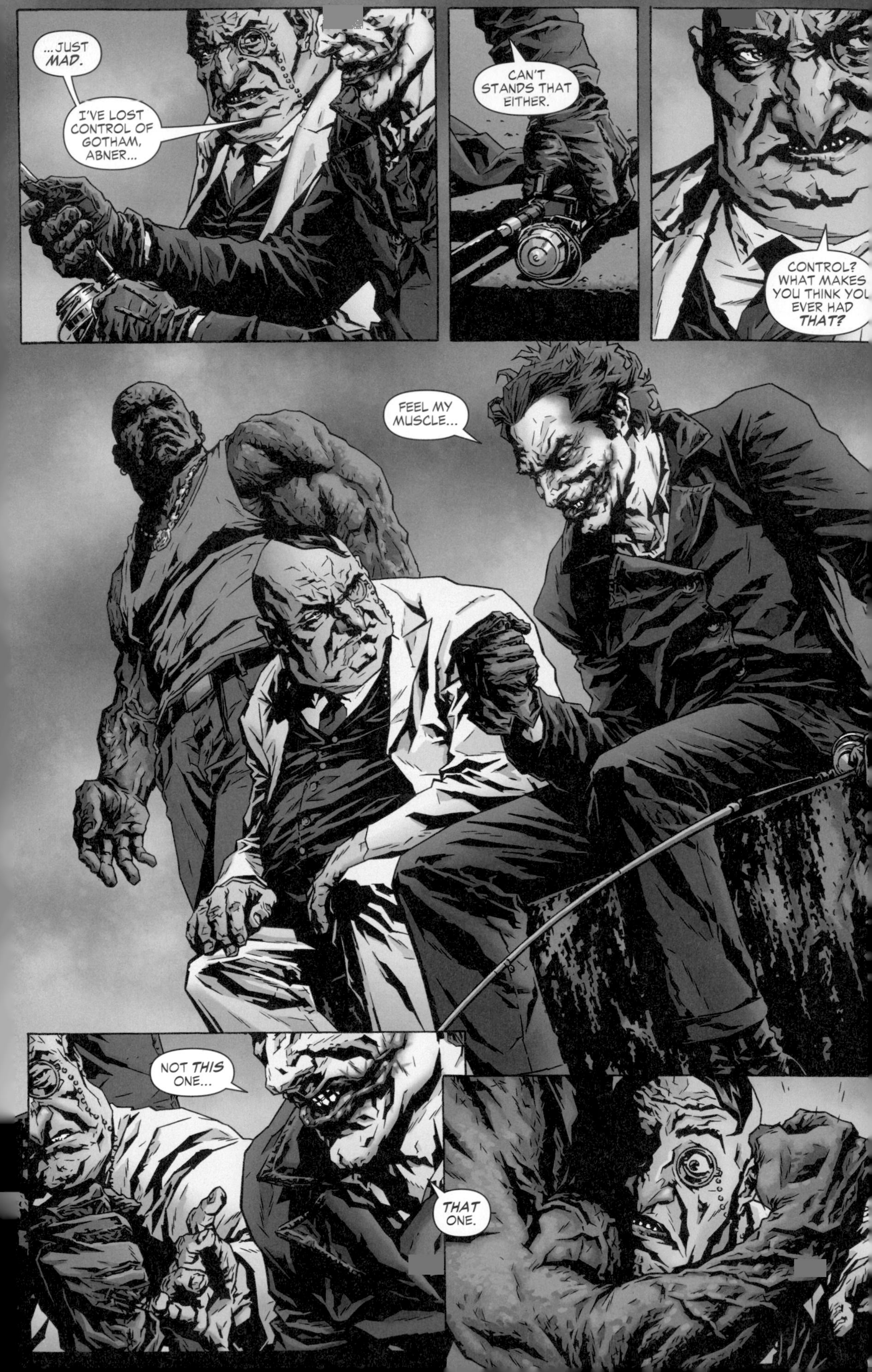
...JUST MAD.
I'VE LOST CONTROL OF GOTHAM, ABNER...
CAN'T STANDS THAT EITHER.
CONTROL? WHAT MAKES YOU THINK YOU EVER HAD THAT?
FEEL MY MUSCLE...
NOT THIS ONE...
THAT ONE.

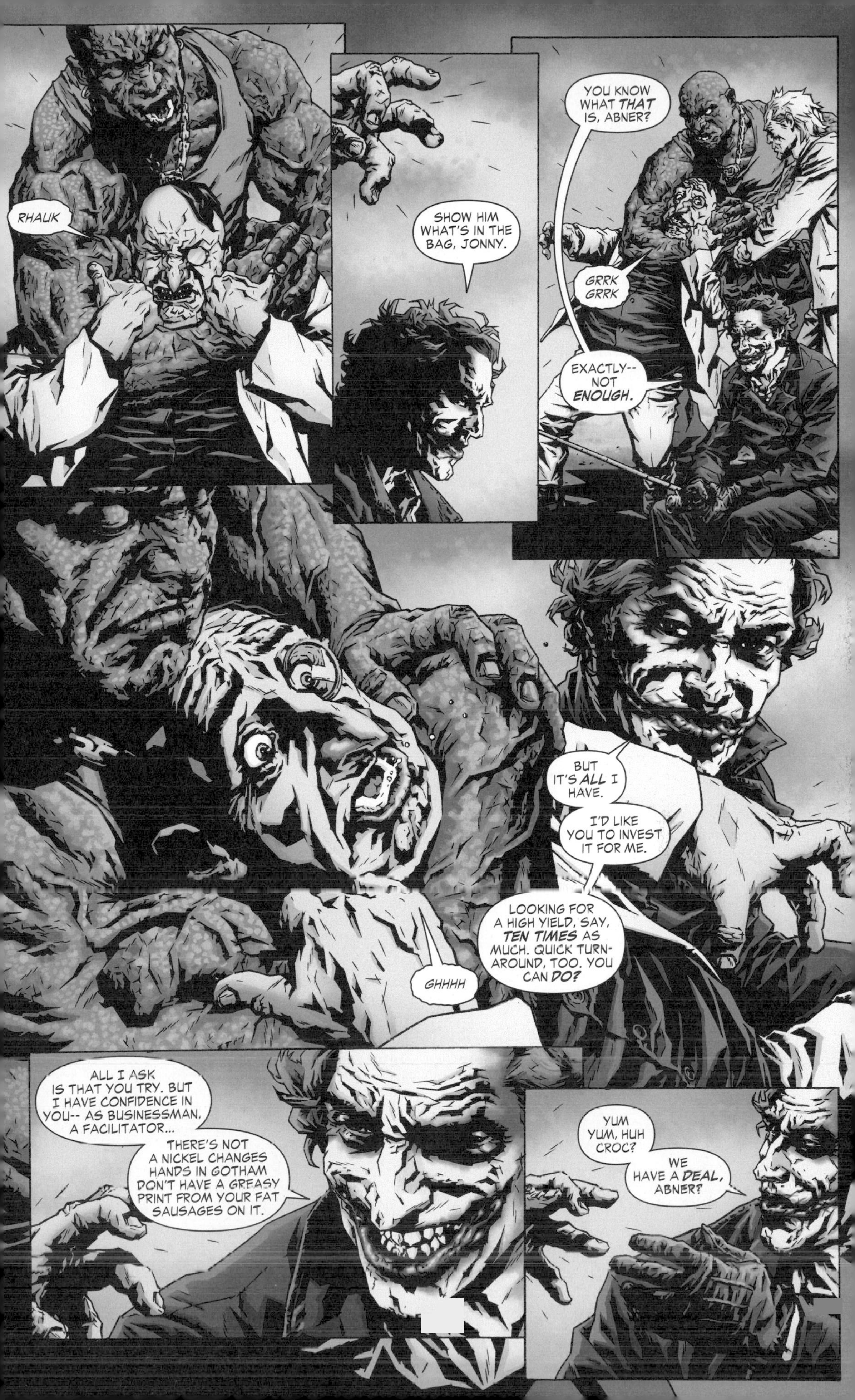
RHAUK
SHOW HIM WHAT'S IN THE BAG, JONNY.
YOU KNOW WHAT THAT IS, ABNER?
GRRK GRRK
EXACTLY-- NOT ENOUGH.
BUT IT'S ALL I HAVE.
I'D LIKE YOU TO INVEST IT FOR ME.
LOOKING FOR A HIGH YIELD, SAY, TEN TIMES AS MUCH. QUICK TURN-AROUND, TOO. YOU CAN DO?
GHHHH
ALL I ASK IS THAT YOU TRY. BUT I HAVE CONFIDENCE IN YOU-- AS BUSINESSMAN, A FACILITATOR...
THERE'S NOT A NICKEL CHANGES HANDS IN GOTHAM DON'T HAVE A GREASY PRINT FROM YOUR FAT SAUSAGES ON IT.
YUM YUM, HUH CROC?
WE HAVE A DEAL, ABNER?

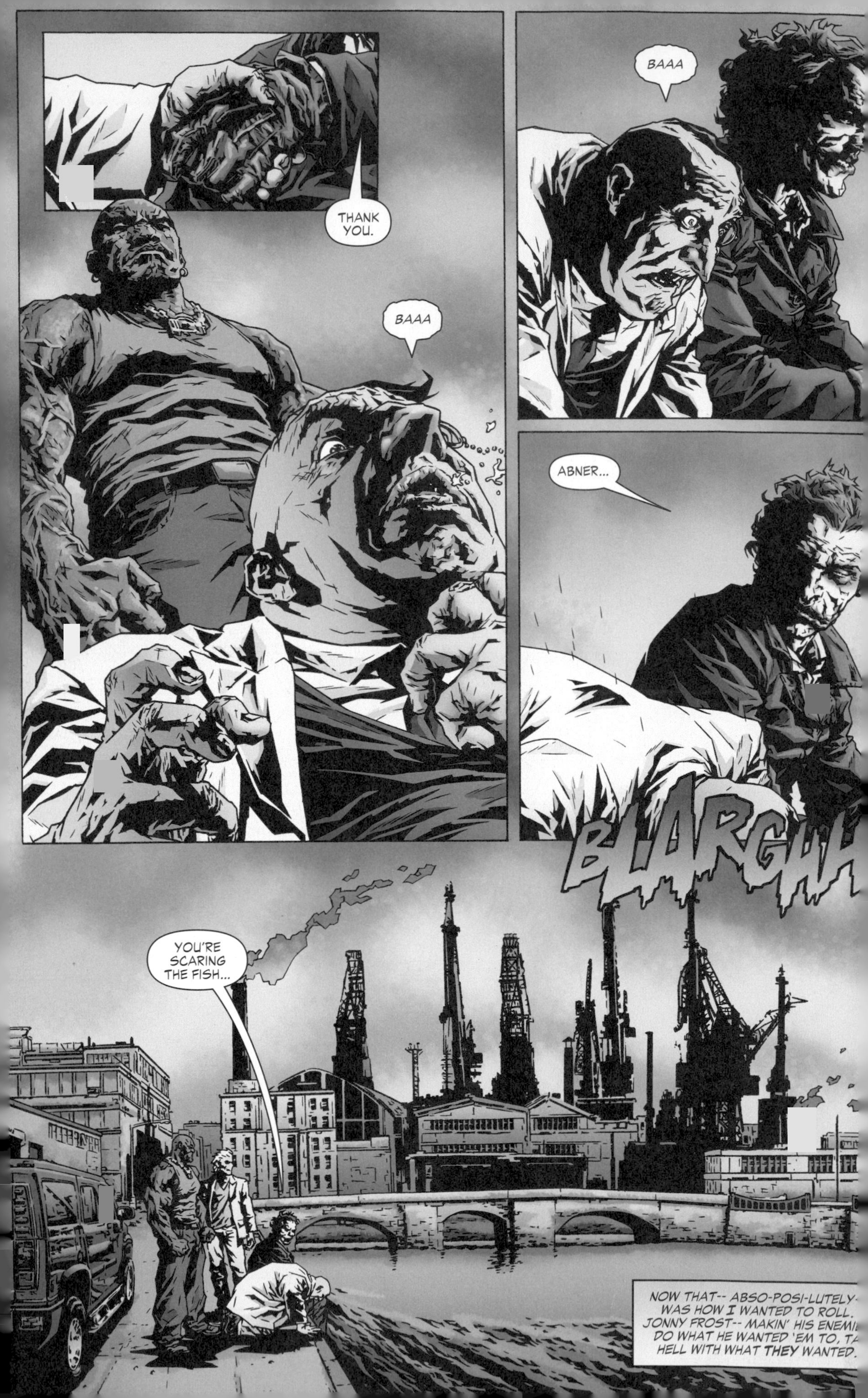
THANK YOU.
BAAA
BAAA
ABNER...
BLARGH
YOU'RE SCARING THE FISH...
NOW THAT-- ABSO-POSI-LUTELY-- WAS HOW I WANTED TO ROLL. JONNY FROST-- MAKIN' HIS ENEMI DO WHAT HE WANTED 'EM TO, TA HELL WITH WHAT THEY WANTED.

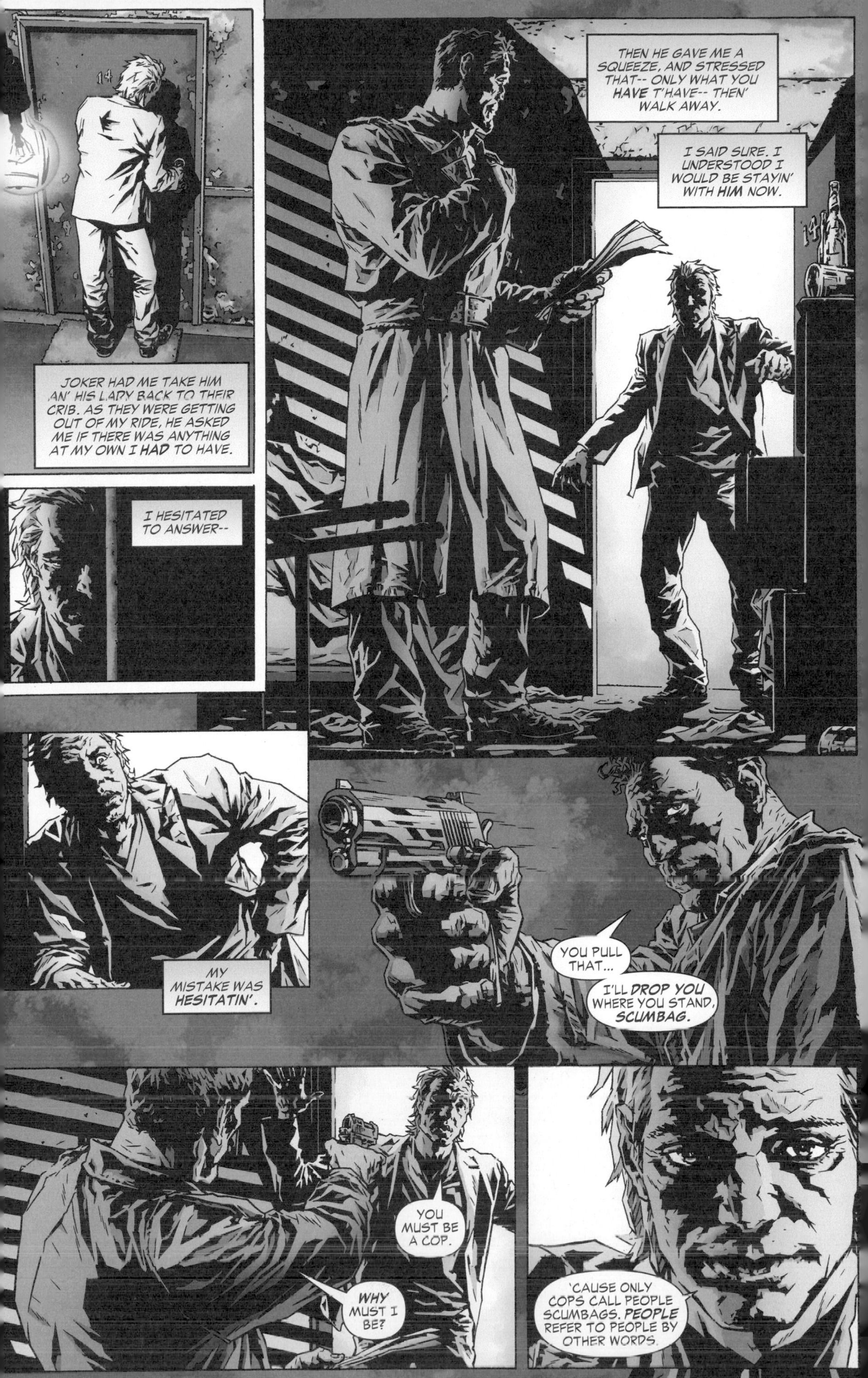
JOKER HAD ME TAKE HIM AN' HIS LADY BACK TO THEIR CRIB. AS THEY WERE GETTING OUT OF MY RIDE, HE ASKED ME IF THERE WAS ANYTHING AT MY OWN I HAD TO HAVE.
I HESITATED TO ANSWER--
THEN HE GAVE ME A SQUEEZE, AND STRESSED THAT-- ONLY WHAT YOU HAVE T'HAVE-- THEN' WALK AWAY.
I SAID SURE. I UNDERSTOOD I WOULD BE STAYIN' WITH HIM NOW.
MY MISTAKE WAS HESITATIN'.
YOU PULL THAT...
I'LL DROP YOU WHERE YOU STAND, SCUMBAG.
YOU MUST BE A COP.
WHY MUST I BE?
'CAUSE ONLY COPS CALL PEOPLE SCUMBAGS. PEOPLE REFER TO PEOPLE BY OTHER WORDS.

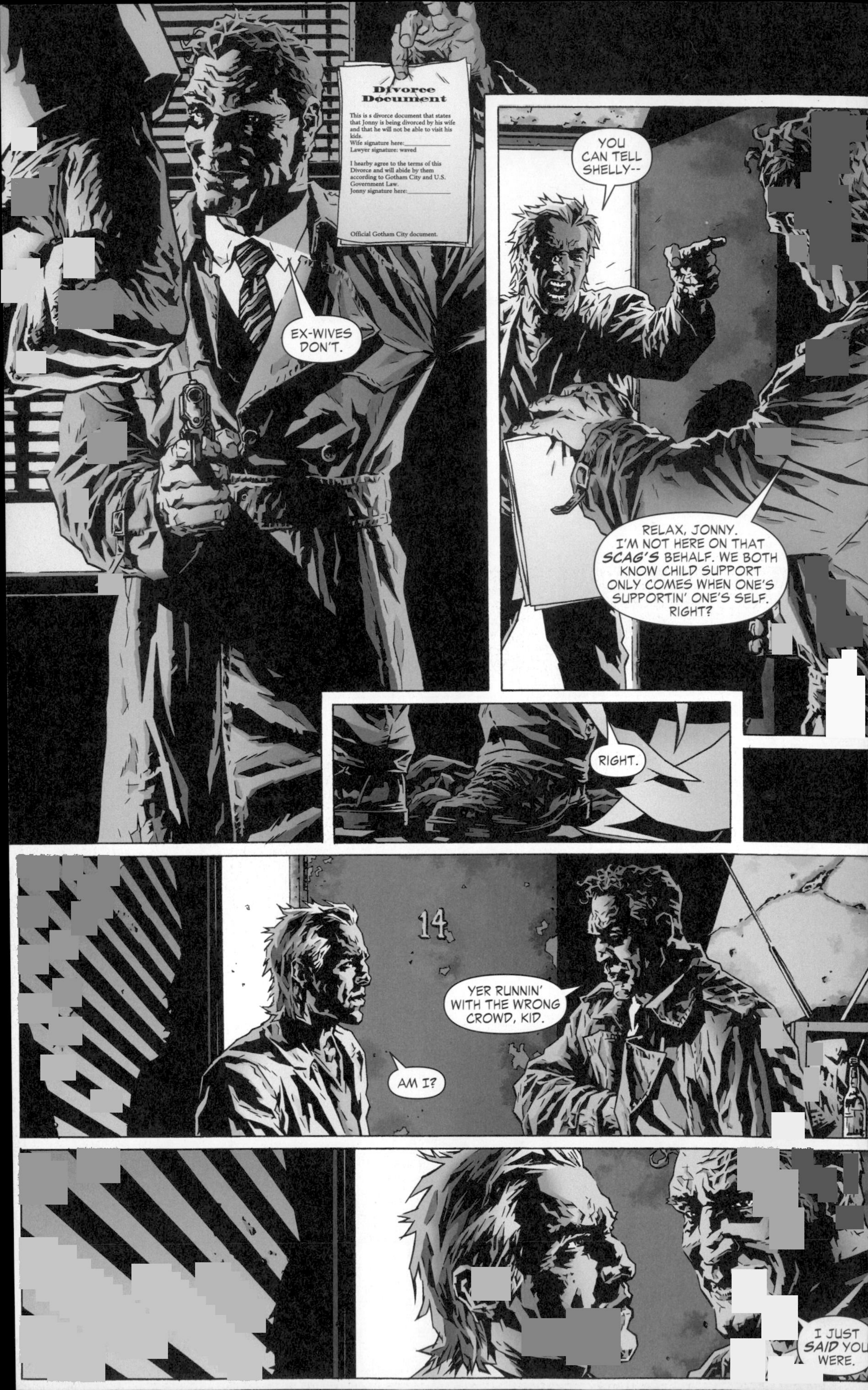
Divorce Document
This is s divorce document that states that Jonny is being divorced by his wife and that he will not be able to visit his kids.
Wife signature here:____________
Lawyer signature: waved
I hearby agree to the terms of this Divorce and will abide by them according to Gotham City and U.S. Government Law.
Jonny signature here:____________
Official Gotham City document.
EX-WIVES DON'T.
YOU CAN TELL SHELLY--
RELAX, JONNY. I'M NOT HERE ON THAT SCAG'S BEHALF. WE BOTH KNOW CHILD SUPPORT ONLY COMES WHEN ONE'S SUPPORTIN' ONE'S SELF. RIGHT?
RIGHT.
14
YER RUNNIN' WITH THE WRONG CROWD, KID.
AM I?
I JUST SAID YOU WERE.

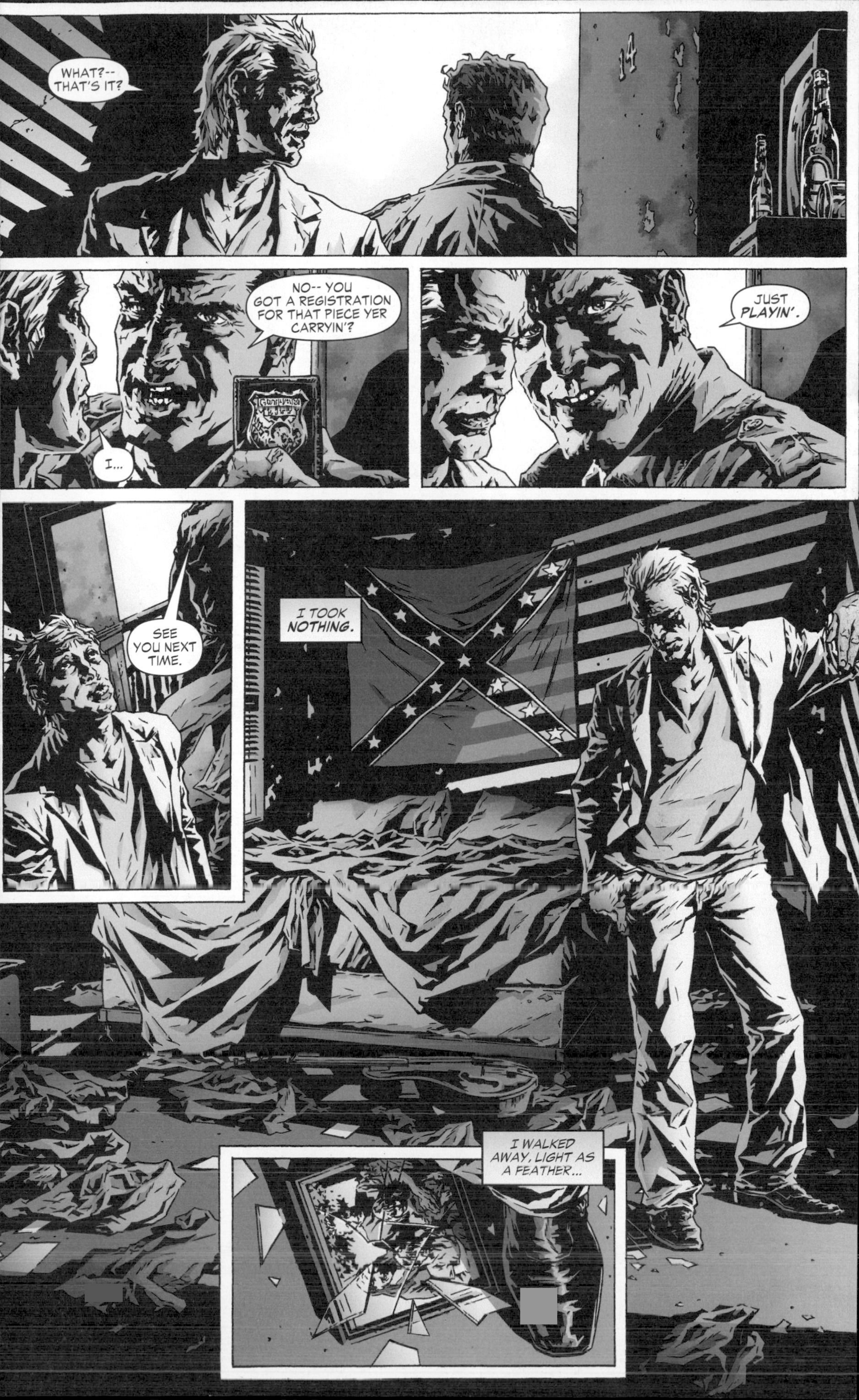
WHAT?-- THAT'S IT?
NO-- YOU GOT A REGISTRATION FOR THAT PIECE YER CARRYIN'?
I...
JUST PLAYIN'.
SEE YOU NEXT TIME.
I TOOK NOTHING.
I WALKED AWAY, LIGHT AS A FEATHER...

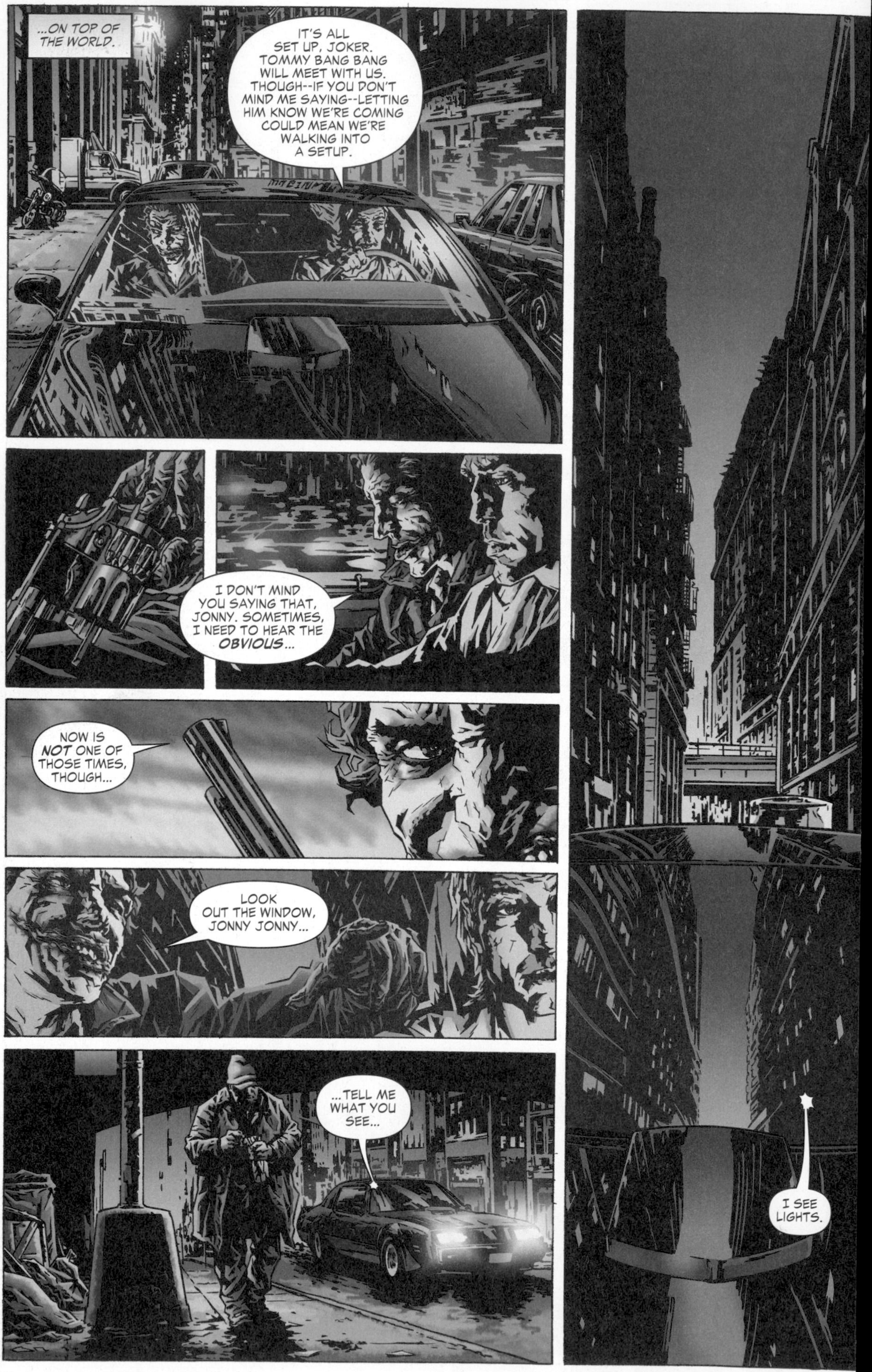
...ON TOP OF THE WORLD.
IT'S ALL SET UP, JOKER. TOMMY BANG BANG WILL MEET WITH US. THOUGH--IF YOU DON'T MIND ME SAYING--LETTING HIM KNOW WE'RE COMING COULD MEAN WE'RE WALKING INTO A SETUP.
I DON'T MIND YOU SAYING THAT, JONNY. SOMETIMES, I NEED TO HEAR THE OBVIOUS...
NOW IS NOT ONE OF THOSE TIMES, THOUGH...
LOOK OUT THE WINDOW, JONNY JONNY...
...TELL ME WHAT YOU SEE...
I SEE LIGHTS.

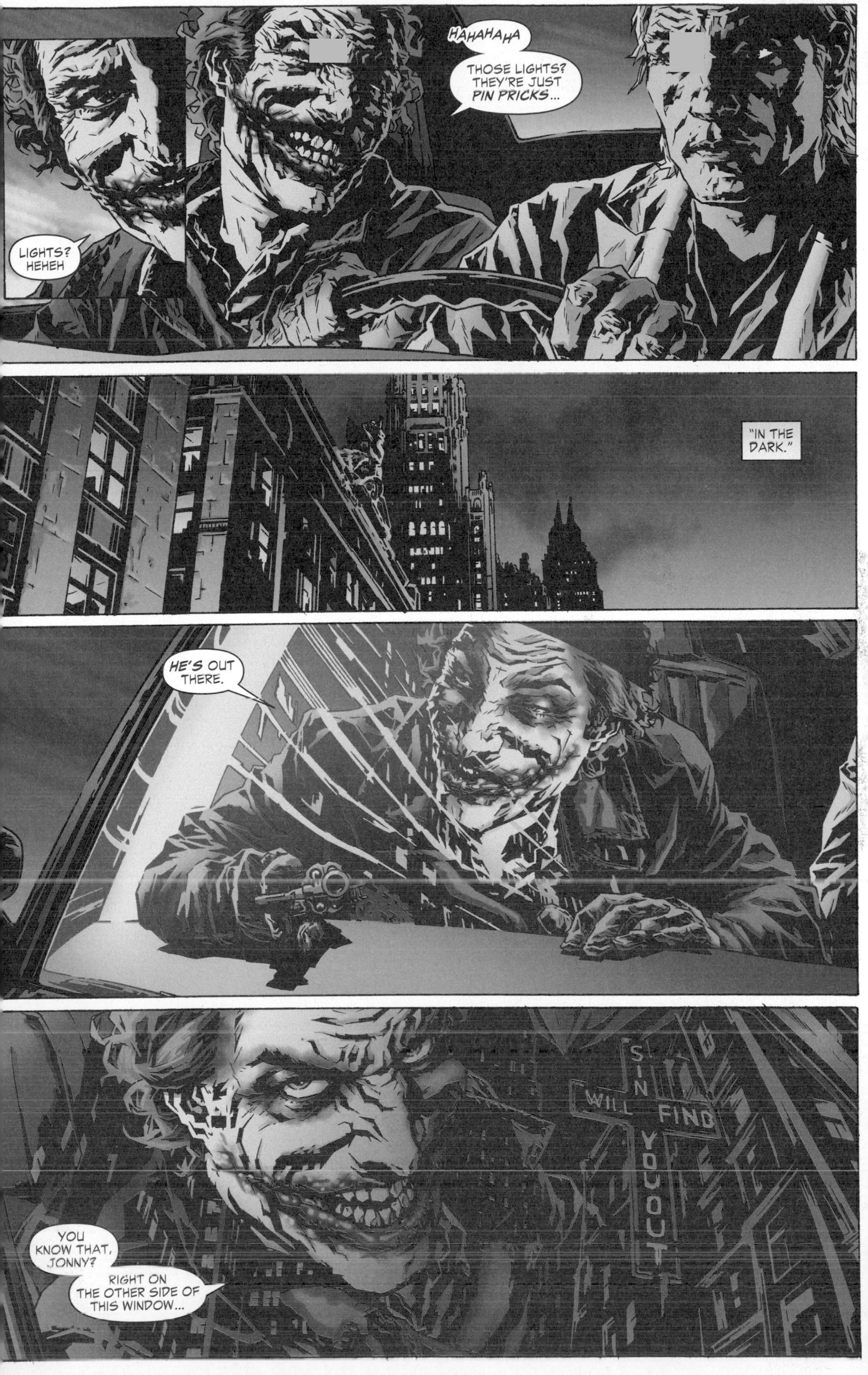
LIGHTS? HEHEH
HAHAHAHA
THOSE LIGHTS? THEY'RE JUST PIN PRICKS...
"IN THE DARK."
HE'S OUT THERE.
SIN WILL FIND YOU OUT
YOU KNOW THAT, JONNY?
RIGHT ON THE OTHER SIDE OF THIS WINDOW...

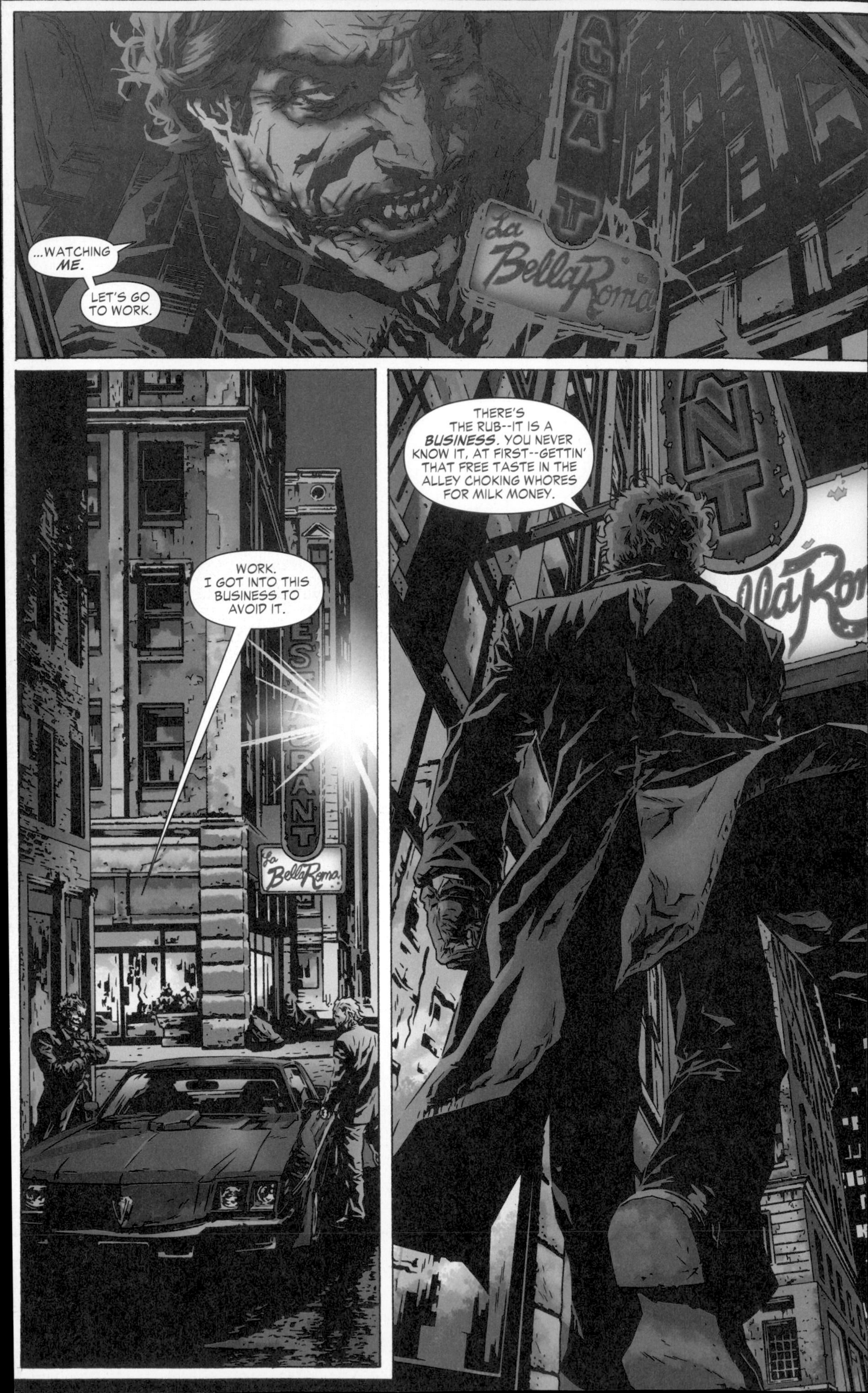
...WATCHING ME.
LET'S GO TO WORK.
La BellaRoma
WORK. I GOT INTO THIS BUSINESS TO AVOID IT.
THERE'S THE RUB--IT IS A BUSINESS. YOU NEVER KNOW IT, AT FIRST--GETTIN' THAT FREE TASTE IN THE ALLEY CHOKING WHORES FOR MILK MONEY.

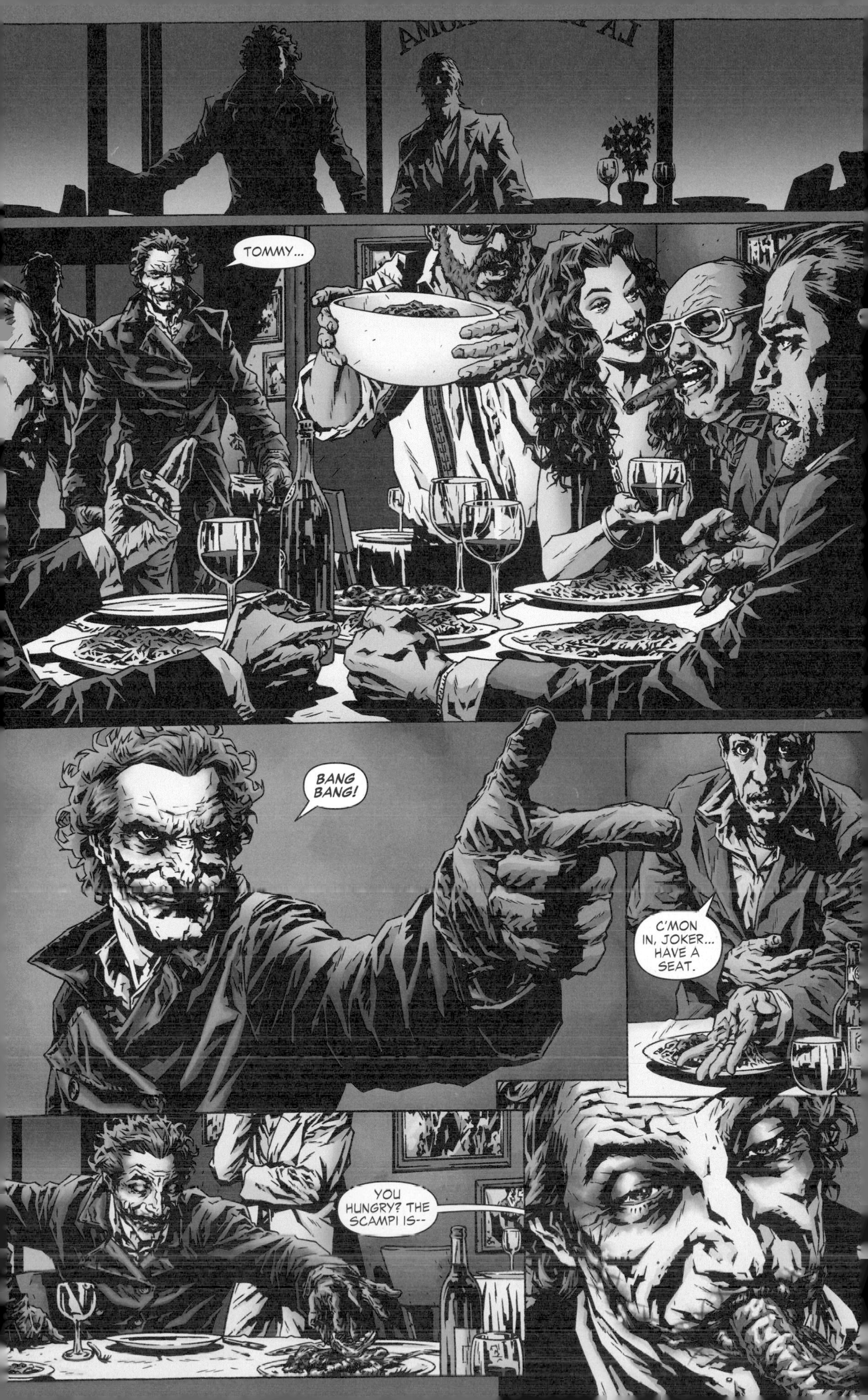
TOMMY...
BANG BANG!
C'MON IN, JOKER... HAVE A SEAT.
YOU HUNGRY? THE SCAMPI IS--

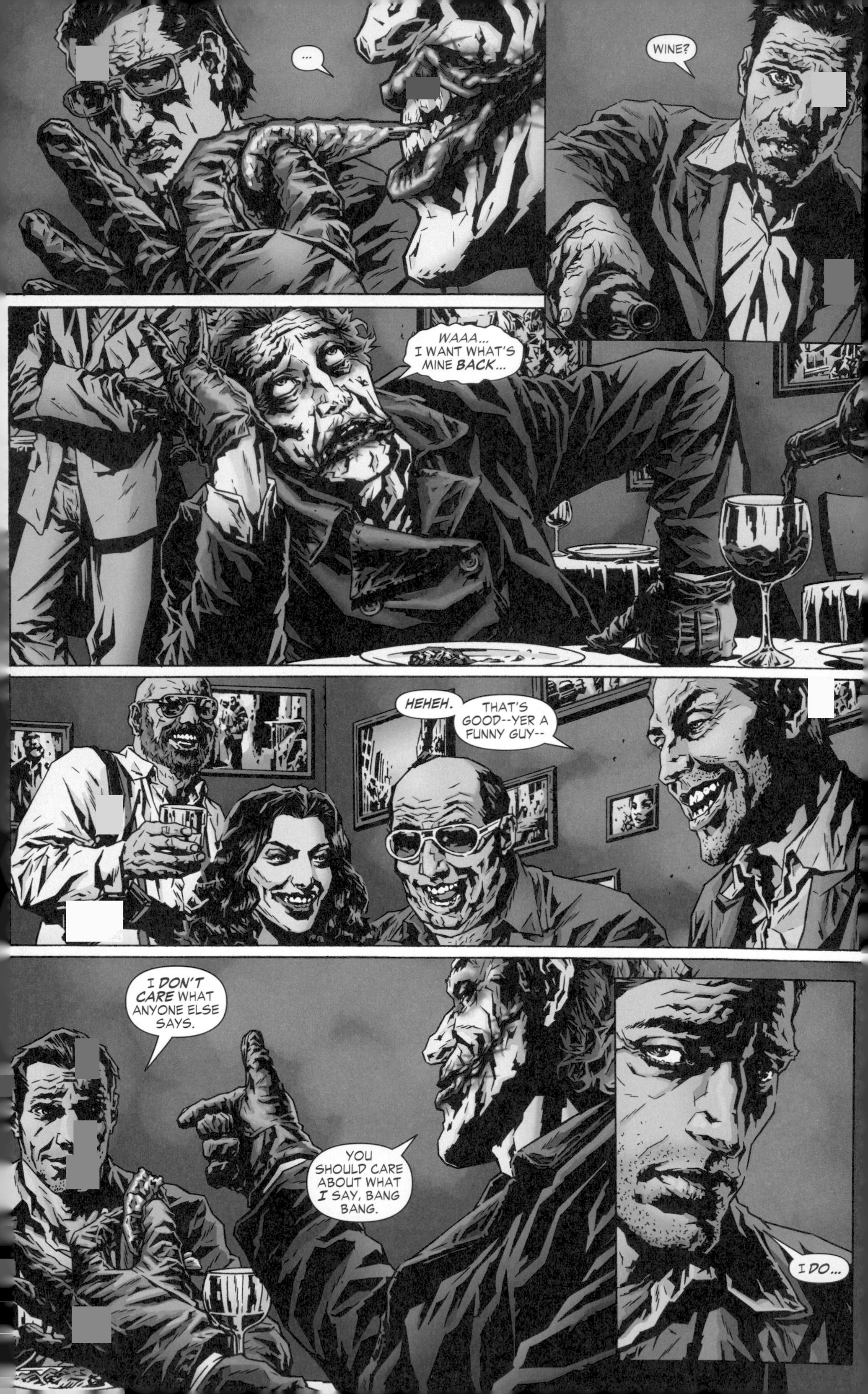
...
WINE?
WAAA... I WANT WHAT'S MINE BACK...
HEHEH.
THAT'S GOOD--YER A FUNNY GUY--
I DON'T CARE WHAT ANYONE ELSE SAYS.
YOU SHOULD CARE ABOUT WHAT I SAY, BANG BANG.
I DO...

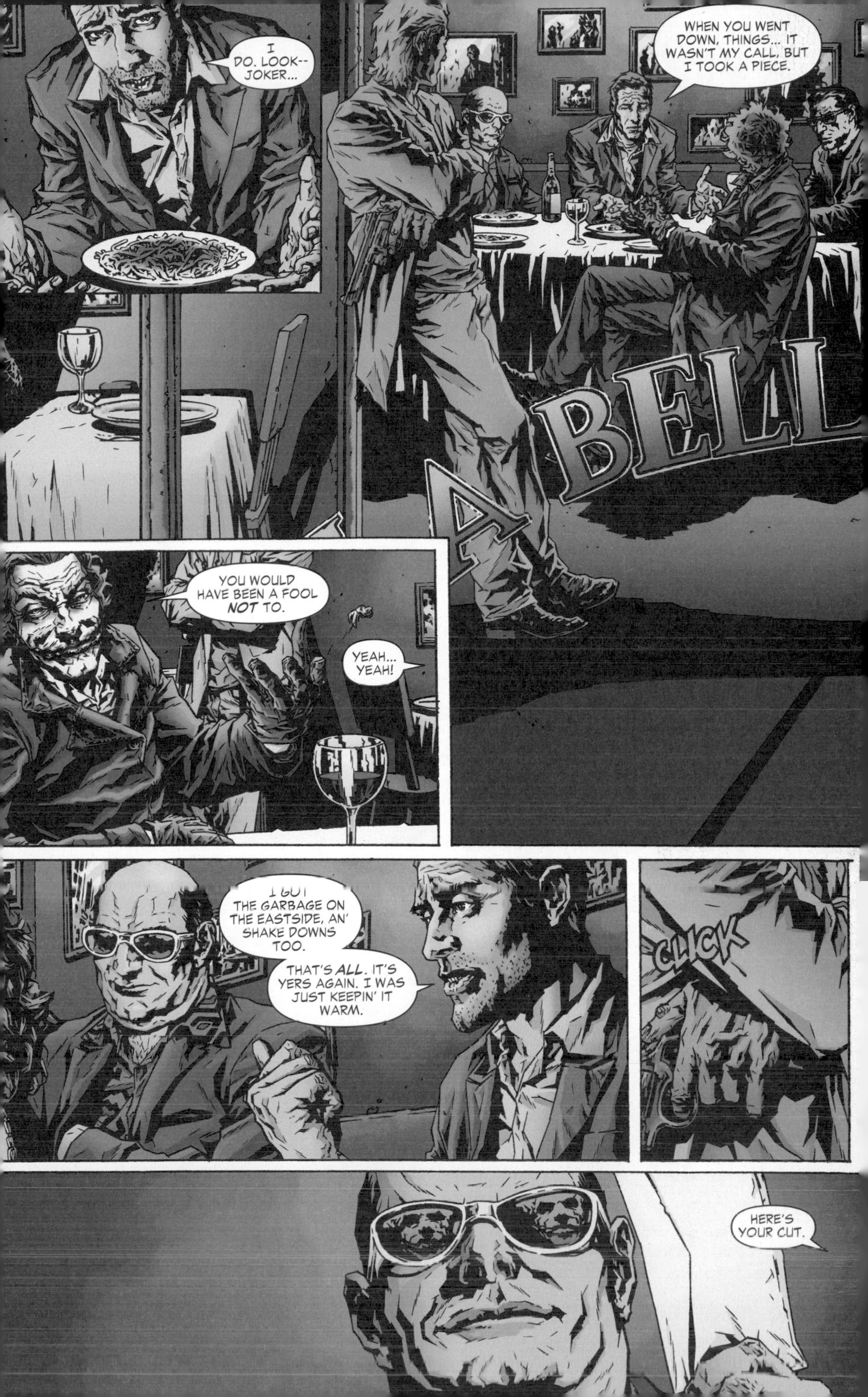
I DO. LOOK-- JOKER...
WHEN YOU WENT DOWN, THINGS... IT WASN'T MY CALL, BUT I TOOK A PIECE.
ABELL
YOU WOULD HAVE BEEN A FOOL *NOT* TO.
YEAH... YEAH!
I GOT THE GARBAGE ON THE EASTSIDE, AN' SHAKE DOWNS TOO.
THAT'S *ALL*. IT'S YERS AGAIN. I WAS JUST KEEPIN' IT WARM.
CLICK
HERE'S YOUR CUT.

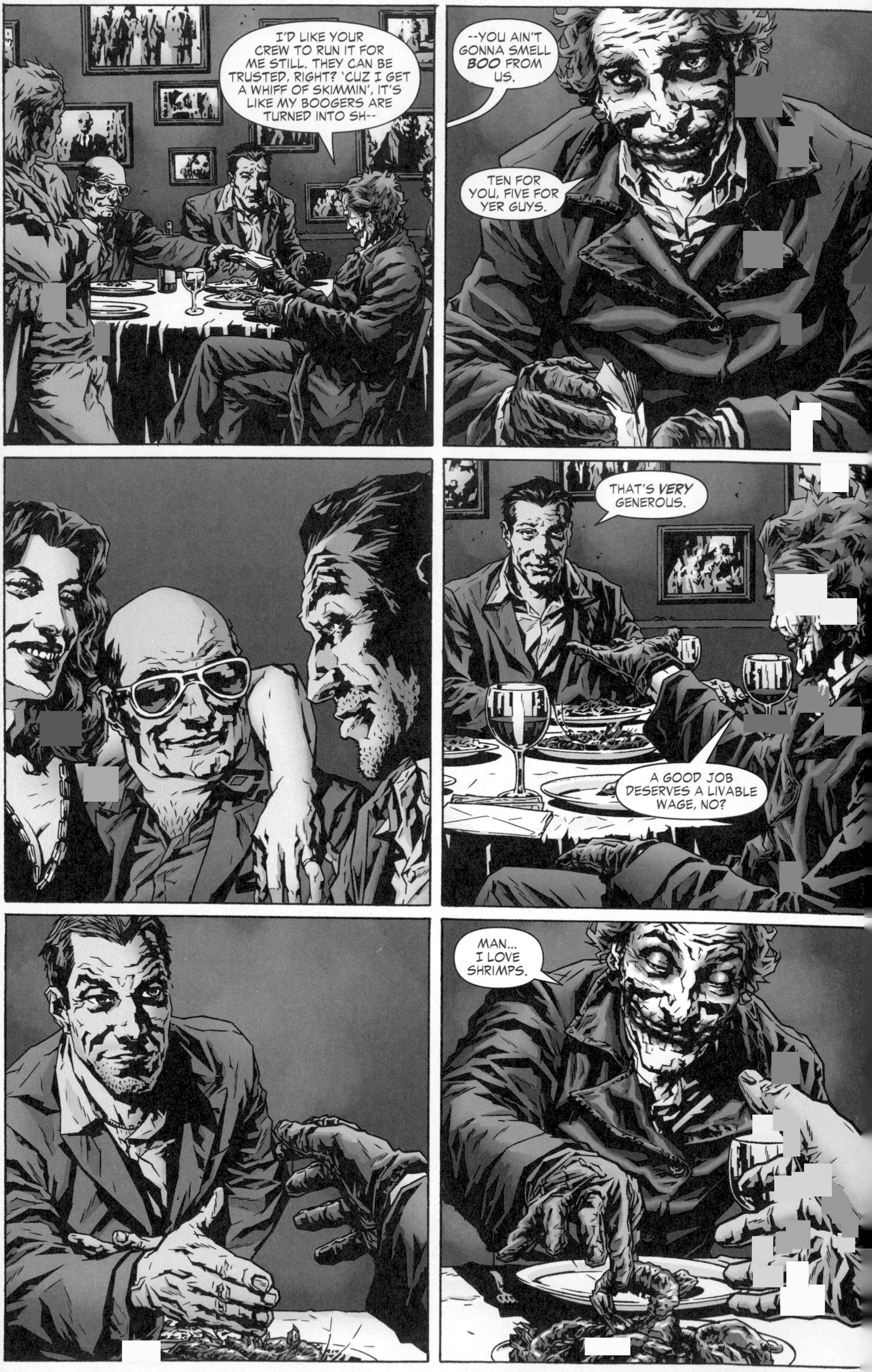
I'D LIKE YOUR CREW TO RUN IT FOR ME STILL. THEY CAN BE TRUSTED, RIGHT? 'CUZ I GET A WHIFF OF SKIMMIN', IT'S LIKE MY BOOGERS ARE TURNED INTO SH--
--YOU AIN'T GONNA SMELL BOO FROM US.
TEN FOR YOU, FIVE FOR YER GUYS.
THAT'S VERY GENEROUS.
A GOOD JOB DESERVES A LIVABLE WAGE, NO?
MAN... I LOVE SHRIMPS.

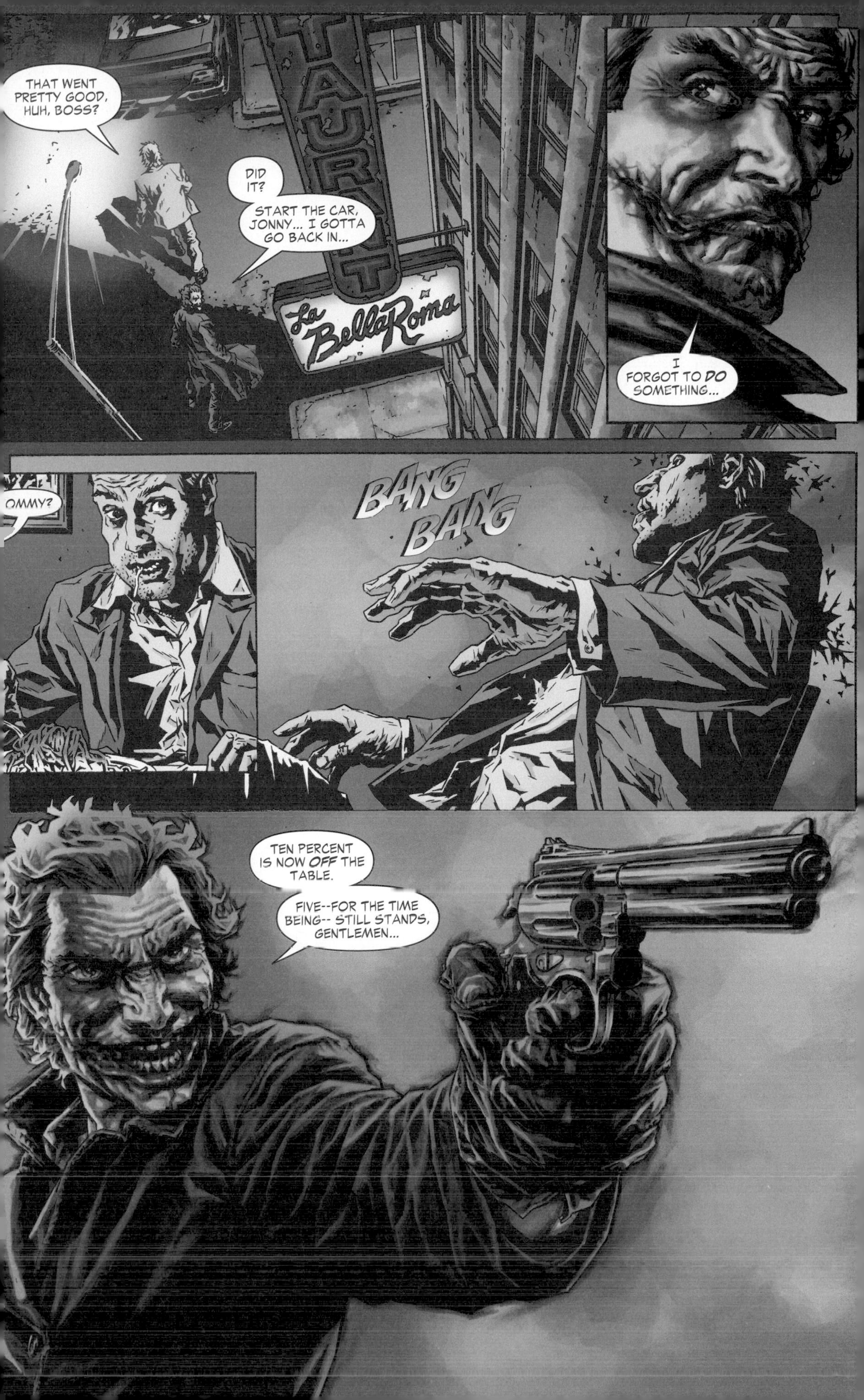
THAT WENT PRETTY GOOD, HUH, BOSS?
DID IT?
START THE CAR, JONNY... I GOTTA GO BACK IN...
La BellaRoma
I FORGOT TO DO SOMETHING...
OMMY?
BANG BANG
TEN PERCENT IS NOW OFF THE TABLE.
FIVE--FOR THE TIME BEING-- STILL STANDS, GENTLEMEN...

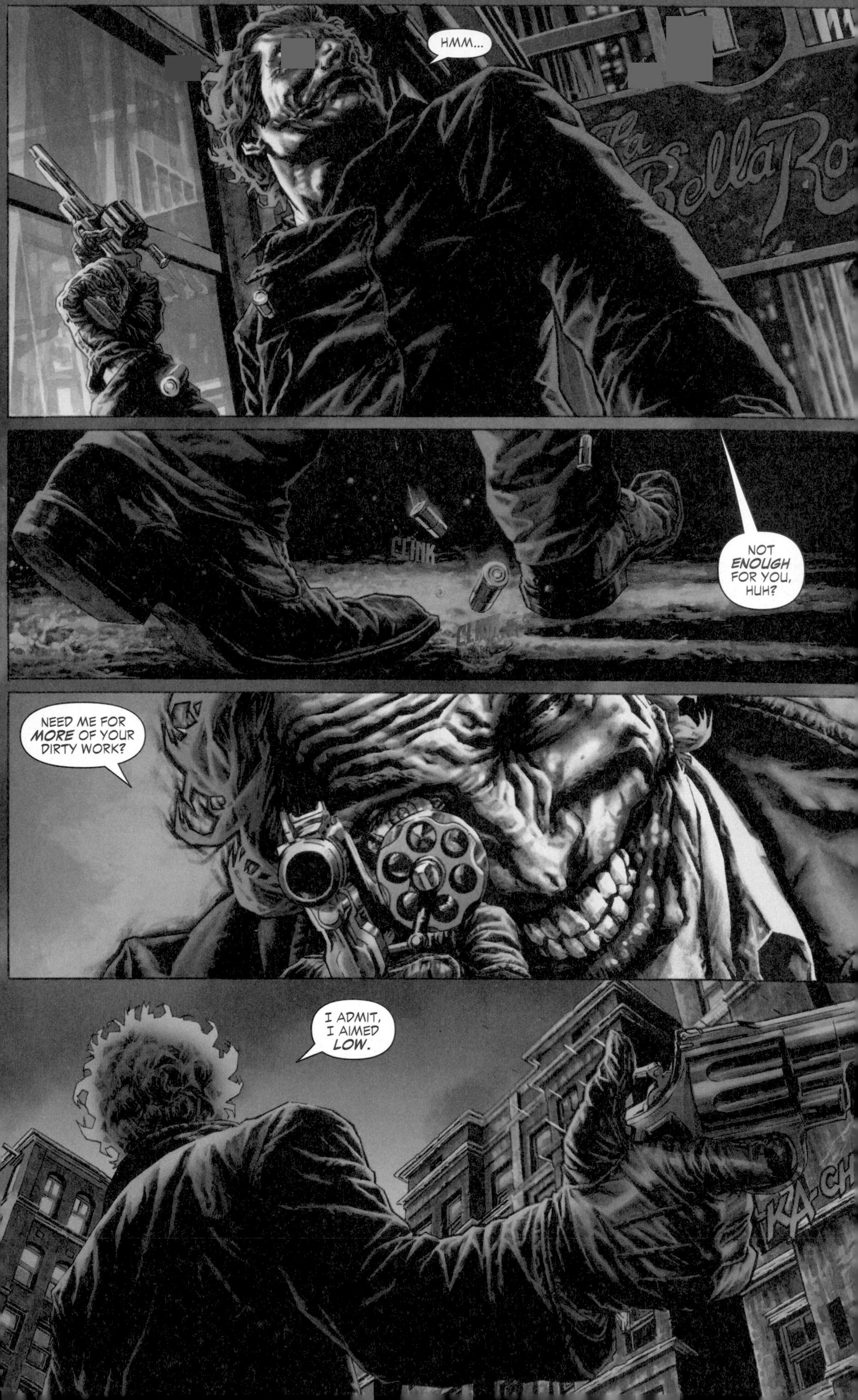
HMM...
NOT ENOUGH FOR YOU, HUH?
CLINK
NEED ME FOR MORE OF YOUR DIRTY WORK?
I ADMIT, I AIMED LOW.

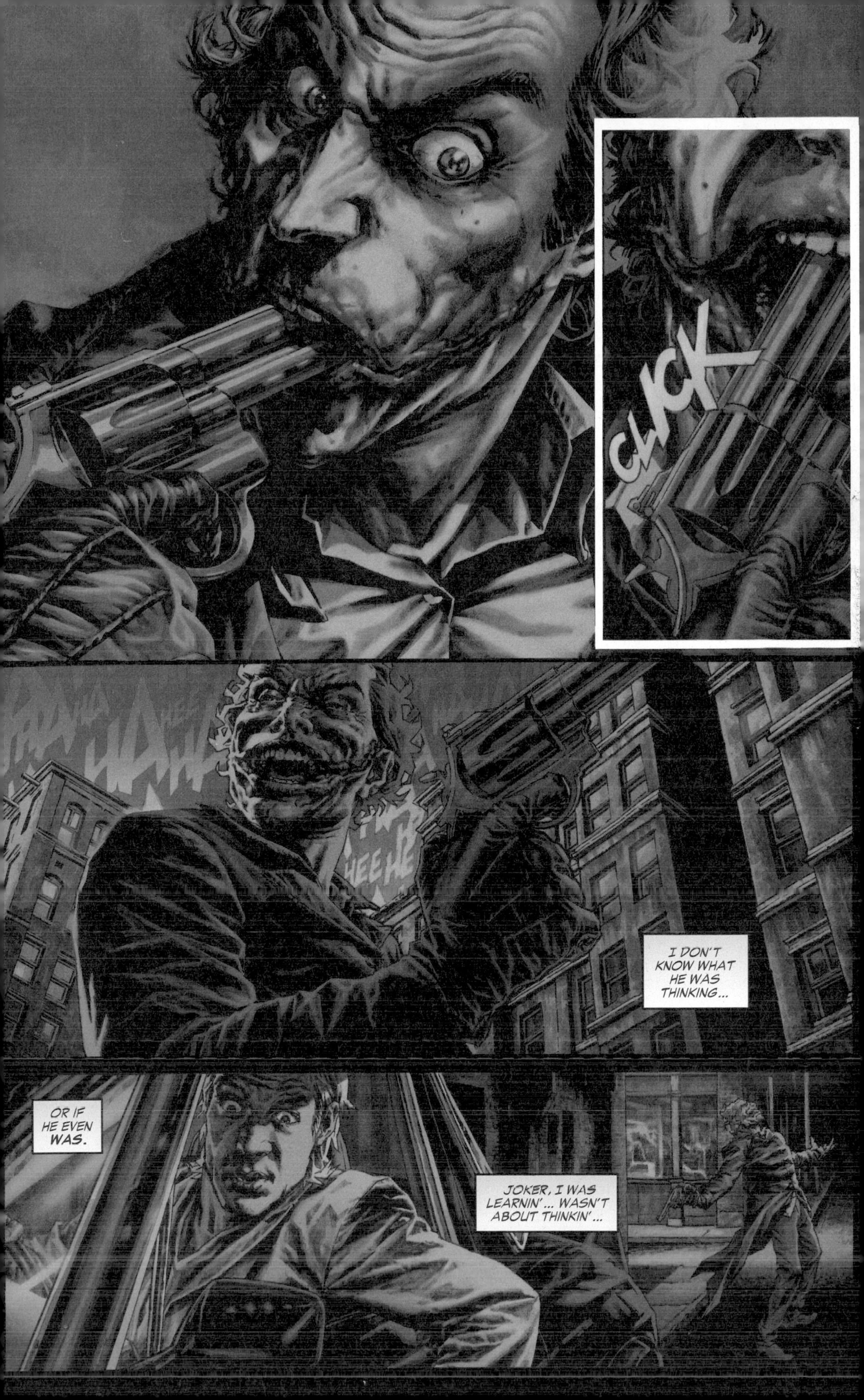
CLICK
I DON'T KNOW WHAT HE WAS THINKING...
OR IF HE EVEN WAS.
JOKER, I WAS LEARNIN'... WASN'T ABOUT THINKIN'...

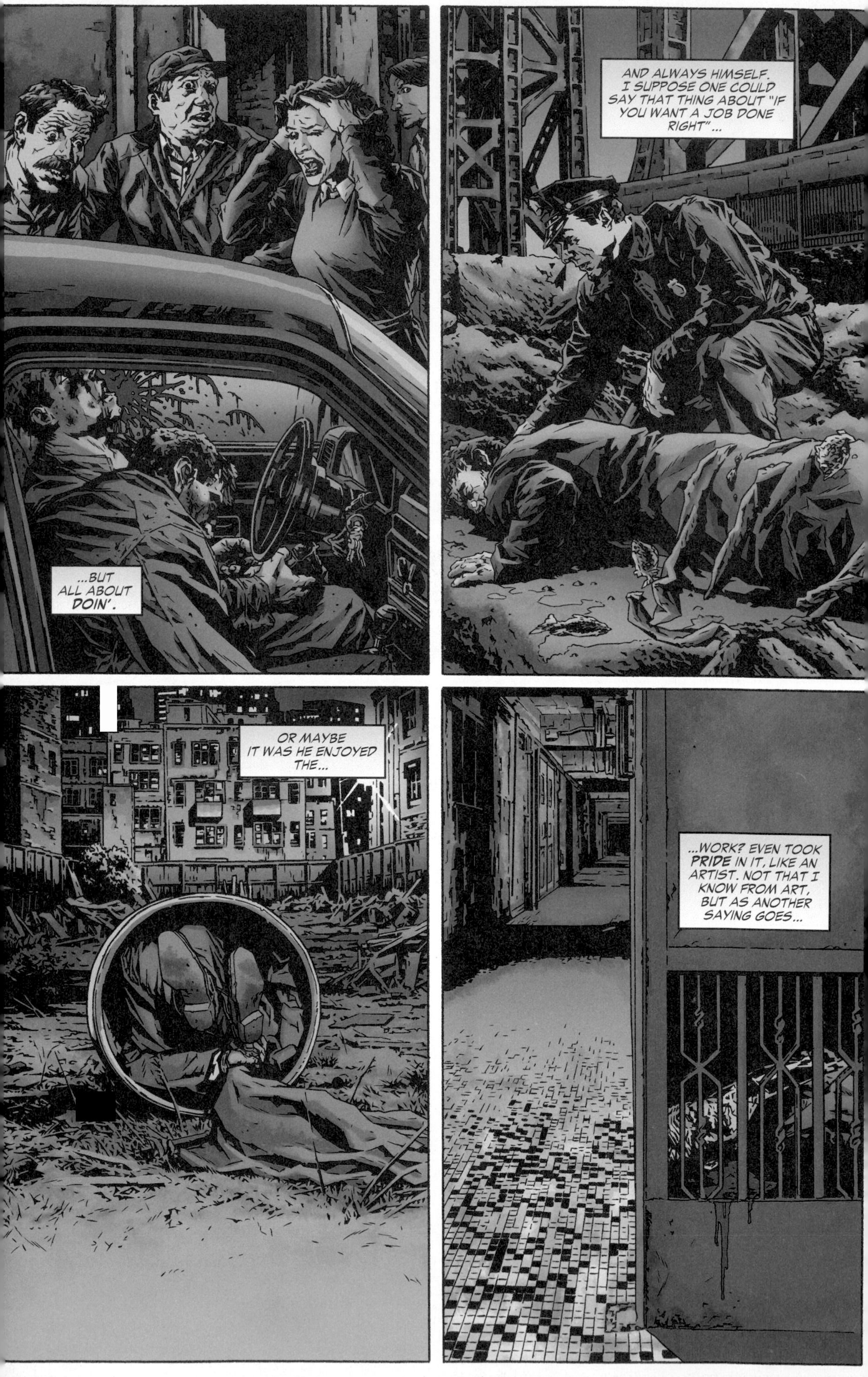
...BUT ALL ABOUT DOIN'.
AND ALWAYS HIMSELF. I SUPPOSE ONE COULD SAY THAT THING ABOUT "IF YOU WANT A JOB DONE RIGHT"...
OR MAYBE IT WAS HE ENJOYED THE...
...WORK? EVEN TOOK PRIDE IN IT, LIKE AN ARTIST. NOT THAT I KNOW FROM ART, BUT AS ANOTHER SAYING GOES...

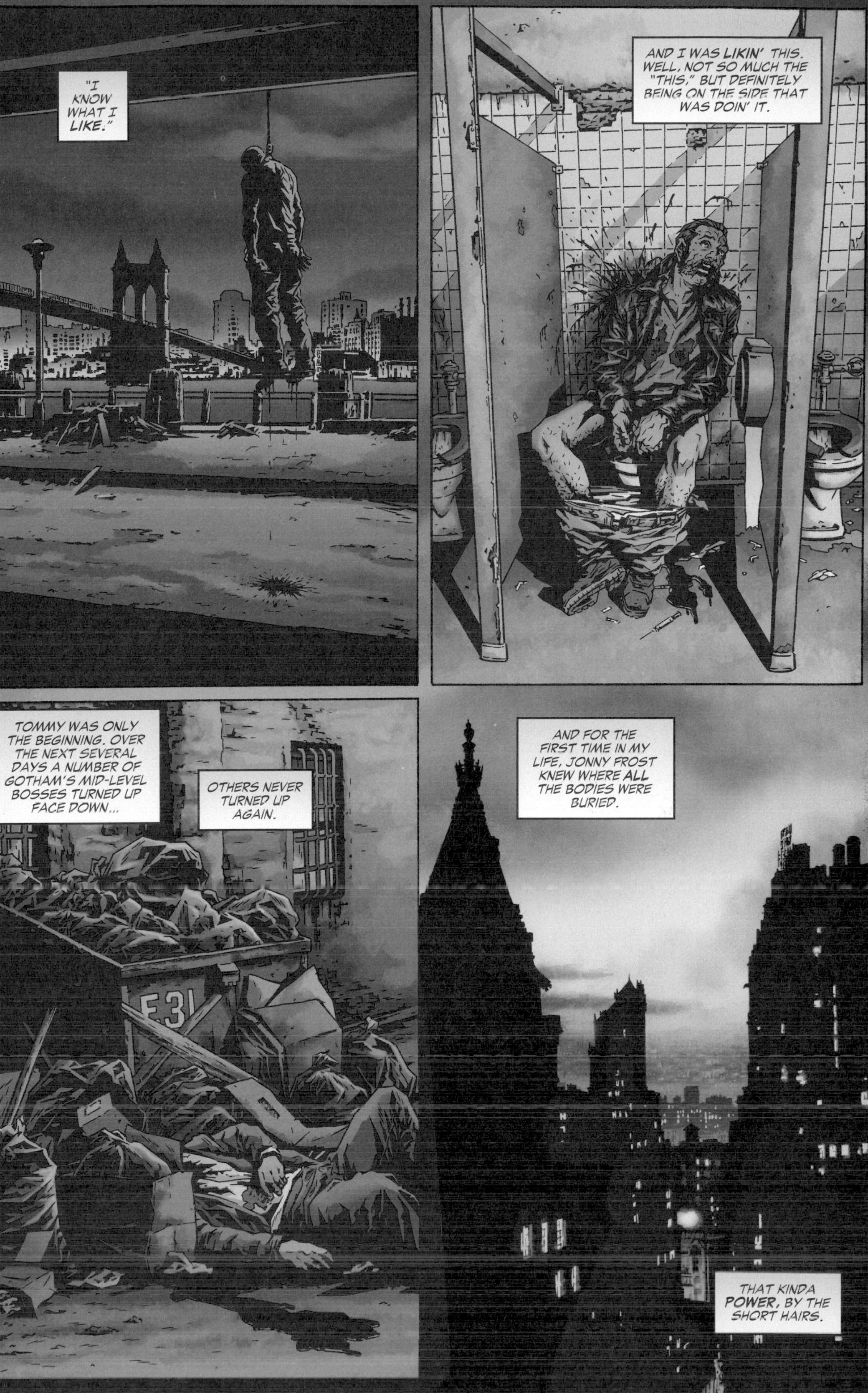
"I KNOW WHAT I LIKE."
AND I WAS LIKIN' THIS. WELL, NOT SO MUCH THE "THIS," BUT DEFINITELY BEING ON THE SIDE THAT WAS DOIN' IT.
TOMMY WAS ONLY THE BEGINNING. OVER THE NEXT SEVERAL DAYS A NUMBER OF GOTHAM'S MID-LEVEL BOSSES TURNED UP FACE DOWN...
OTHERS NEVER TURNED UP AGAIN.
E31
AND FOR THE FIRST TIME IN MY LIFE, JONNY FROST KNEW WHERE ALL THE BODIES WERE BURIED.
THAT KINDA POWER, BY THE SHORT HAIRS.

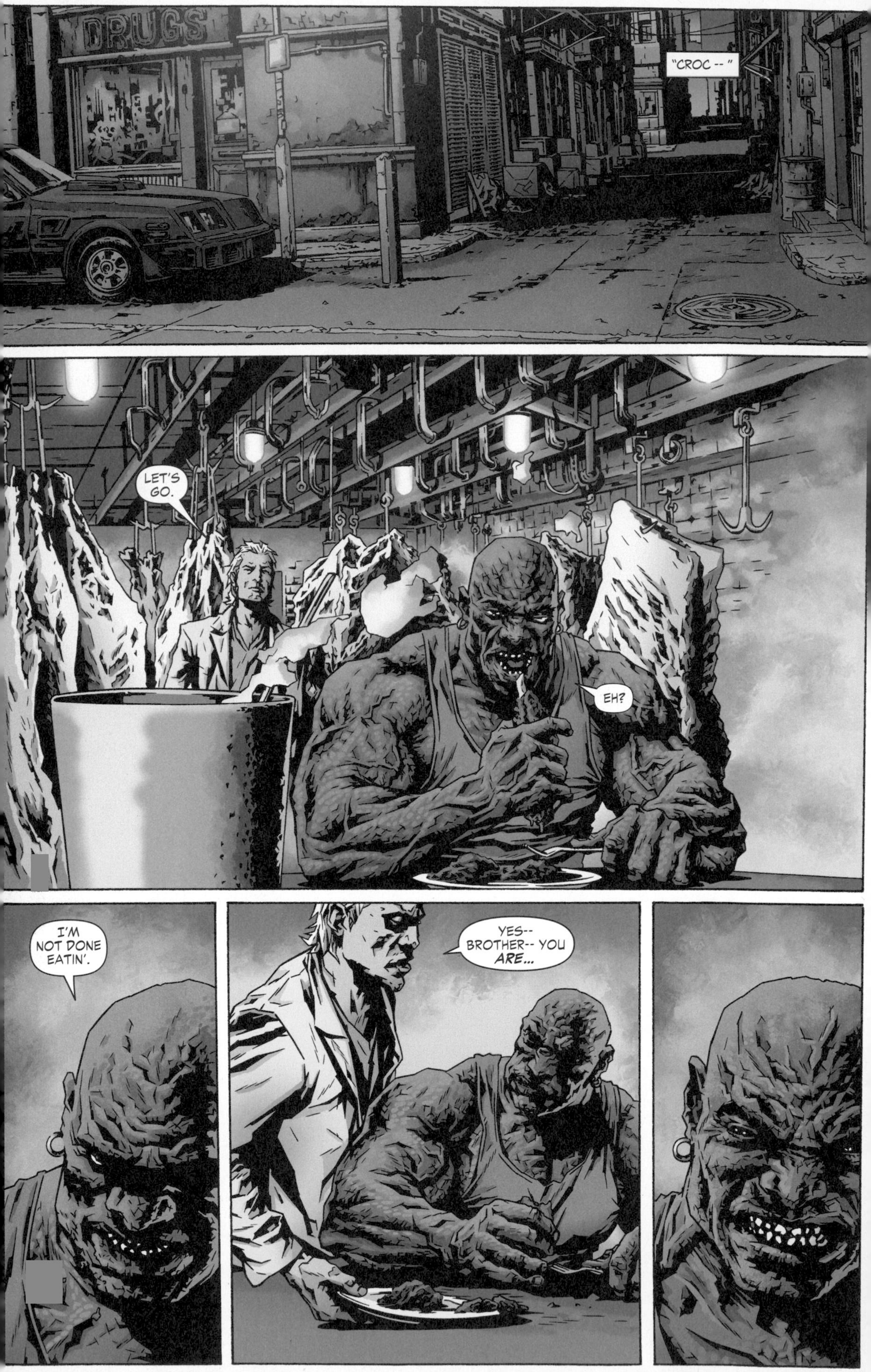
"CROC -- "
LET'S GO.
EH?
I'M NOT DONE EATIN'.
YES-- BROTHER-- YOU ARE...

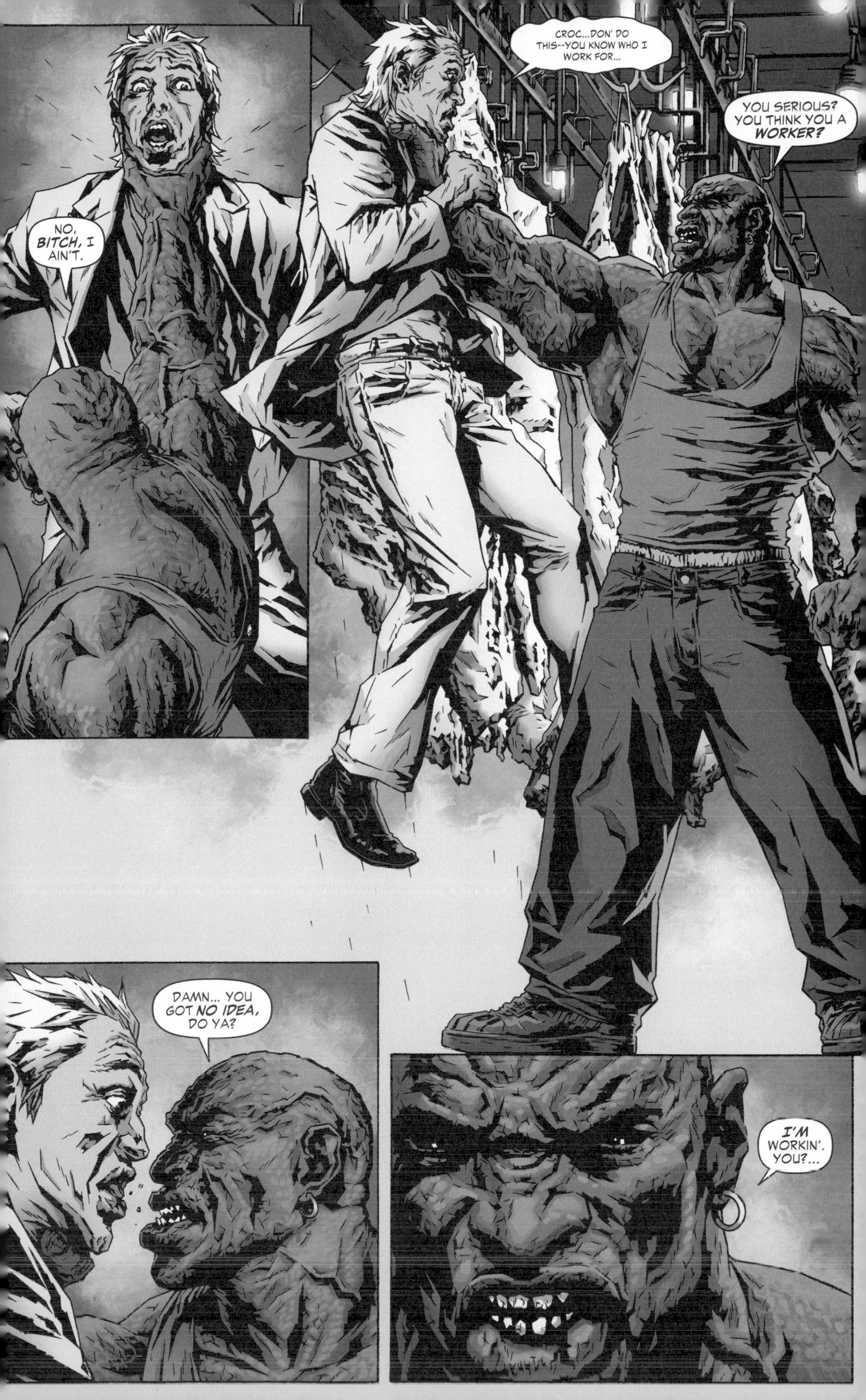
CROC...DON' DO THIS--YOU KNOW WHO I WORK FOR...
YOU SERIOUS? YOU THINK YOU A WORKER?
NO, BITCH, I AIN'T.
DAMN... YOU GOT NO IDEA, DO YA?
I'M WORKIN'. YOU?...

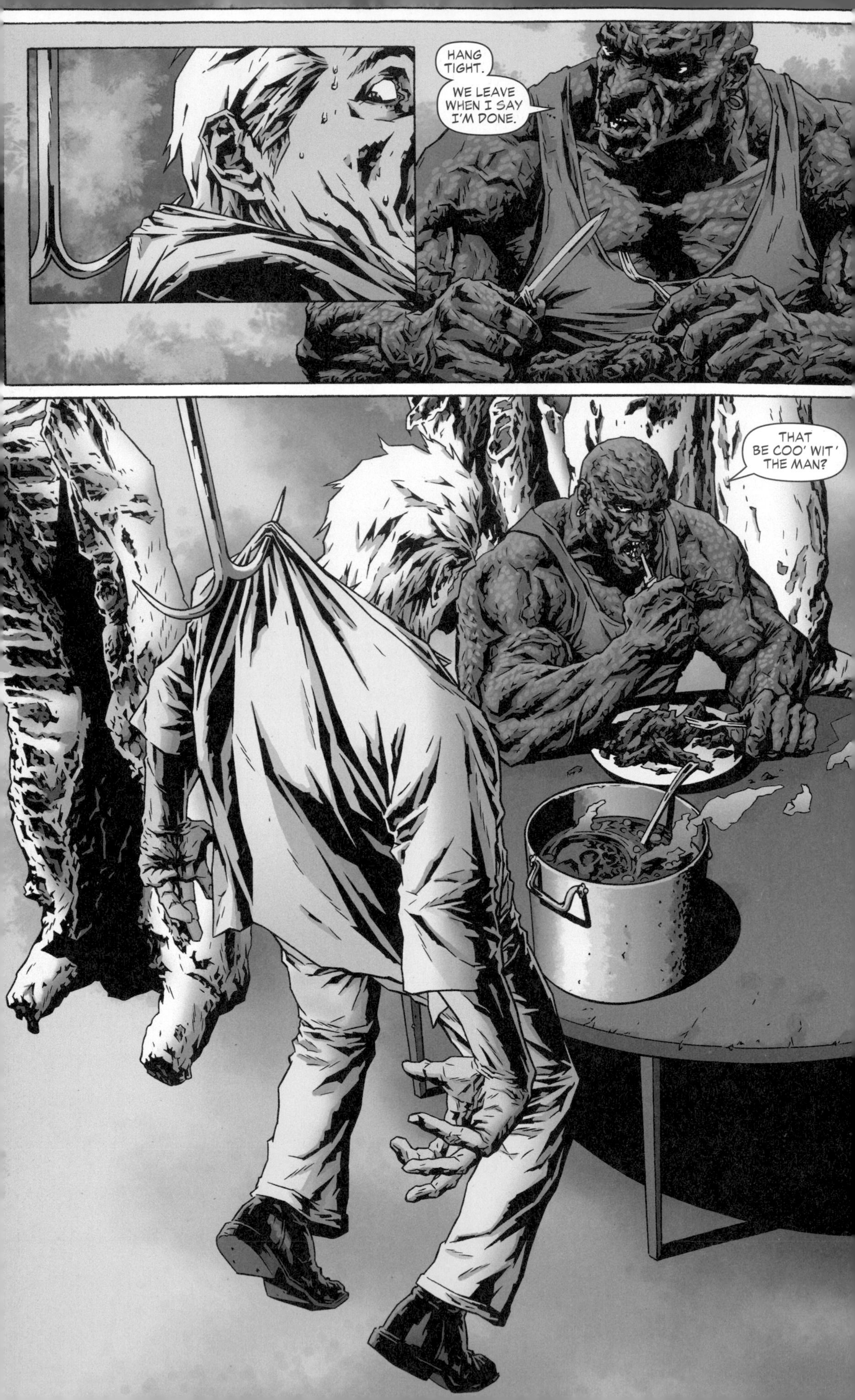
HANG TIGHT.
WE LEAVE WHEN I SAY I'M DONE.
THAT BE COO' WIT' THE MAN?

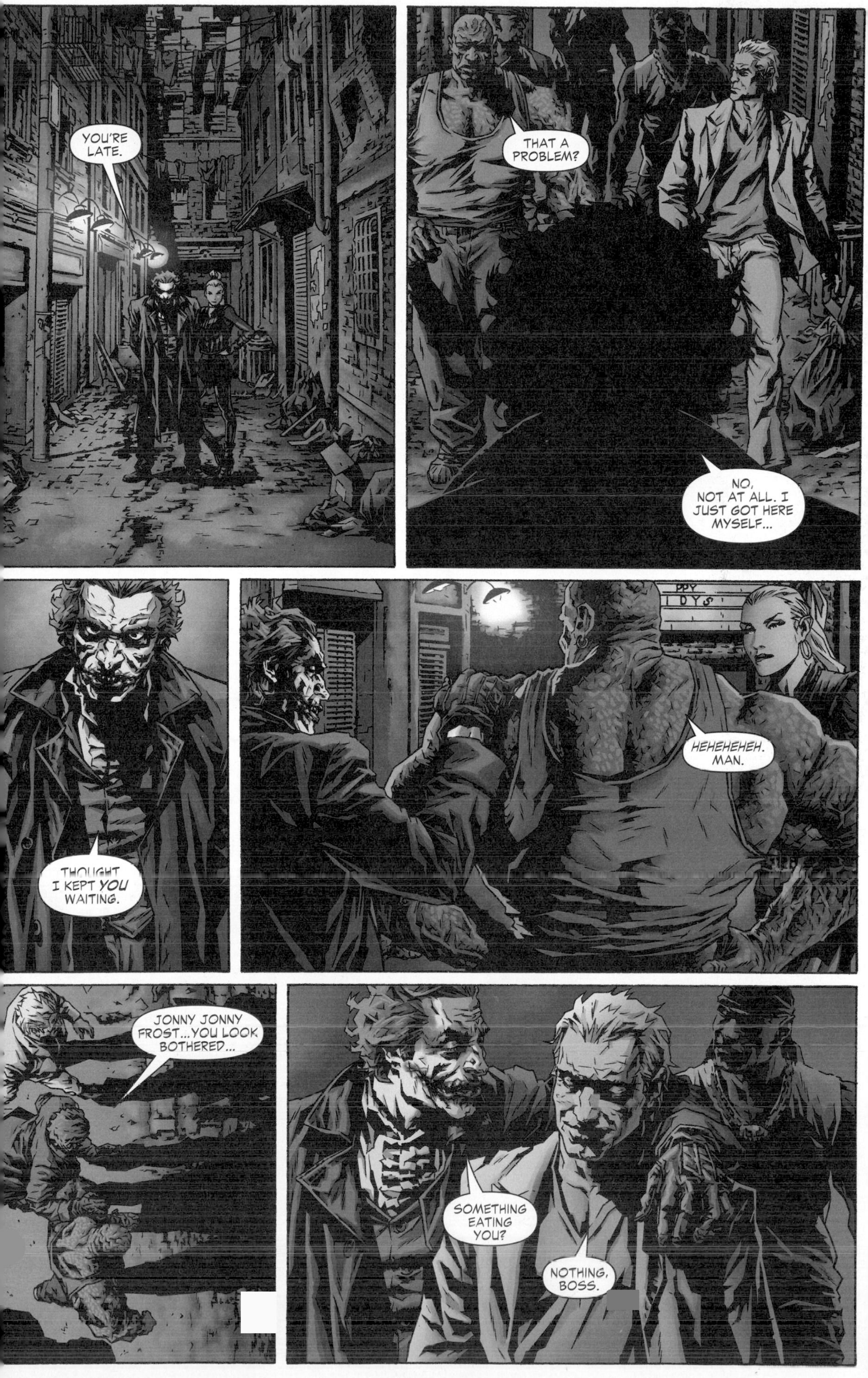
YOU'RE LATE.
THAT A PROBLEM?
NO, NOT AT ALL. I JUST GOT HERE MYSELF...
THOUGHT I KEPT *YOU* WAITING.
HEHEHEHEH. MAN.
JONNY JONNY FROST...YOU LOOK BOTHERED...
SOMETHING EATING YOU?
NOTHING, BOSS.

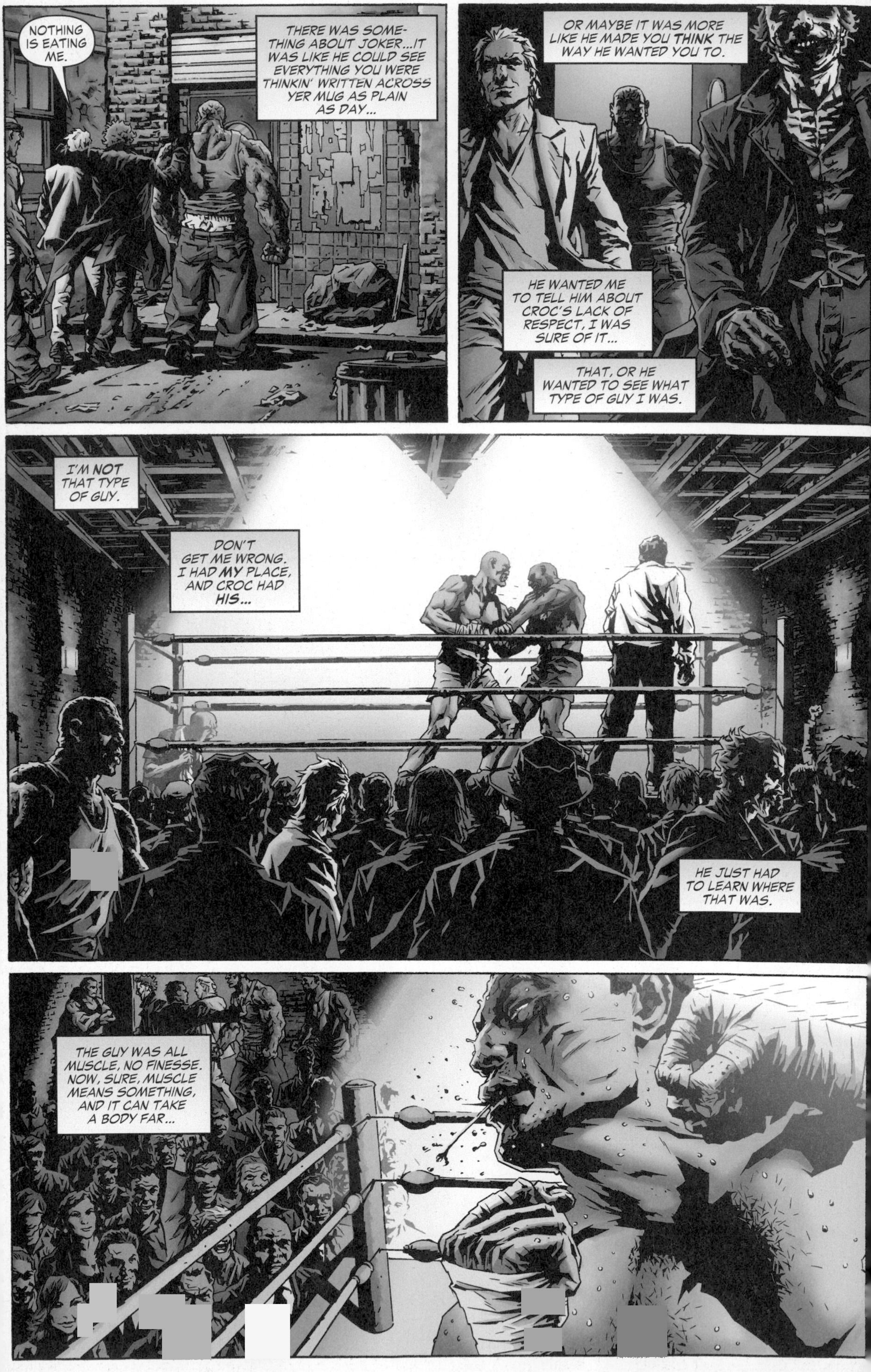
NOTHING IS EATING ME.
THERE WAS SOMETHING ABOUT JOKER... IT WAS LIKE HE COULD SEE EVERYTHING YOU WERE THINKIN' WRITTEN ACROSS YER MUG AS PLAIN AS DAY...
OR MAYBE IT WAS MORE LIKE HE MADE YOU THINK THE WAY HE WANTED YOU TO.
HE WANTED ME TO TELL HIM ABOUT CROC'S LACK OF RESPECT, I WAS SURE OF IT...
THAT, OR HE WANTED TO SEE WHAT TYPE OF GUY I WAS.
I'M NOT THAT TYPE OF GUY.
DON'T GET ME WRONG. I HAD MY PLACE, AND CROC HAD HIS...
HE JUST HAD TO LEARN WHERE THAT WAS.
THE GUY WAS ALL MUSCLE, NO FINESSE. NOW, SURE, MUSCLE MEANS SOMETHING, AND IT CAN TAKE A BODY FAR...

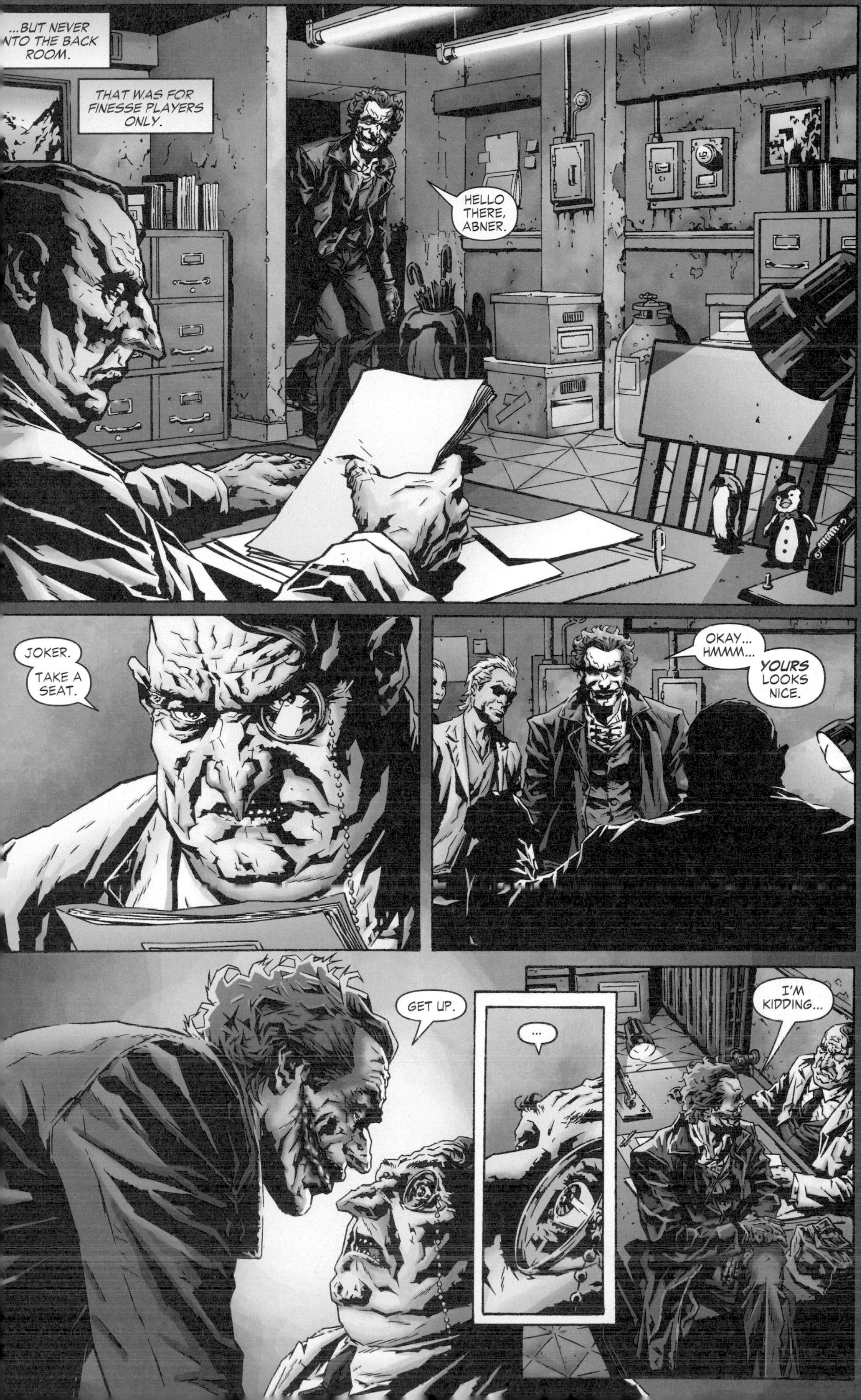
...BUT NEVER INTO THE BACK ROOM.
THAT WAS FOR FINESSE PLAYERS ONLY.
HELLO THERE, ABNER.
JOKER. TAKE A SEAT.
OKAY... HMMM... YOURS LOOKS NICE.
GET UP.
...
I'M KIDDING...

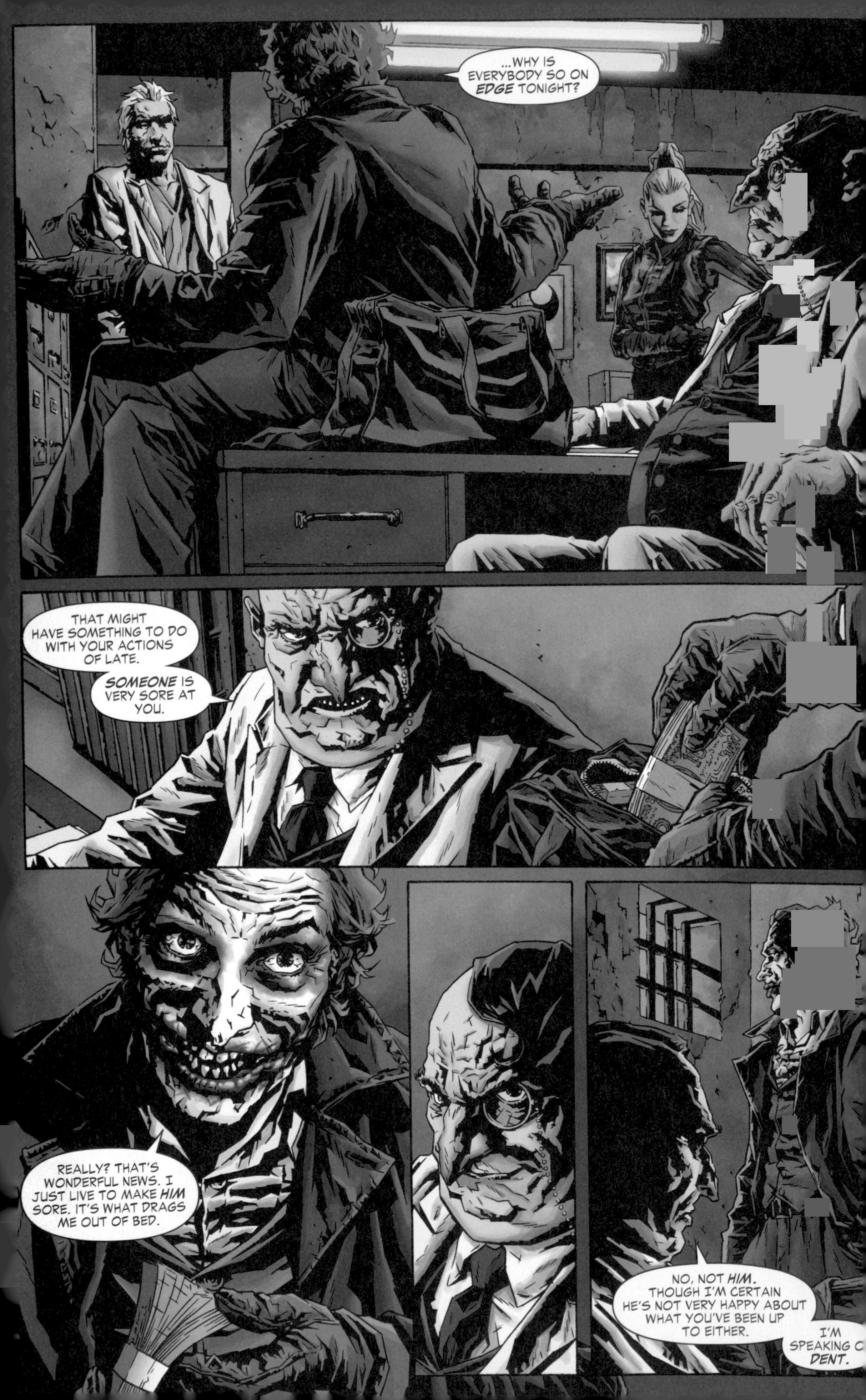
...WHY IS EVERYBODY SO ON *EDGE* TONIGHT?
THAT MIGHT HAVE SOMETHING TO DO WITH YOUR ACTIONS OF LATE.
SOMEONE IS VERY SORE AT YOU.
REALLY? THAT'S WONDERFUL NEWS. I JUST LIVE TO MAKE *HIM* SORE. IT'S WHAT DRAGS ME OUT OF BED.
NO, NOT *HIM*. THOUGH I'M CERTAIN HE'S NOT VERY HAPPY ABOUT WHAT YOU'VE BEEN UP TO EITHER.
I'M SPEAKING C *DENT.*

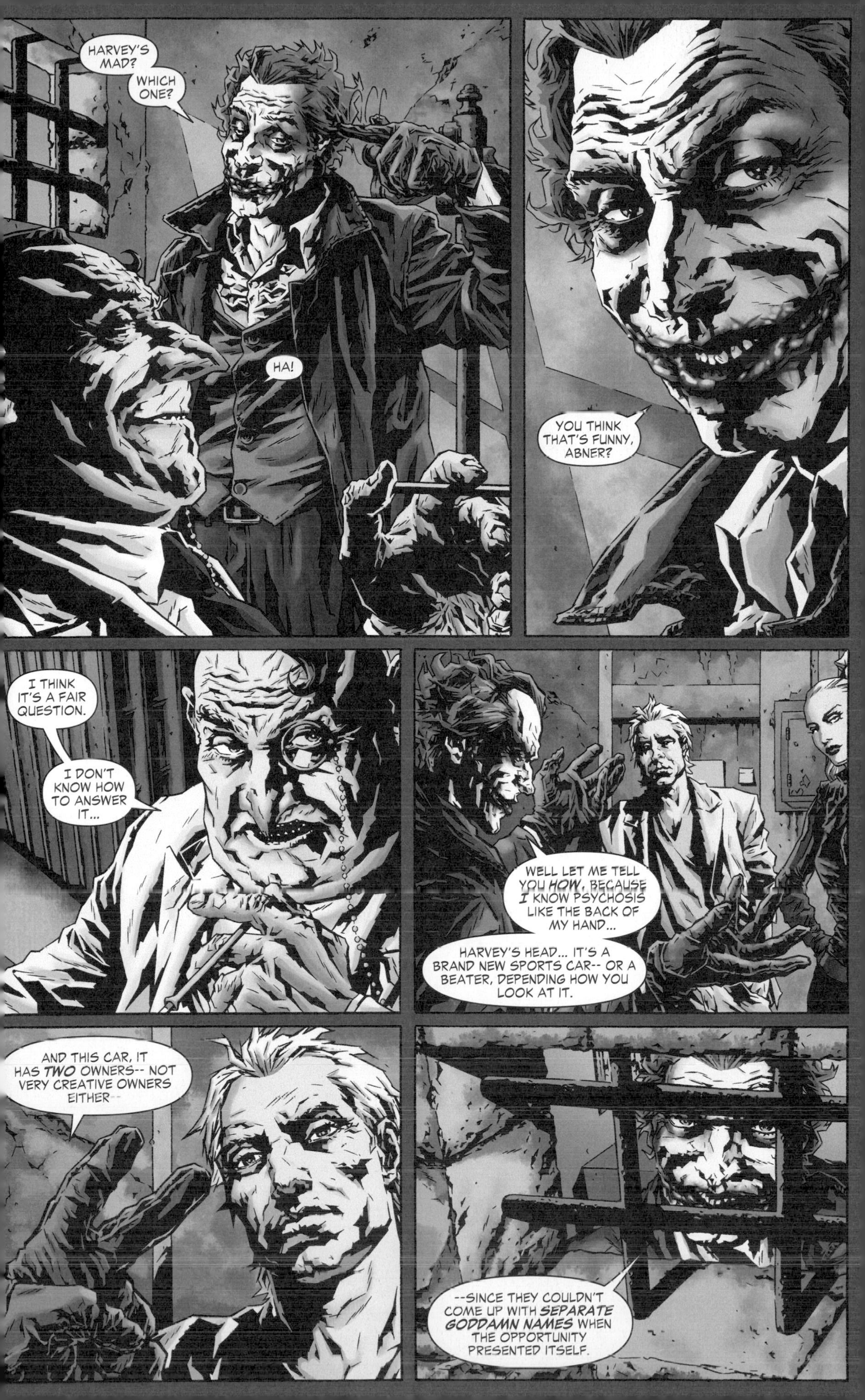
HARVEY'S MAD?
WHICH ONE?
HA!
YOU THINK THAT'S FUNNY, ABNER?
I THINK IT'S A FAIR QUESTION.
I DON'T KNOW HOW TO ANSWER IT...
WELL LET ME TELL YOU HOW, BECAUSE I KNOW PSYCHOSIS LIKE THE BACK OF MY HAND...
HARVEY'S HEAD... IT'S A BRAND NEW SPORTS CAR-- OR A BEATER, DEPENDING HOW YOU LOOK AT IT.
AND THIS CAR, IT HAS TWO OWNERS-- NOT VERY CREATIVE OWNERS EITHER--
--SINCE THEY COULDN'T COME UP WITH SEPARATE GODDAMN NAMES WHEN THE OPPORTUNITY PRESENTED ITSELF.

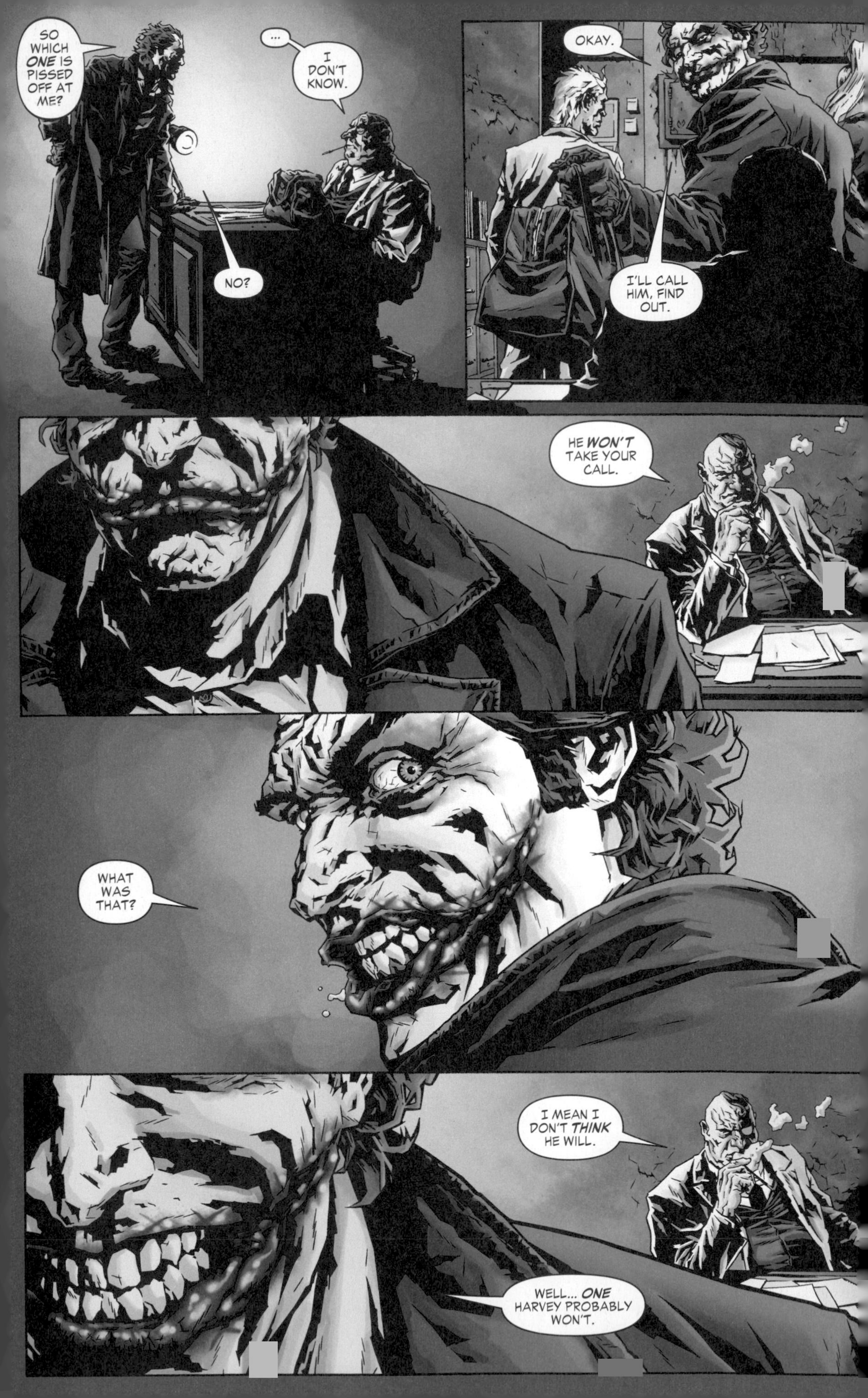
SO WHICH *ONE* IS PISSED OFF AT ME?
...
I DON'T KNOW.
NO?
OKAY.
I'LL CALL HIM, FIND OUT.
HE *WON'T* TAKE YOUR CALL.
WHAT WAS THAT?
I MEAN I DON'T *THINK* HE WILL.
WELL... *ONE* HARVEY PROBABLY WON'T.

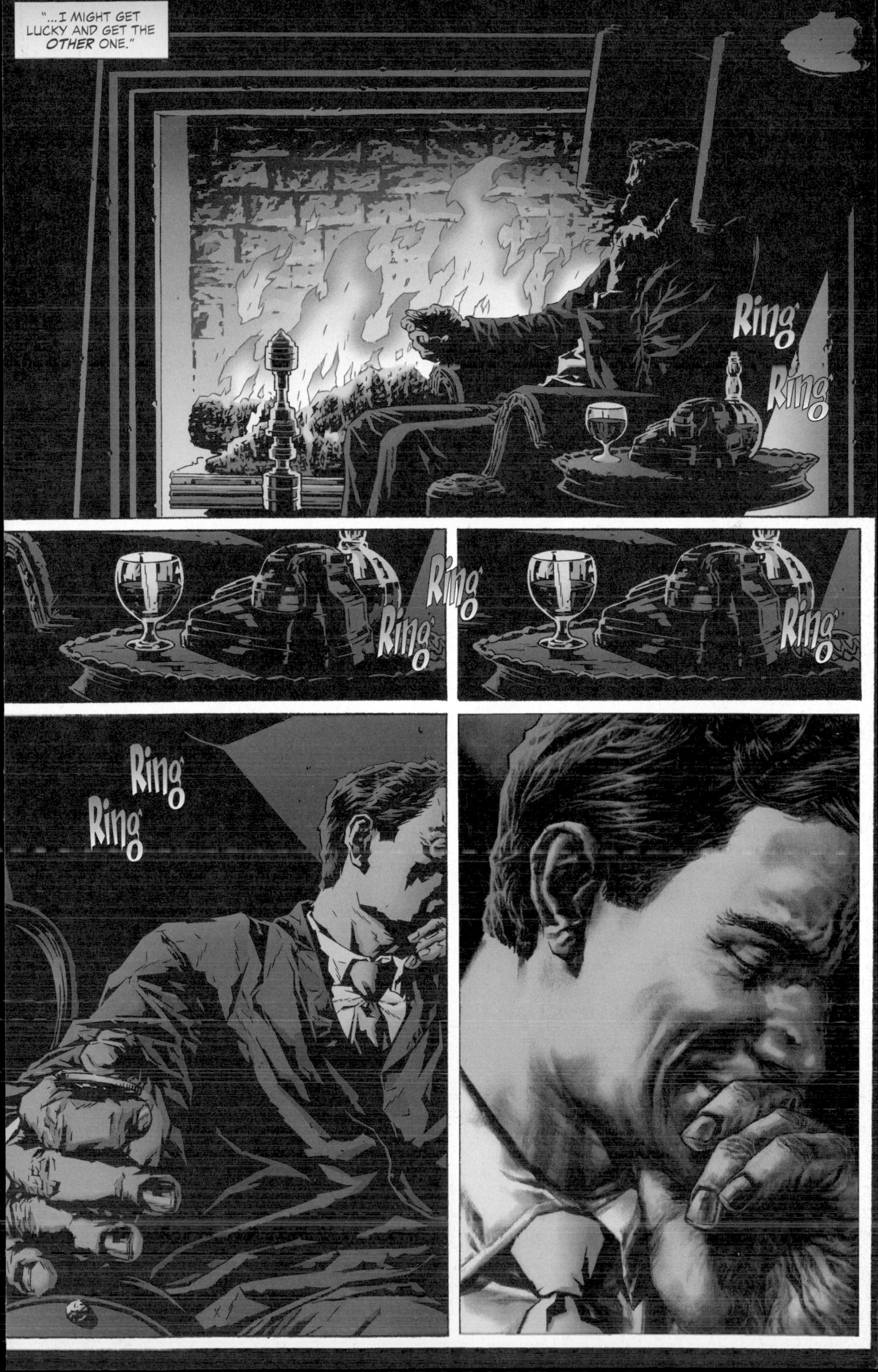
"...I MIGHT GET LUCKY AND GET THE *OTHER* ONE."
Ring
Ring
Ring
Ring
Ring
Ring
Ring

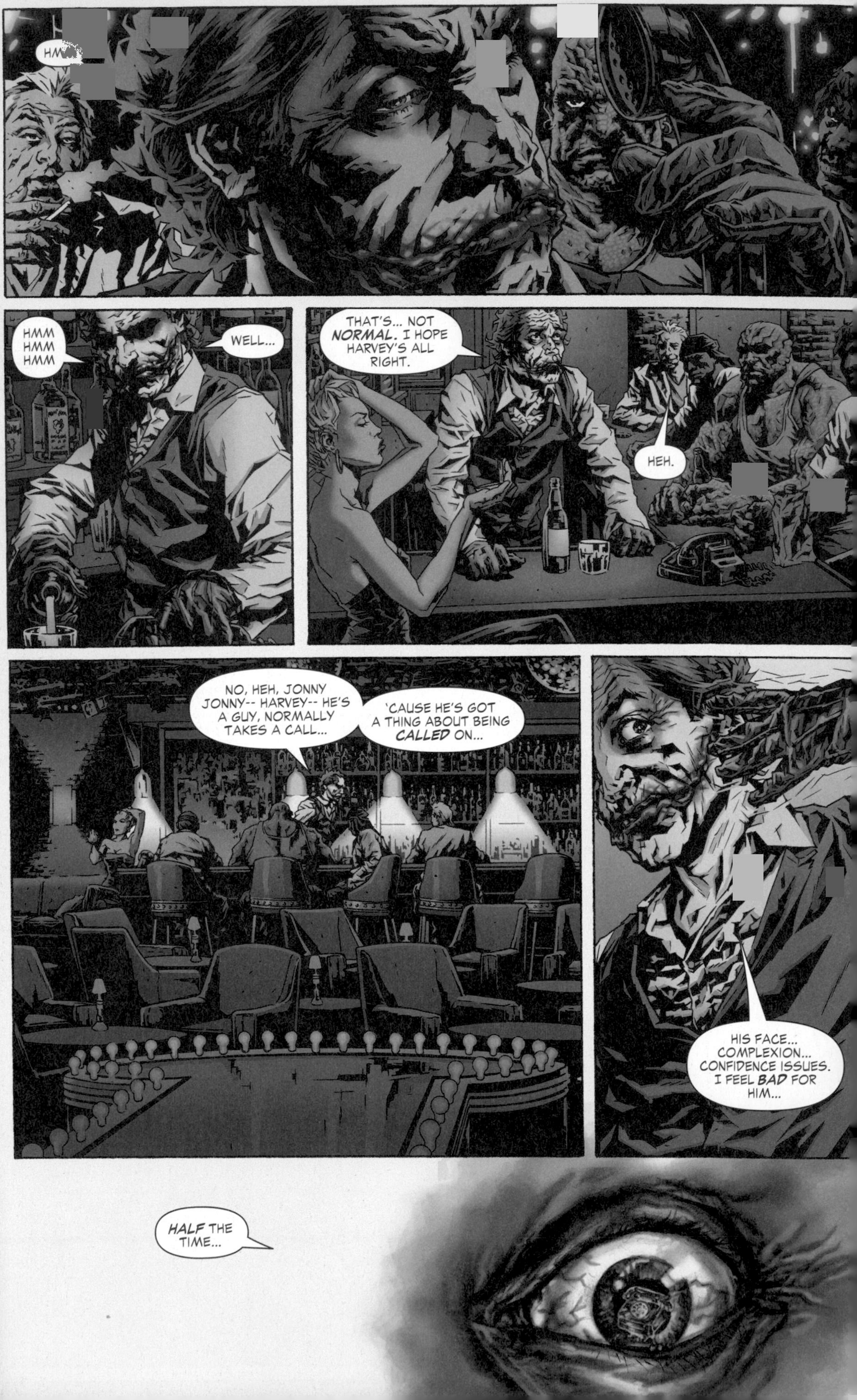
HM
HMM HMM HMM
WELL...
THAT'S... NOT NORMAL. I HOPE HARVEY'S ALL RIGHT.
HEH.
NO, HEH, JONNY JONNY-- HARVEY-- HE'S A GUY, NORMALLY TAKES A CALL...
'CAUSE HE'S GOT A THING ABOUT BEING CALLED ON...
HIS FACE... COMPLEXION... CONFIDENCE ISSUES. I FEEL BAD FOR HIM...
HALF THE TIME...

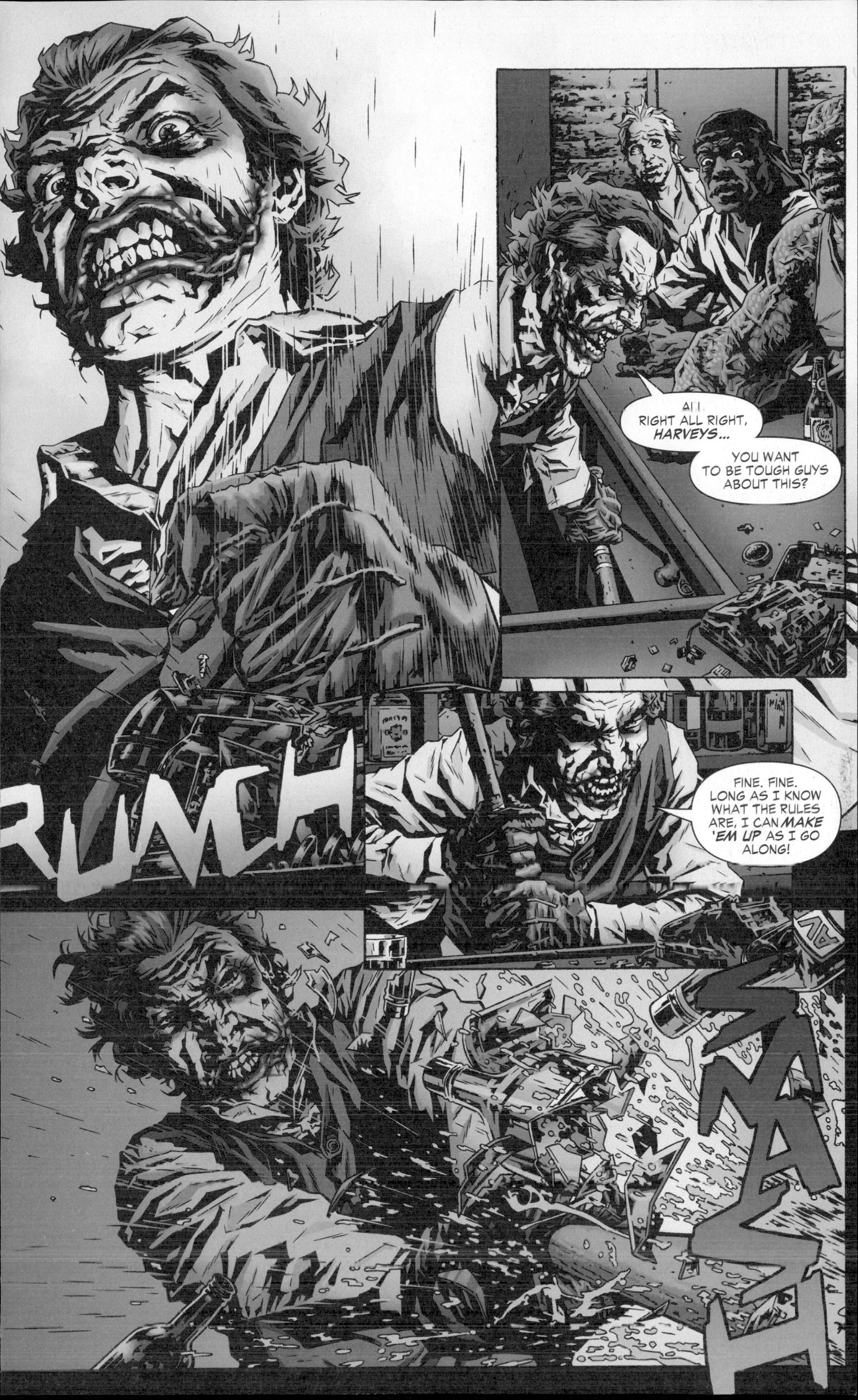
ALL RIGHT ALL RIGHT, *HARVEYS...*
YOU WANT TO BE TOUGH GUYS ABOUT THIS?
FINE. FINE. LONG AS I KNOW WHAT THE RULES ARE, I CAN *MAKE 'EM UP* AS I GO ALONG!

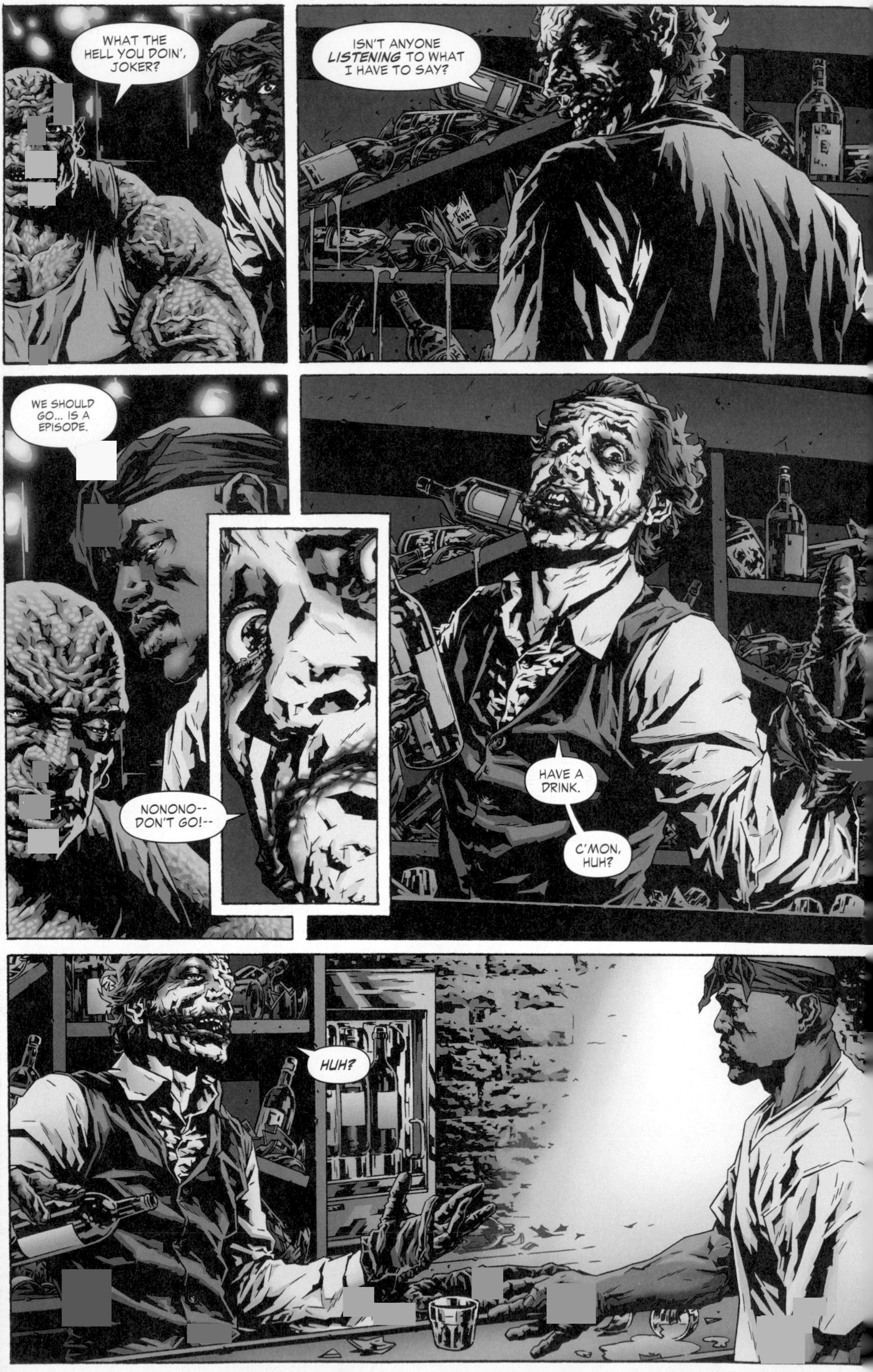
WHAT THE HELL YOU DOIN', JOKER?
ISN'T ANYONE *LISTENING* TO WHAT I HAVE TO SAY?
WE SHOULD GO... IS A EPISODE.
NONONO-- DON'T GO!--
HAVE A DRINK.
C'MON, HUH?
HUH?

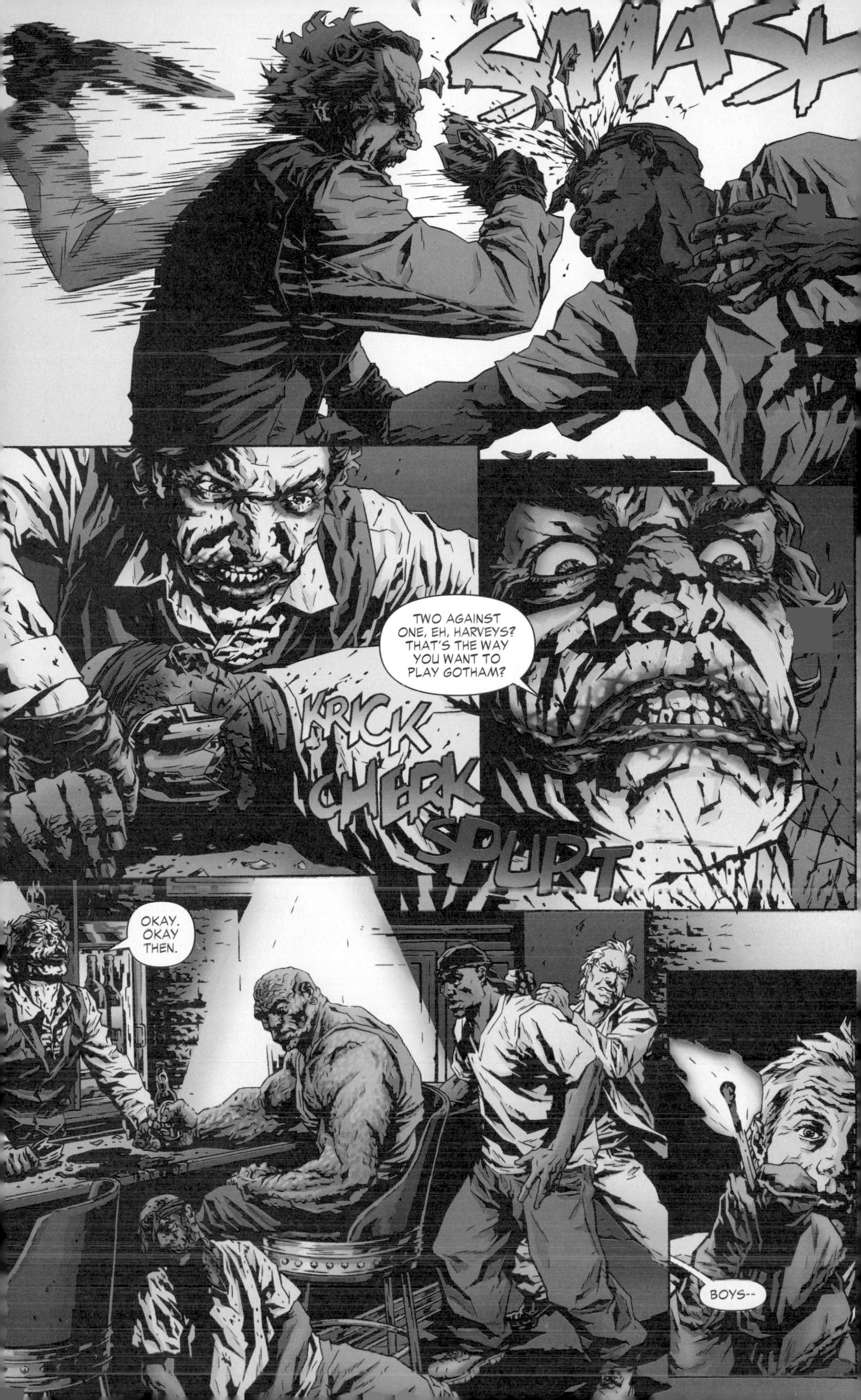
SMASH
TWO AGAINST ONE, EH, HARVEYS? THAT'S THE WAY YOU WANT TO PLAY GOTHAM?
KRICK
CHERK
SPURT
OKAY. OKAY THEN.
BOYS--

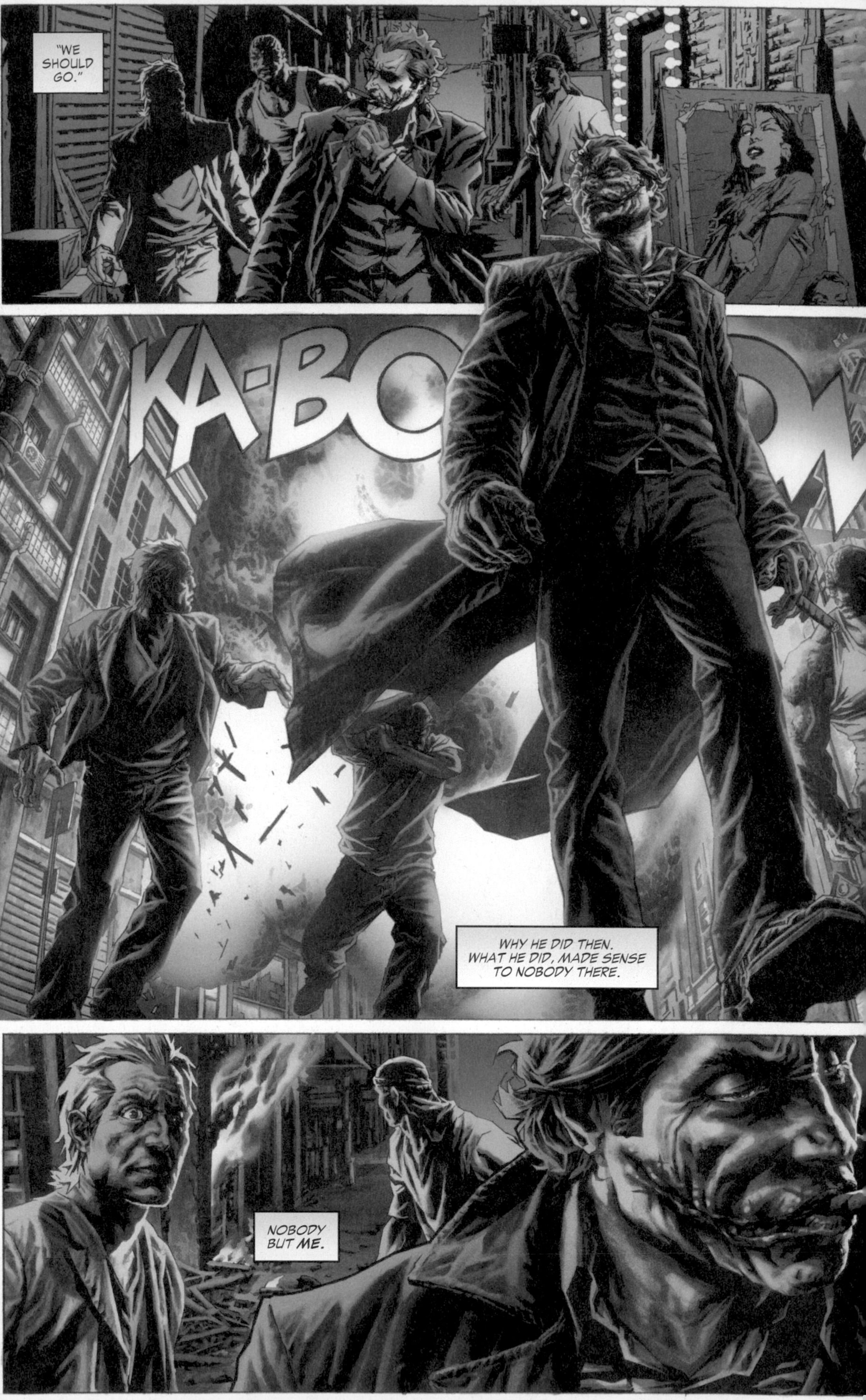
"WE SHOULD GO."
KA-BOOOM
WHY HE DID THEN. WHAT HE DID, MADE SENSE TO NOBODY THERE.
NOBODY BUT **ME**.

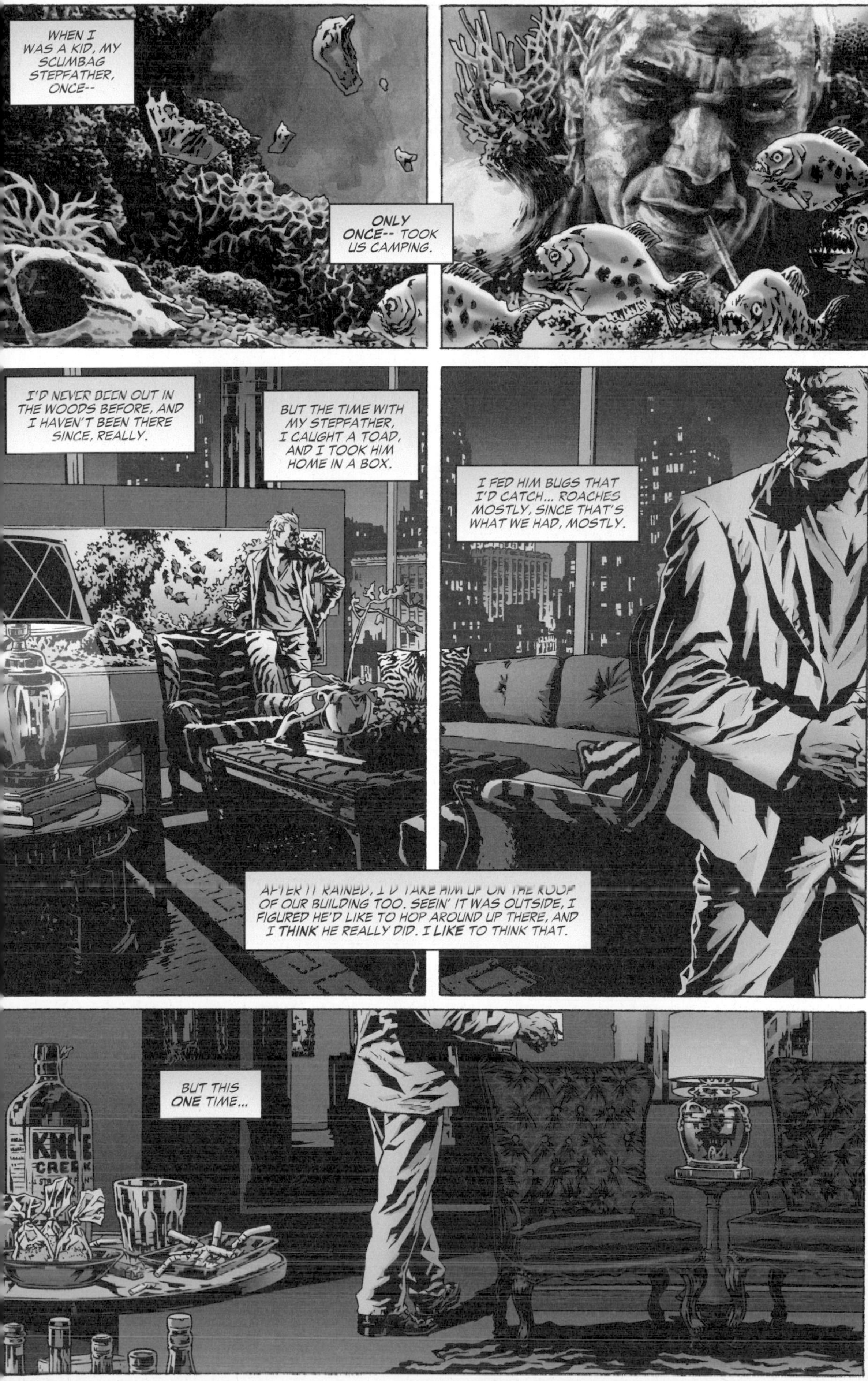

WHEN I WAS A KID, MY SCUMBAG STEPFATHER, ONCE--
ONLY ONCE-- TOOK US CAMPING.
I'D NEVER BEEN OUT IN THE WOODS BEFORE, AND I HAVEN'T BEEN THERE SINCE, REALLY.
BUT THE TIME WITH MY STEPFATHER, I CAUGHT A TOAD, AND I TOOK HIM HOME IN A BOX.
I FED HIM BUGS THAT I'D CATCH... ROACHES MOSTLY, SINCE THAT'S WHAT WE HAD, MOSTLY.
AFTER IT RAINED, I'D TAKE HIM UP ON THE ROOF OF OUR BUILDING TOO. SEEIN' IT WAS OUTSIDE, I FIGURED HE'D LIKE TO HOP AROUND UP THERE, AND I THINK HE REALLY DID. I LIKE TO THINK THAT.
BUT THIS ONE TIME...

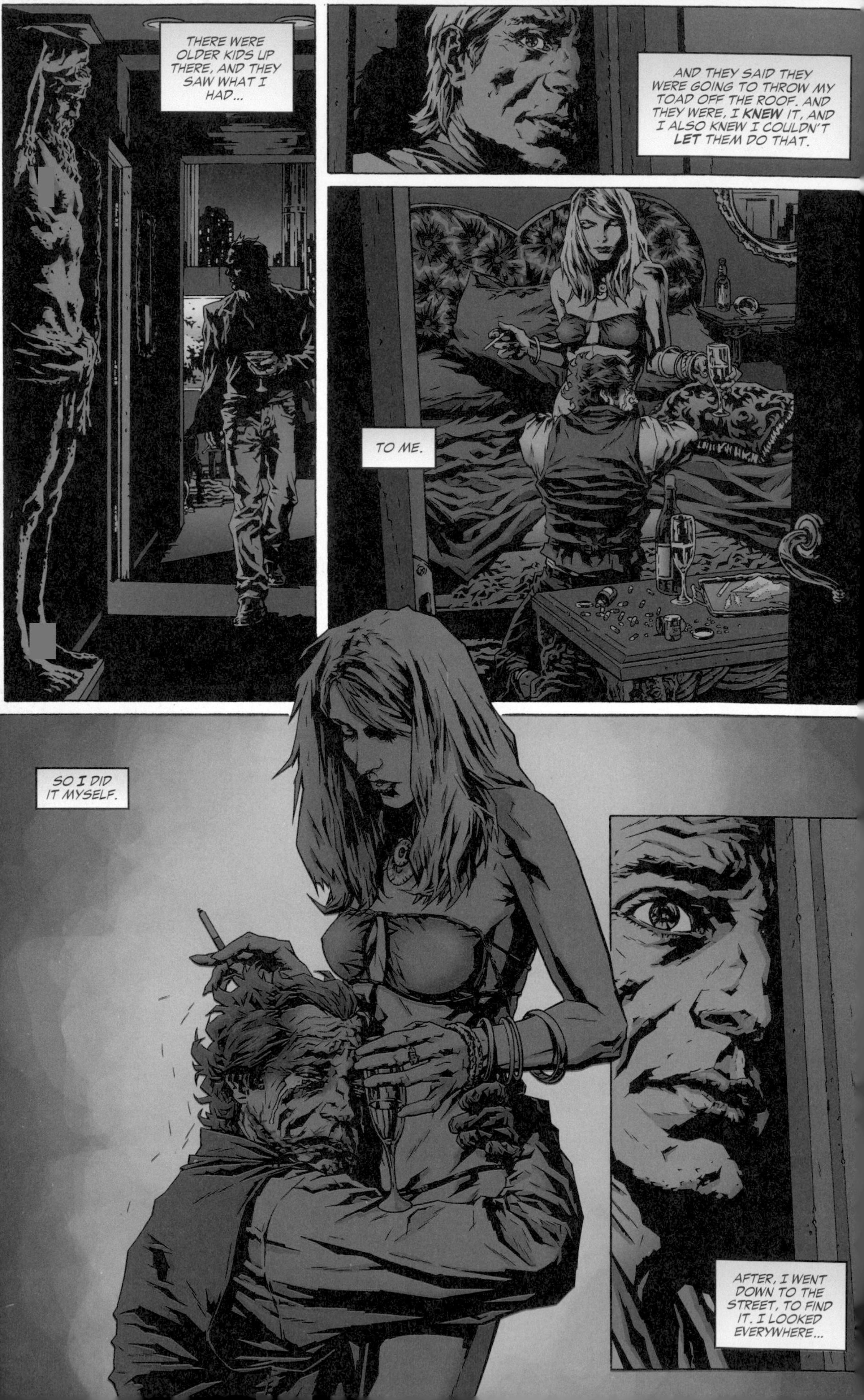
THERE WERE OLDER KIDS UP THERE, AND THEY SAW WHAT I HAD...
AND THEY SAID THEY WERE GOING TO THROW MY TOAD OFF THE ROOF. AND THEY WERE, I KNEW IT, AND I ALSO KNEW I COULDN'T LET THEM DO THAT.
TO ME.
SO I DID IT MYSELF.
AFTER, I WENT DOWN TO THE STREET, TO FIND IT. I LOOKED EVERYWHERE...

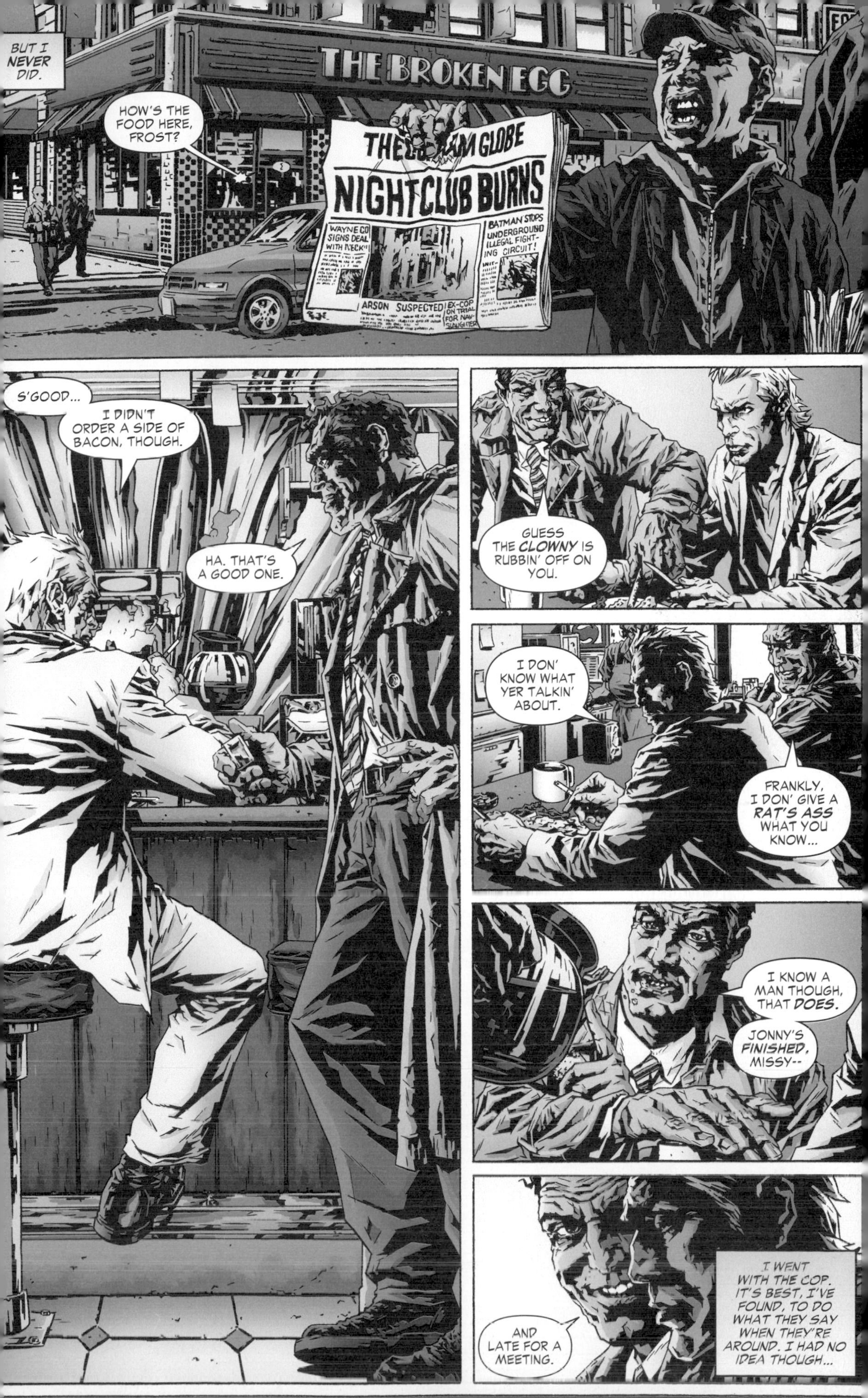
BUT I NEVER DID.
THE BROKEN EGG
HOW'S THE FOOD HERE, FROST?
NIGHTCLUB BURNS
BATMAN STOPS UNDERGROUND ILLEGAL FIGHTING CIRCUIT!
ARSON SUSPECTED
S'GOOD...
I DIDN'T ORDER A SIDE OF BACON, THOUGH.
HA. THAT'S A GOOD ONE.
GUESS THE CLOWNY IS RUBBIN' OFF ON YOU.
I DON' KNOW WHAT YER TALKIN' ABOUT.
FRANKLY, I DON' GIVE A RAT'S ASS WHAT YOU KNOW...
I KNOW A MAN THOUGH, THAT DOES.
JONNY'S FINISHED, MISSY--
AND LATE FOR A MEETING.
I WENT WITH THE COP. IT'S BEST, I'VE FOUND, TO DO WHAT THEY SAY WHEN THEY'RE AROUND. I HAD NO IDEA THOUGH...

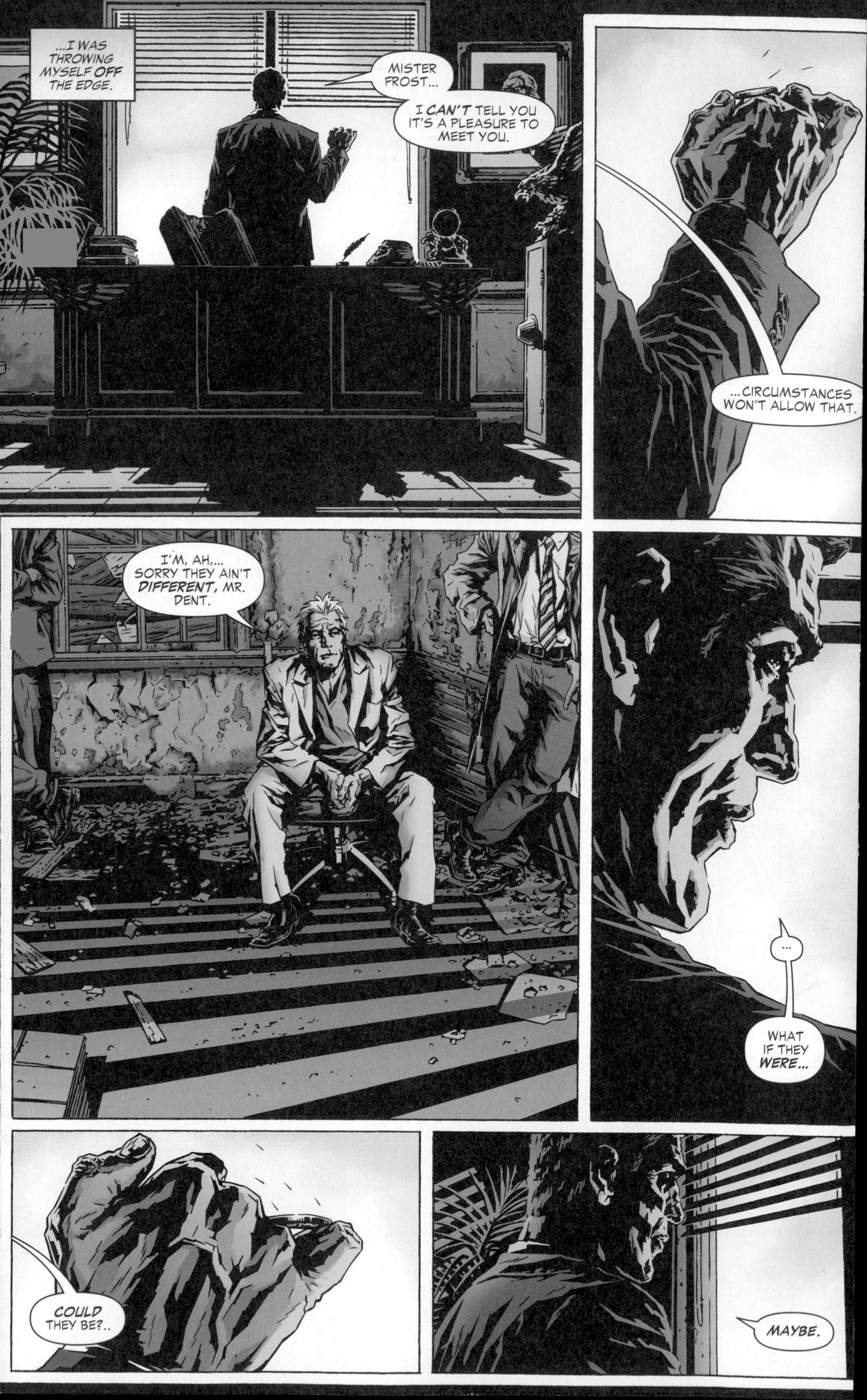
...I WAS THROWING MYSELF OFF THE EDGE.
MISTER FROST...
I CAN'T TELL YOU IT'S A PLEASURE TO MEET YOU.
...CIRCUMSTANCES WON'T ALLOW THAT.
I'M, AH,... SORRY THEY AIN'T DIFFERENT, MR. DENT.
...
WHAT IF THEY WERE...
COULD THEY BE?..
MAYBE.

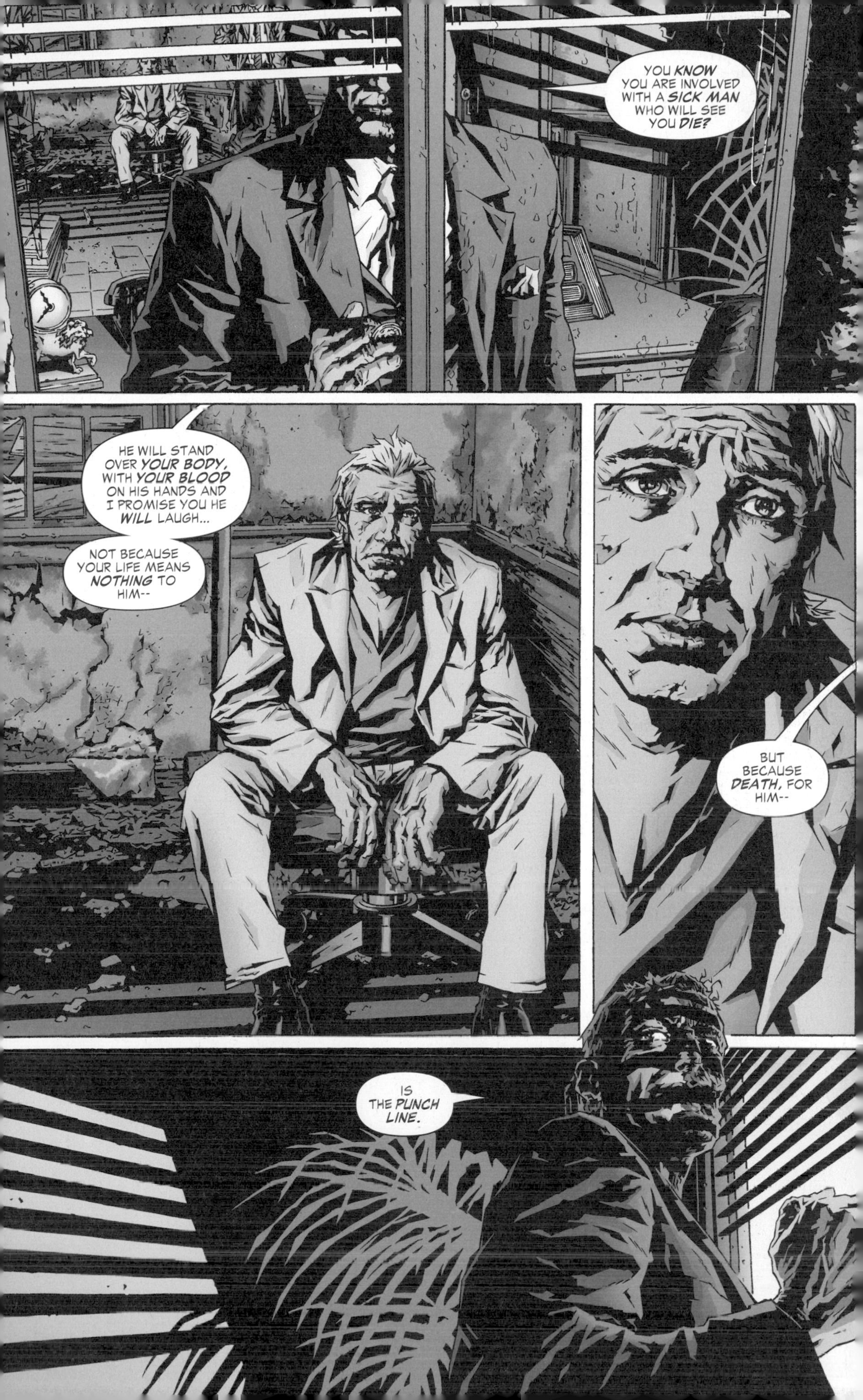
YOU KNOW YOU ARE INVOLVED WITH A SICK MAN WHO WILL SEE YOU DIE?
HE WILL STAND OVER YOUR BODY, WITH YOUR BLOOD ON HIS HANDS AND I PROMISE YOU HE WILL LAUGH...
NOT BECAUSE YOUR LIFE MEANS NOTHING TO HIM--
BUT BECAUSE DEATH, FOR HIM--
IS THE PUNCH LINE.

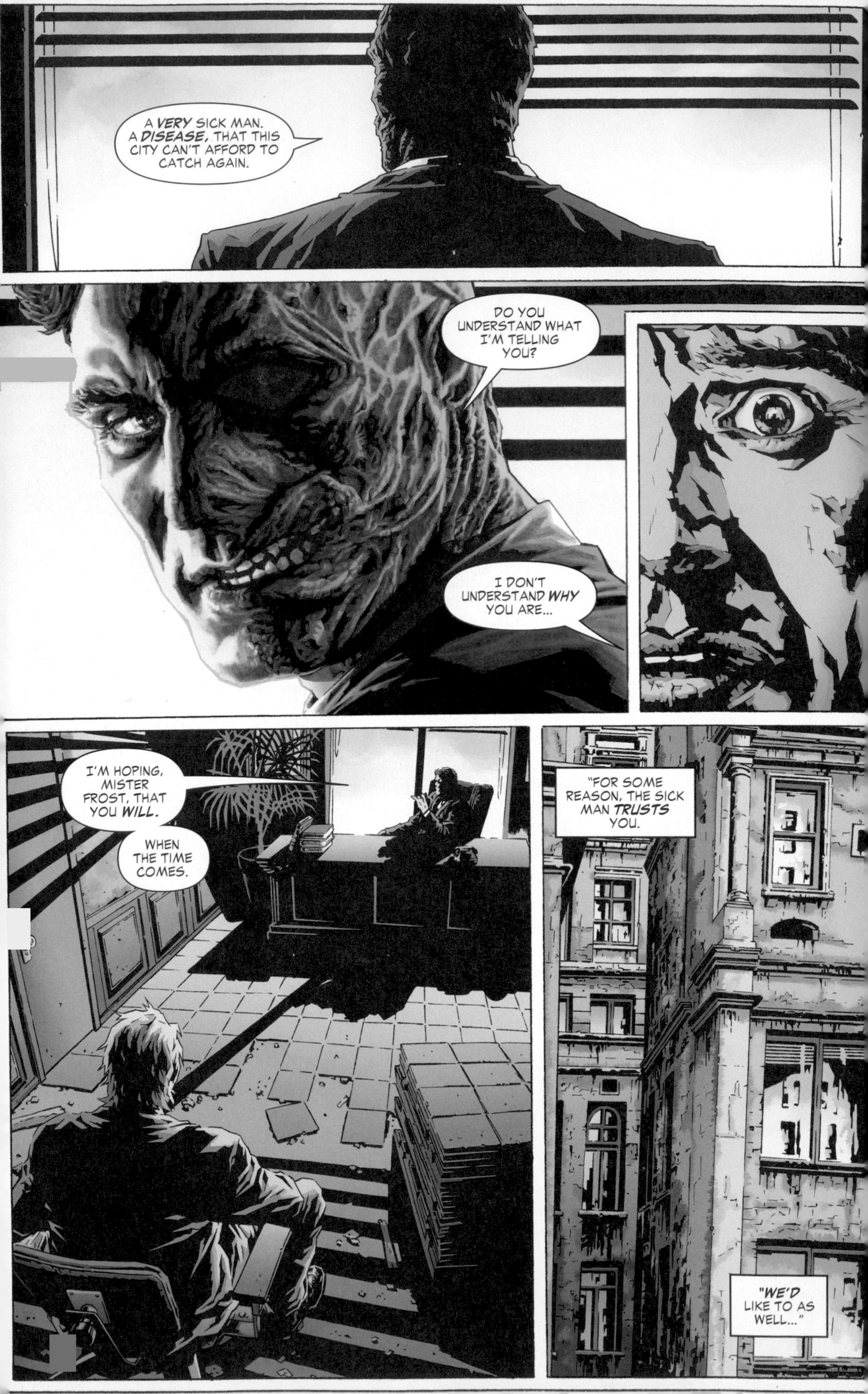
A VERY SICK MAN. A DISEASE, THAT THIS CITY CAN'T AFFORD TO CATCH AGAIN.
DO YOU UNDERSTAND WHAT I'M TELLING YOU?
I DON'T UNDERSTAND WHY YOU ARE...
I'M HOPING, MISTER FROST, THAT YOU WILL.
WHEN THE TIME COMES.
"FOR SOME REASON, THE SICK MAN TRUSTS YOU.
"WE'D LIKE TO AS WELL..."

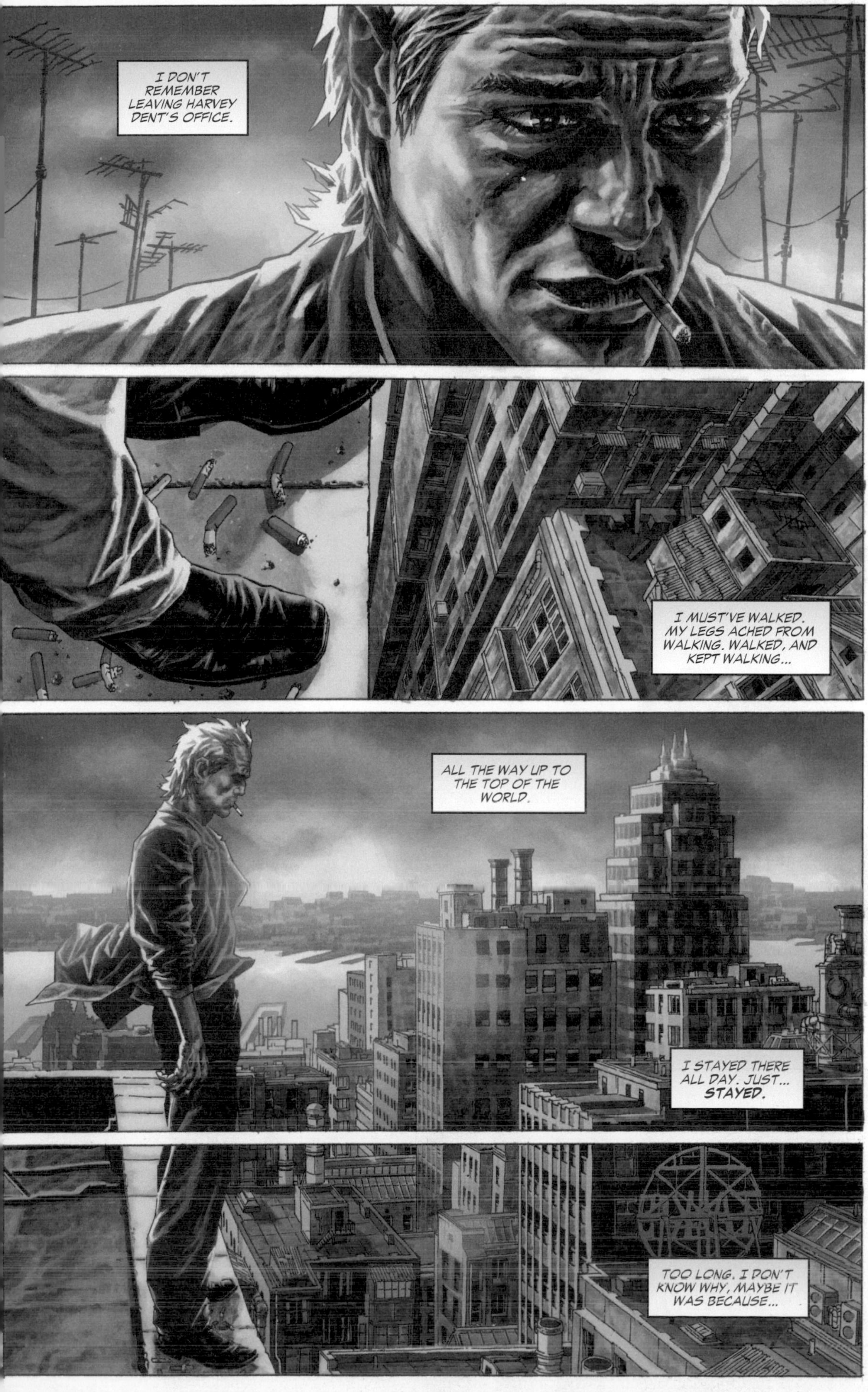
I DON'T REMEMBER LEAVING HARVEY DENT'S OFFICE.
I MUST'VE WALKED. MY LEGS ACHED FROM WALKING. WALKED, AND KEPT WALKING...
ALL THE WAY UP TO THE TOP OF THE WORLD.
I STAYED THERE ALL DAY. JUST... **STAYED.**
TOO LONG. I DON'T KNOW WHY, MAYBE IT WAS BECAUSE...

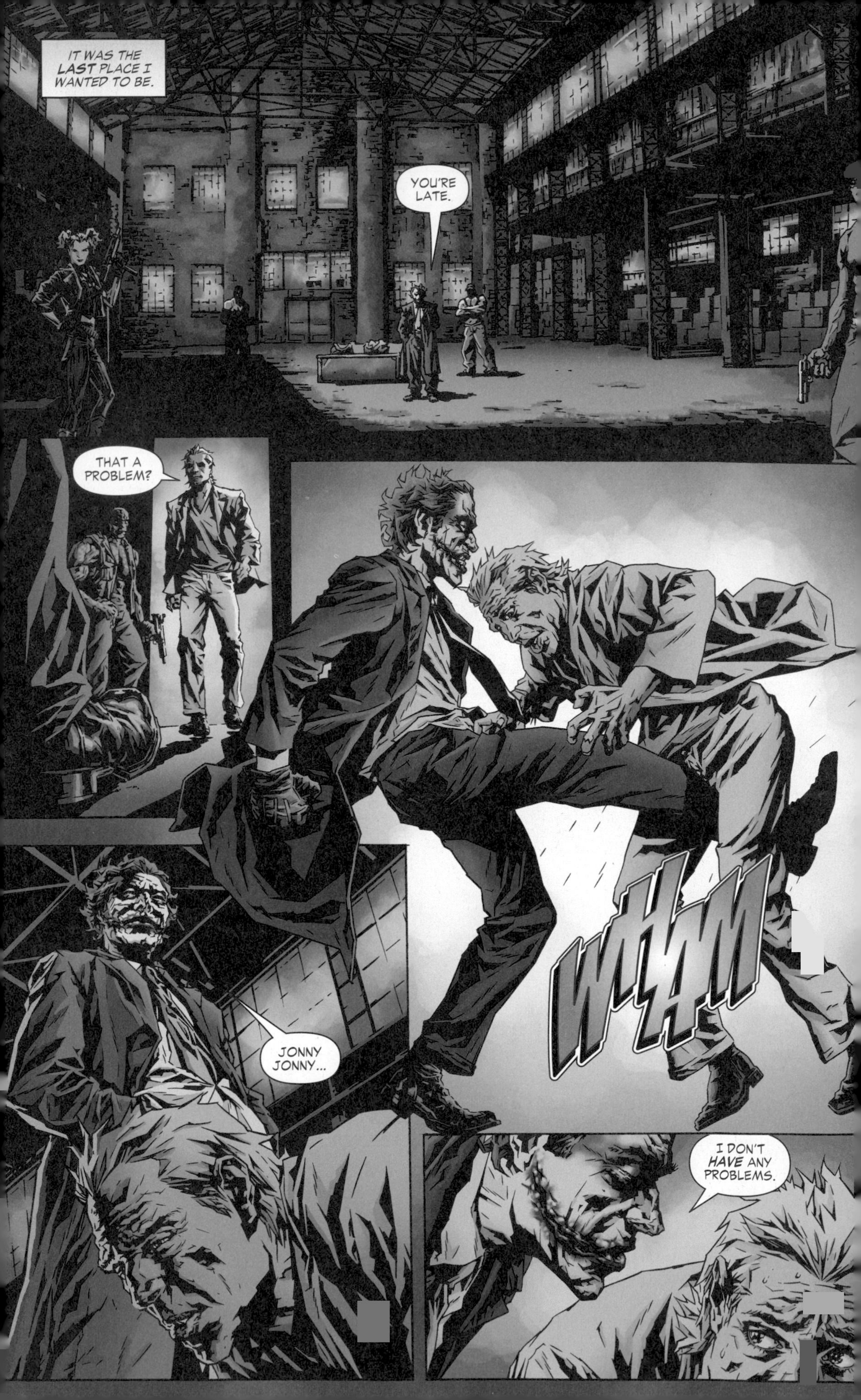
IT WAS THE *LAST* PLACE I WANTED TO BE.
YOU'RE LATE.
THAT A PROBLEM?
WHAM
JONNY JONNY...
I DON'T *HAVE* ANY PROBLEMS.

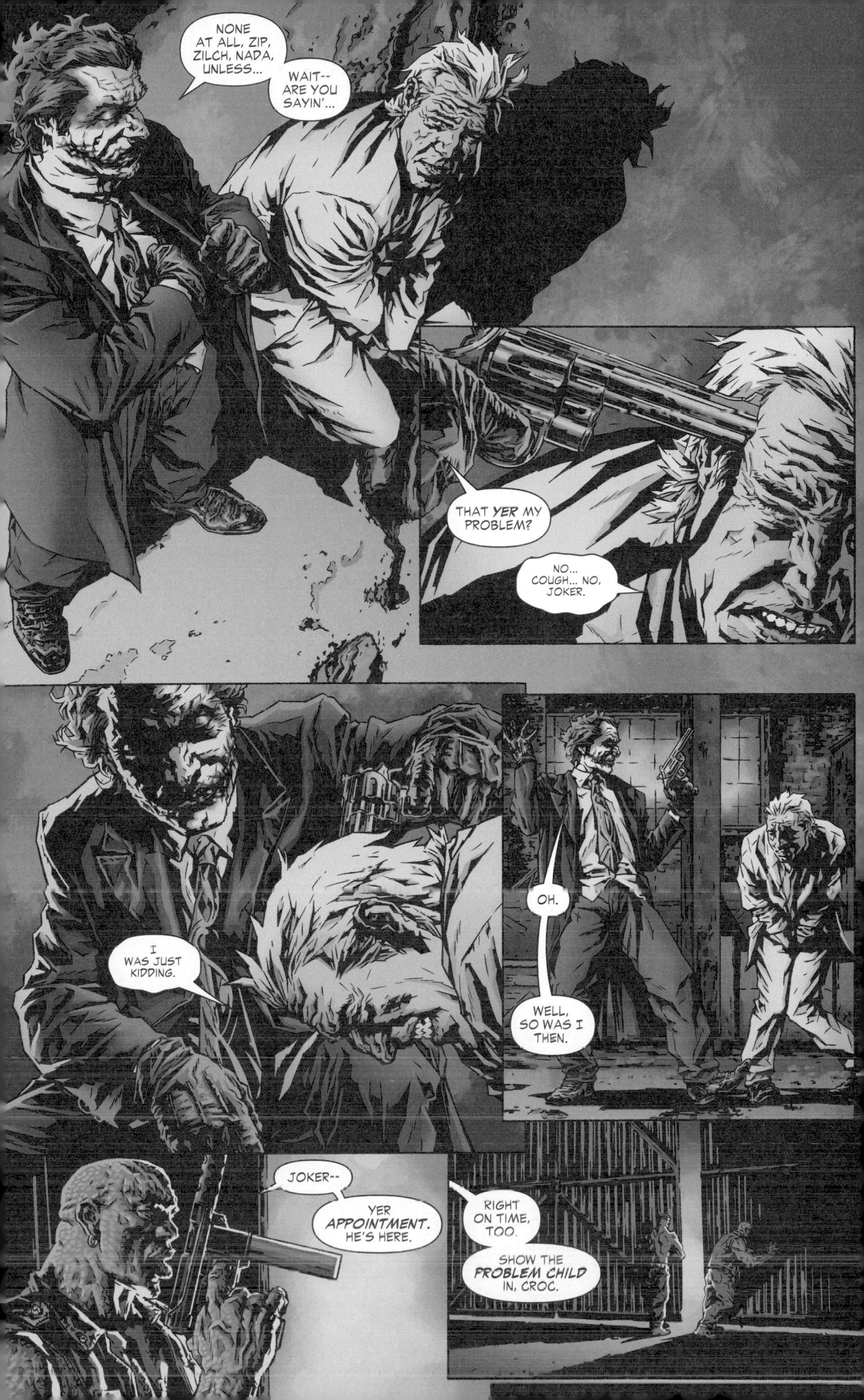
NONE AT ALL, ZIP, ZILCH, NADA, UNLESS...
WAIT-- ARE YOU SAYIN'...
THAT *YER* MY PROBLEM?
NO... COUGH... NO, JOKER.
I WAS JUST KIDDING.
OH.
WELL, SO WAS I THEN.
JOKER--
YER *APPOINTMENT*. HE'S HERE.
RIGHT ON TIME, TOO.
SHOW THE *PROBLEM CHILD* IN, CROC.

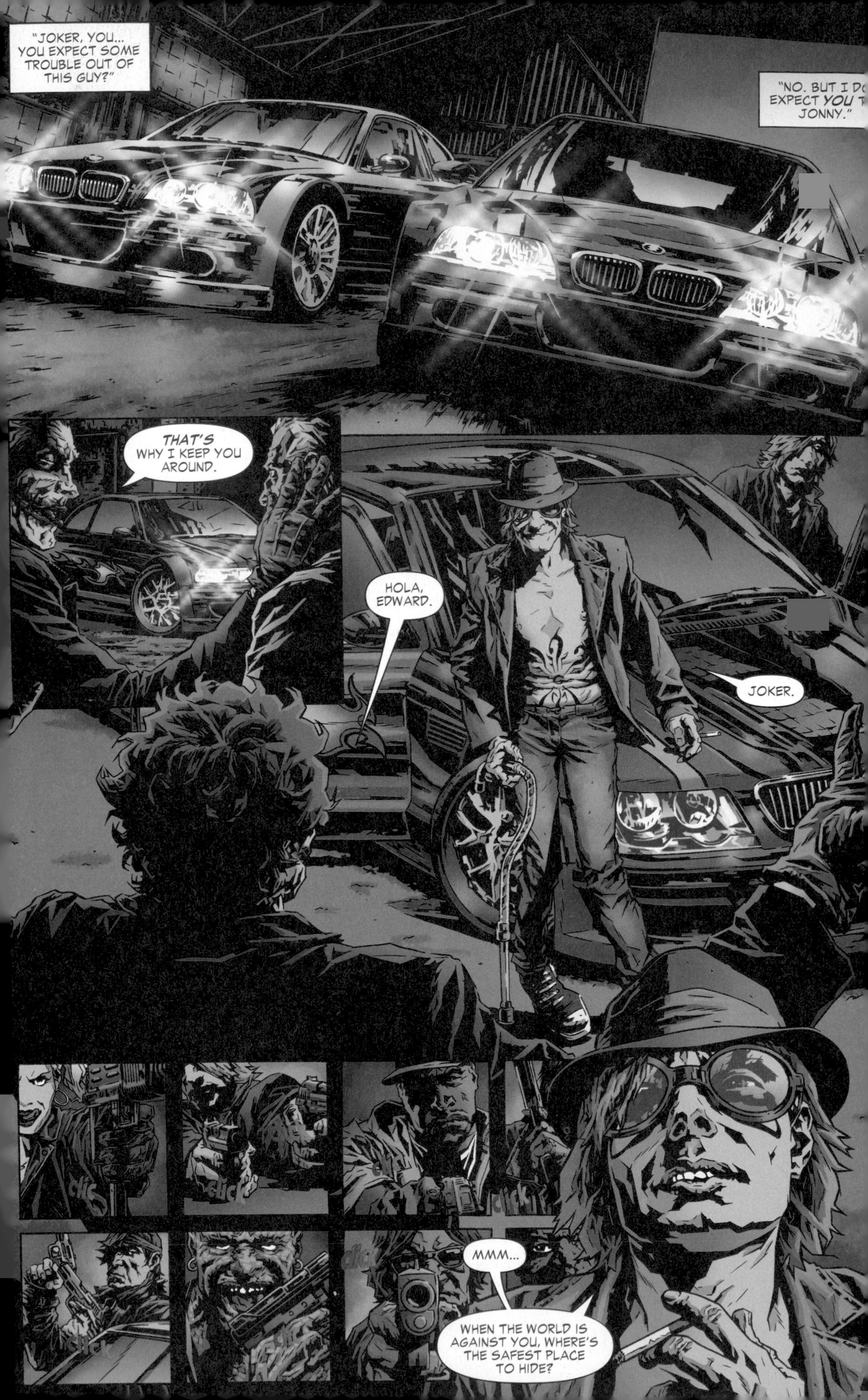
"JOKER, YOU... YOU EXPECT SOME TROUBLE OUT OF THIS GUY?"
"NO. BUT I D
EXPECT YOU T
JONNY."
THAT'S WHY I KEEP YOU AROUND.
HOLA, EDWARD.
JOKER.
MMM...
WHEN THE WORLD IS AGAINST YOU, WHERE'S THE SAFEST PLACE TO HIDE?

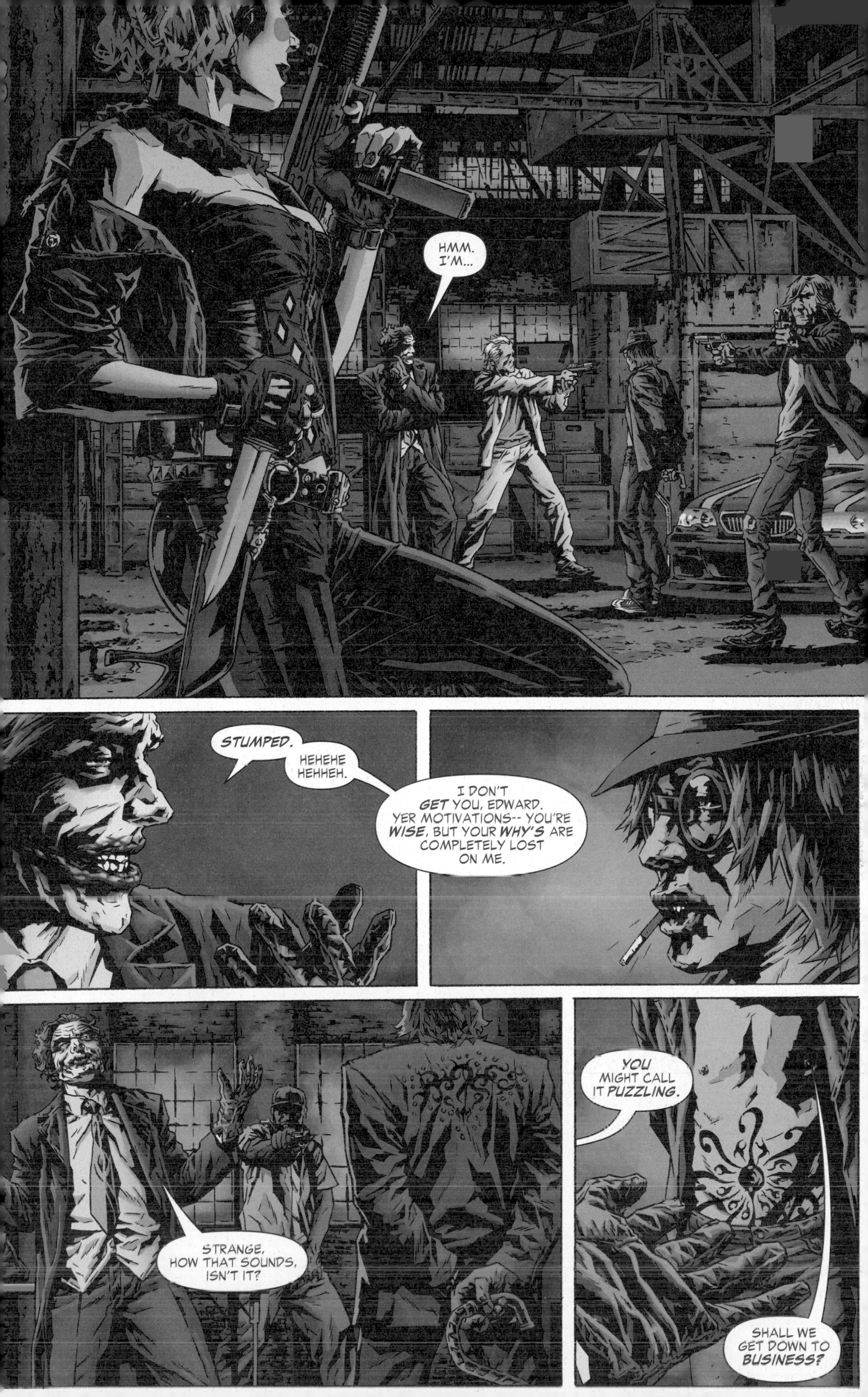
HMM. I'M...
STUMPED.
HEHEHE HEHHEH.
I DON'T GET YOU, EDWARD. YER MOTIVATIONS-- YOU'RE WISE, BUT YOUR WHY'S ARE COMPLETELY LOST ON ME.
STRANGE, HOW THAT SOUNDS, ISN'T IT?
YOU MIGHT CALL IT PUZZLING.
SHALL WE GET DOWN TO BUSINESS?

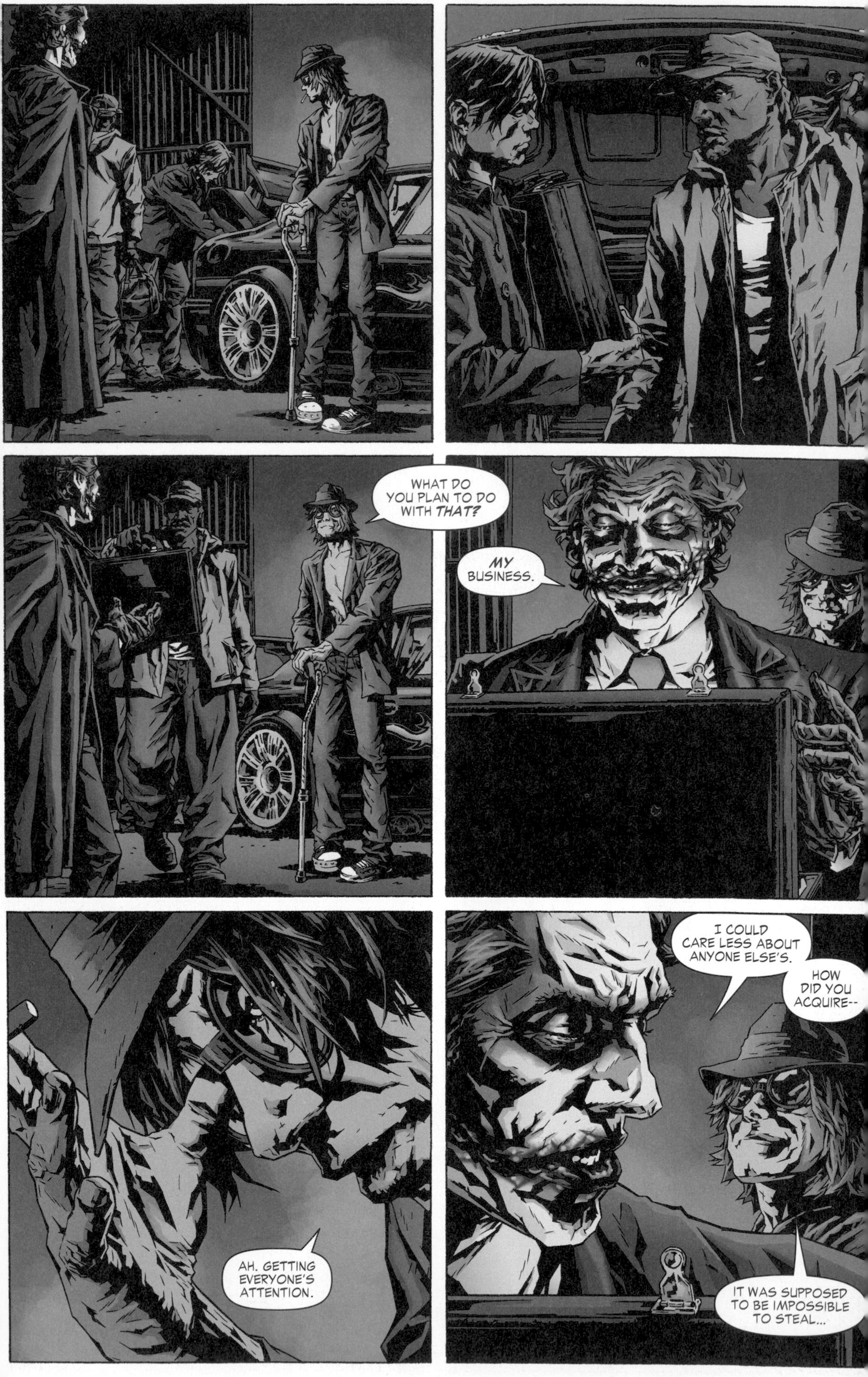
WHAT DO YOU PLAN TO DO WITH *THAT?*
MY BUSINESS.
AH. GETTING EVERYONE'S ATTENTION.
I COULD CARE LESS ABOUT ANYONE ELSE'S.
HOW DID YOU ACQUIRE--
IT WAS SUPPOSED TO BE IMPOSSIBLE TO STEAL...

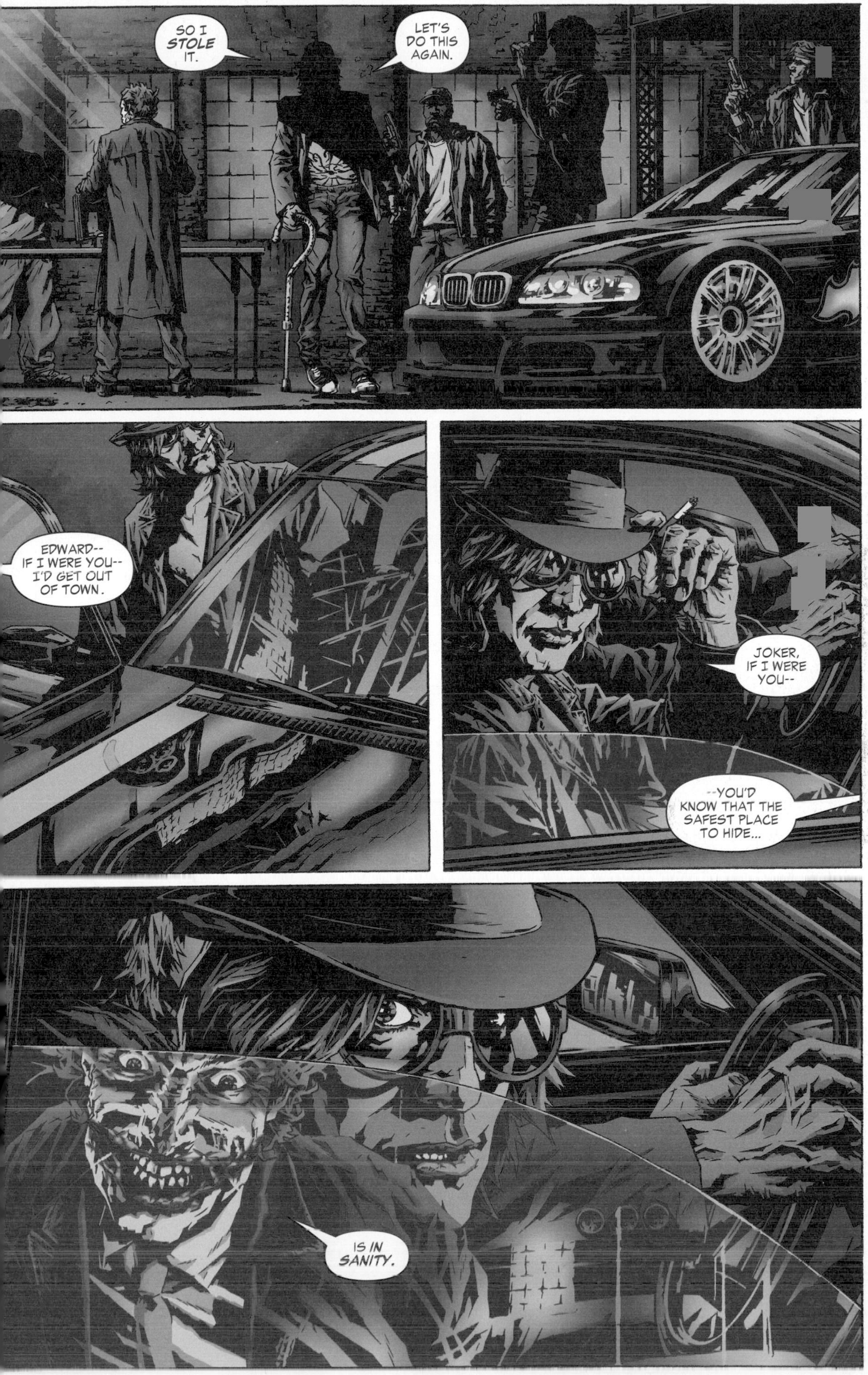
SO I STOLE IT.
LET'S DO THIS AGAIN.
EDWARD-- IF I WERE YOU-- I'D GET OUT OF TOWN.
JOKER, IF I WERE YOU--
--YOU'D KNOW THAT THE SAFEST PLACE TO HIDE...
IS IN SANITY.

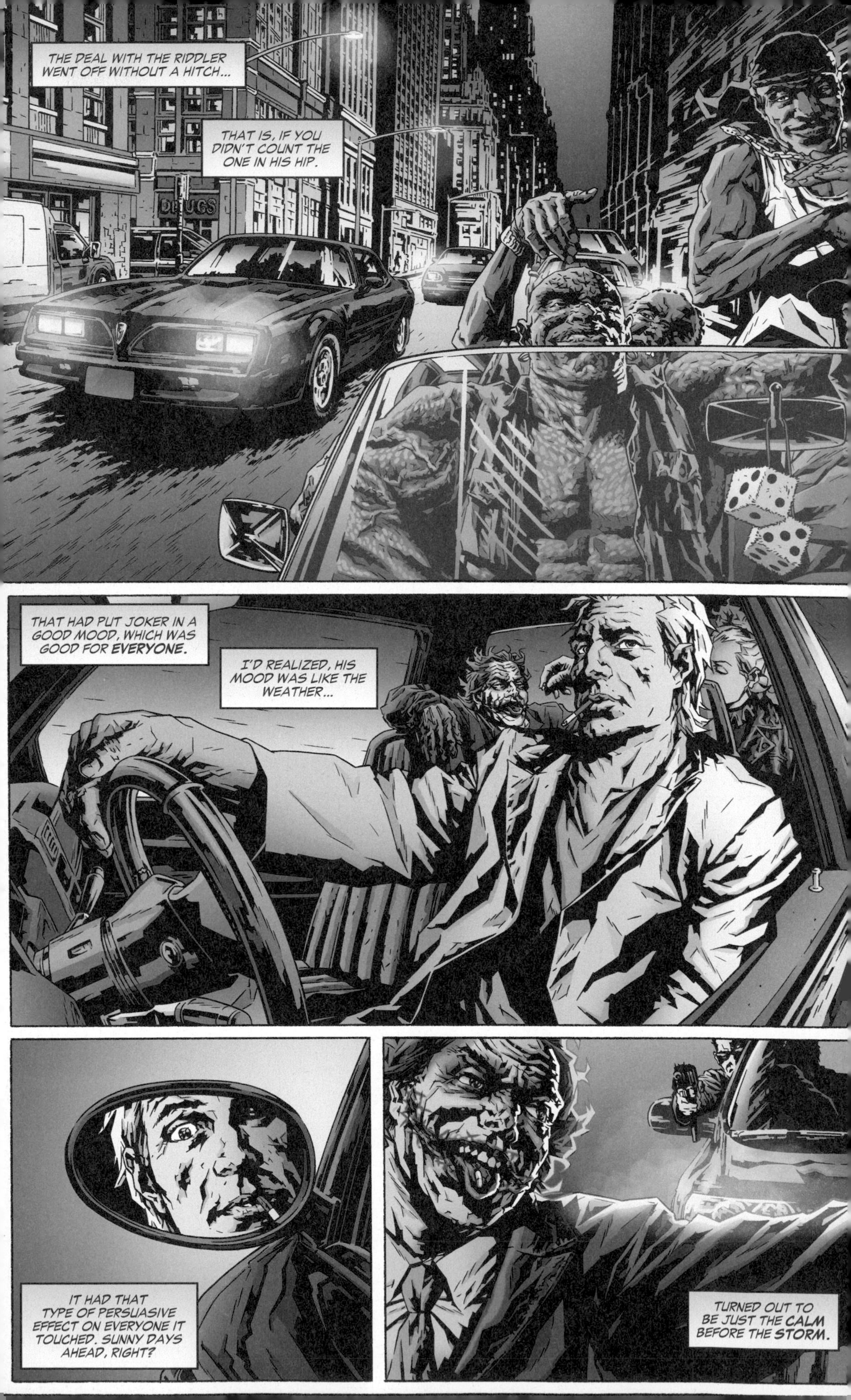
THE DEAL WITH THE RIDDLER WENT OFF WITHOUT A HITCH...
THAT IS, IF YOU DIDN'T COUNT THE ONE IN HIS HIP.
DRUGS
THAT HAD PUT JOKER IN A GOOD MOOD, WHICH WAS GOOD FOR EVERYONE.
I'D REALIZED, HIS MOOD WAS LIKE THE WEATHER...
IT HAD THAT TYPE OF PERSUASIVE EFFECT ON EVERYONE IT TOUCHED. SUNNY DAYS AHEAD, RIGHT?
TURNED OUT TO BE JUST THE CALM BEFORE THE STORM.

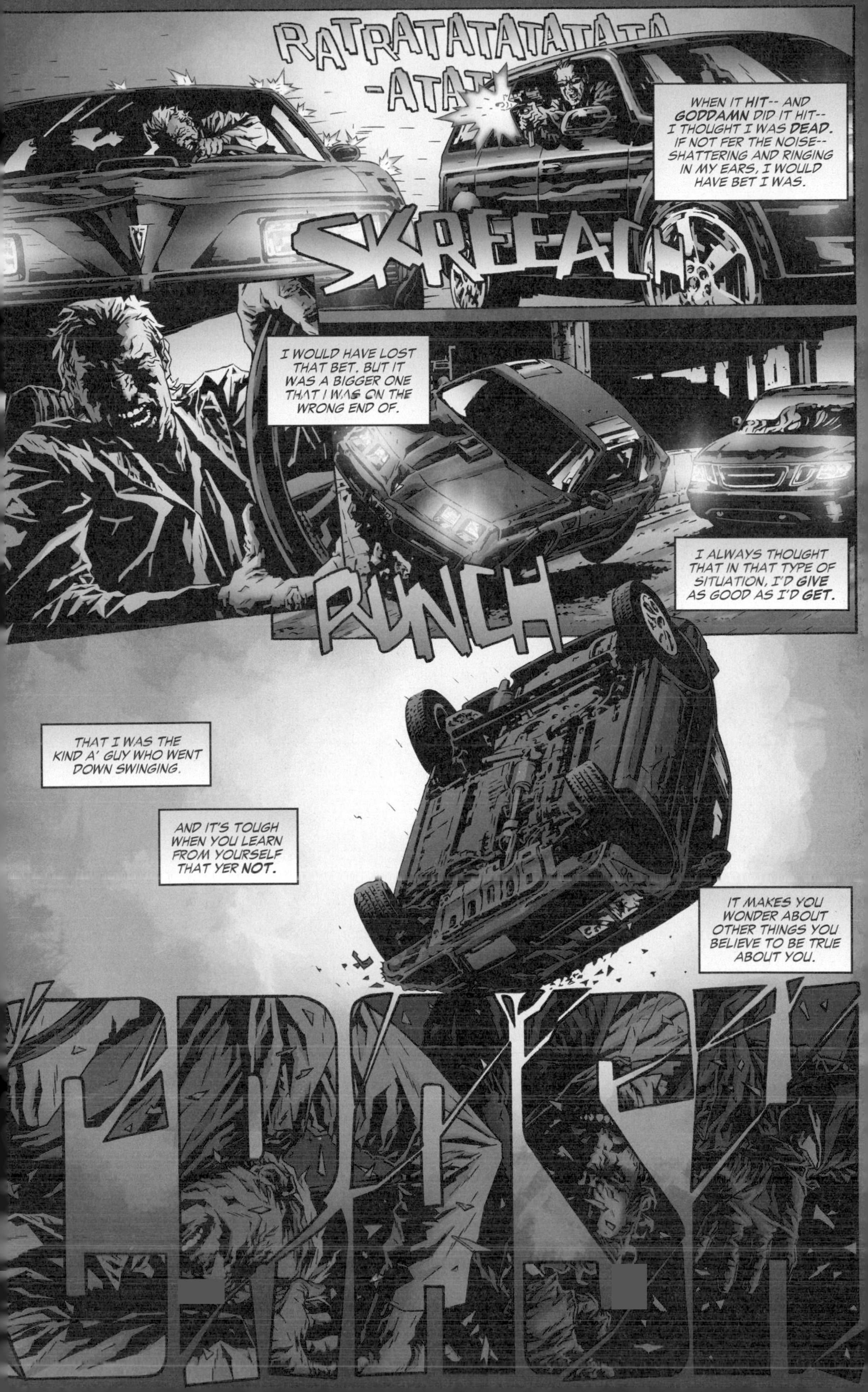
RATRATATATATATATA
-ATAT
WHEN IT HIT-- AND GODDAMN DID IT HIT-- I THOUGHT I WAS DEAD. IF NOT FER THE NOISE-- SHATTERING AND RINGING IN MY EARS, I WOULD HAVE BET I WAS.
SKREEACH
I WOULD HAVE LOST THAT BET. BUT IT WAS A BIGGER ONE THAT I WAS ON THE WRONG END OF.
I ALWAYS THOUGHT THAT IN THAT TYPE OF SITUATION, I'D GIVE AS GOOD AS I'D GET.
PUNCH
THAT I WAS THE KIND A' GUY WHO WENT DOWN SWINGING.
AND IT'S TOUGH WHEN YOU LEARN FROM YOURSELF THAT YER NOT.
IT MAKES YOU WONDER ABOUT OTHER THINGS YOU BELIEVE TO BE TRUE ABOUT YOU.

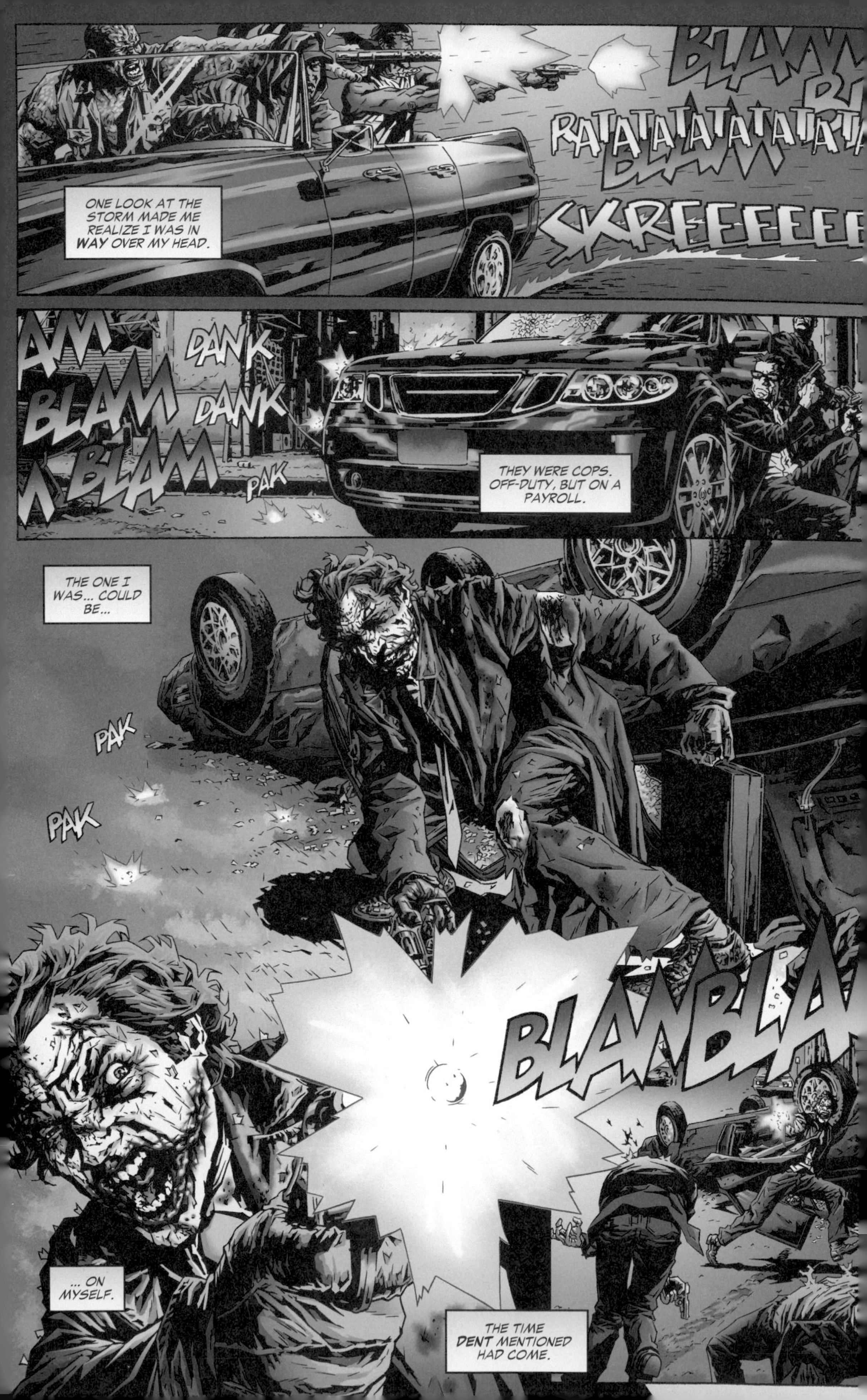

BLAAM
RATATATATATATATA
BLAM
ONE LOOK AT THE STORM MADE ME REALIZE I WAS IN WAY OVER MY HEAD.
SKREEEEEE
BLAM
DANK
DANK
BLAM
PAK
THEY WERE COPS. OFF-DUTY, BUT ON A PAYROLL.
THE ONE I WAS... COULD BE...
PAK
PAK
BLAMBLAM
... ON MYSELF.
THE TIME DENT MENTIONED HAD COME.

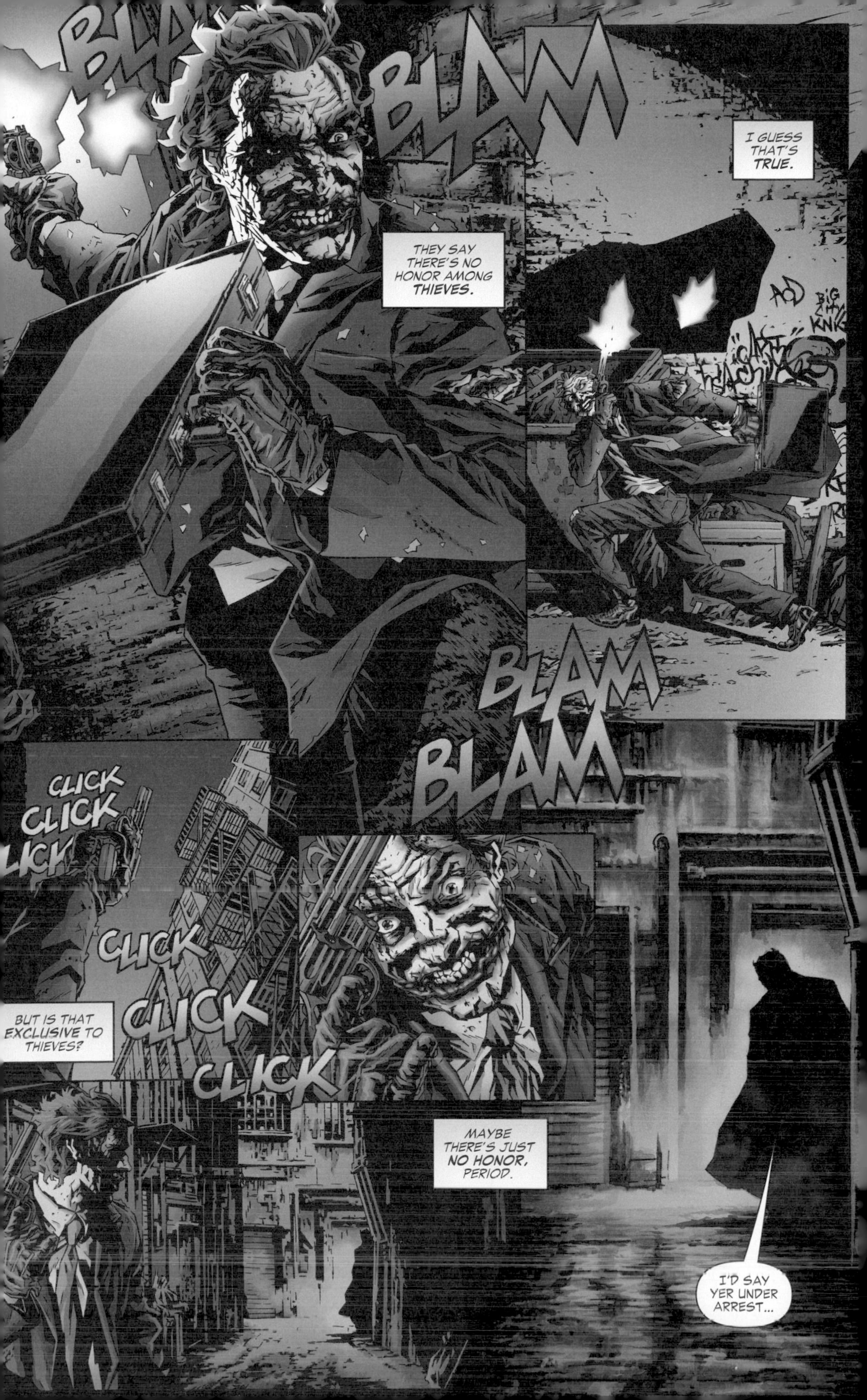
BLAM
BLAM
THEY SAY THERE'S NO HONOR AMONG THIEVES.
I GUESS THAT'S TRUE.
BLAM
BLAM
CLICK
CLICK
CLICK
CLICK
CLICK
CLICK
BUT IS THAT EXCLUSIVE TO THIEVES?
MAYBE THERE'S JUST NO HONOR, PERIOD.
I'D SAY YER UNDER ARREST...

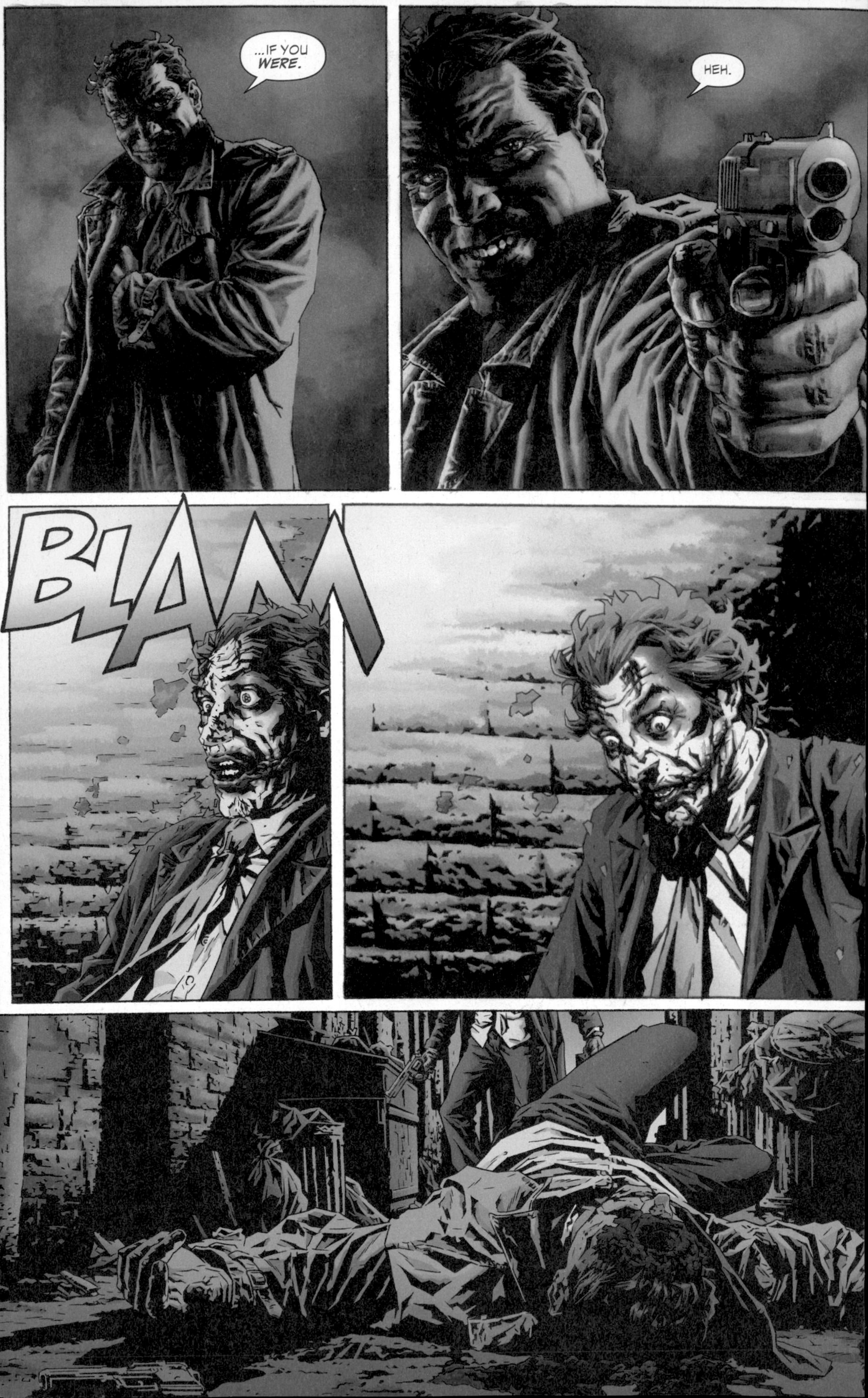
...IF YOU WERE.
HEH.
BLAM

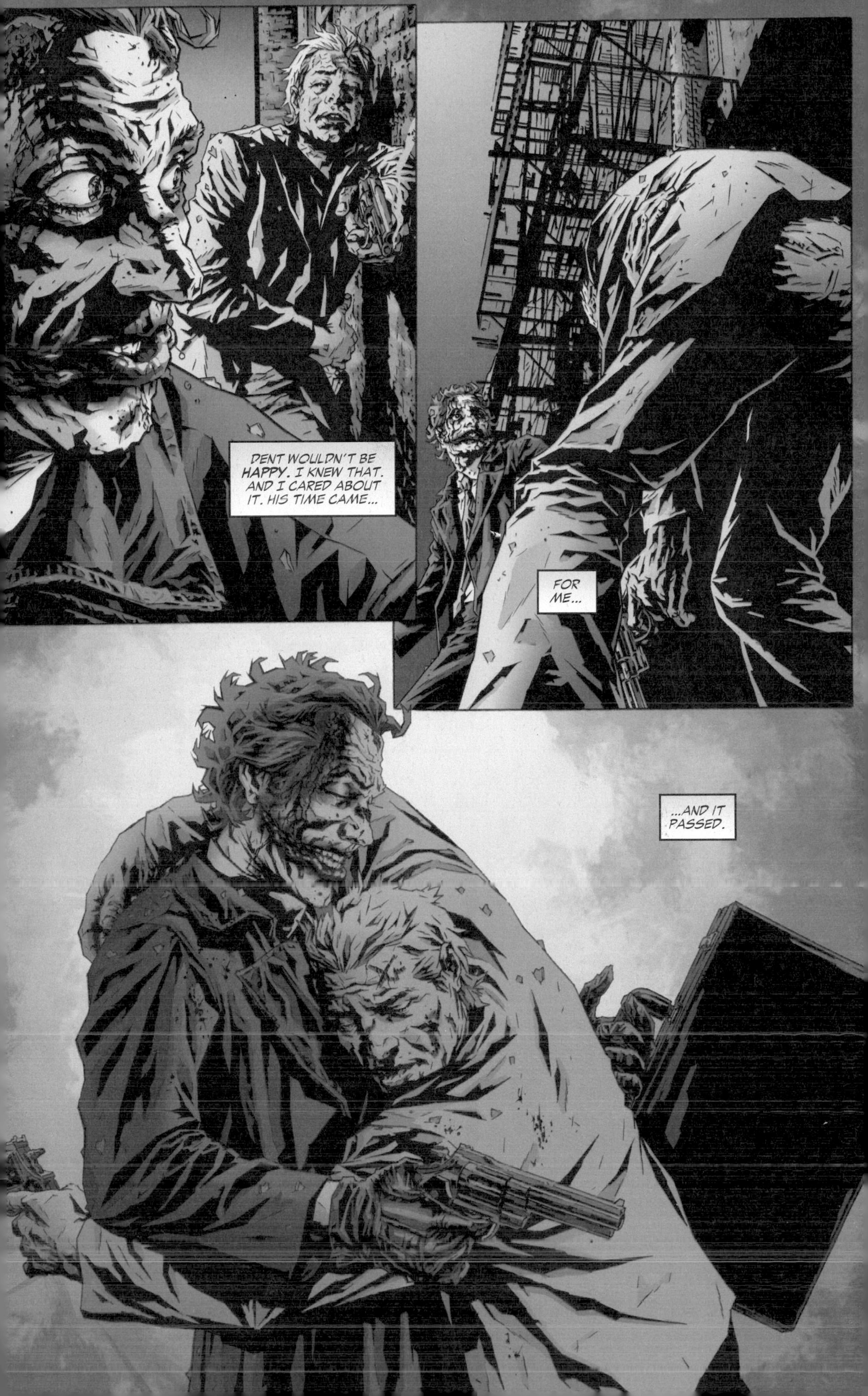
DENT WOULDN'T BE HAPPY. I KNEW THAT. AND I CARED ABOUT IT. HIS TIME CAME...
FOR ME...
...AND IT PASSED.

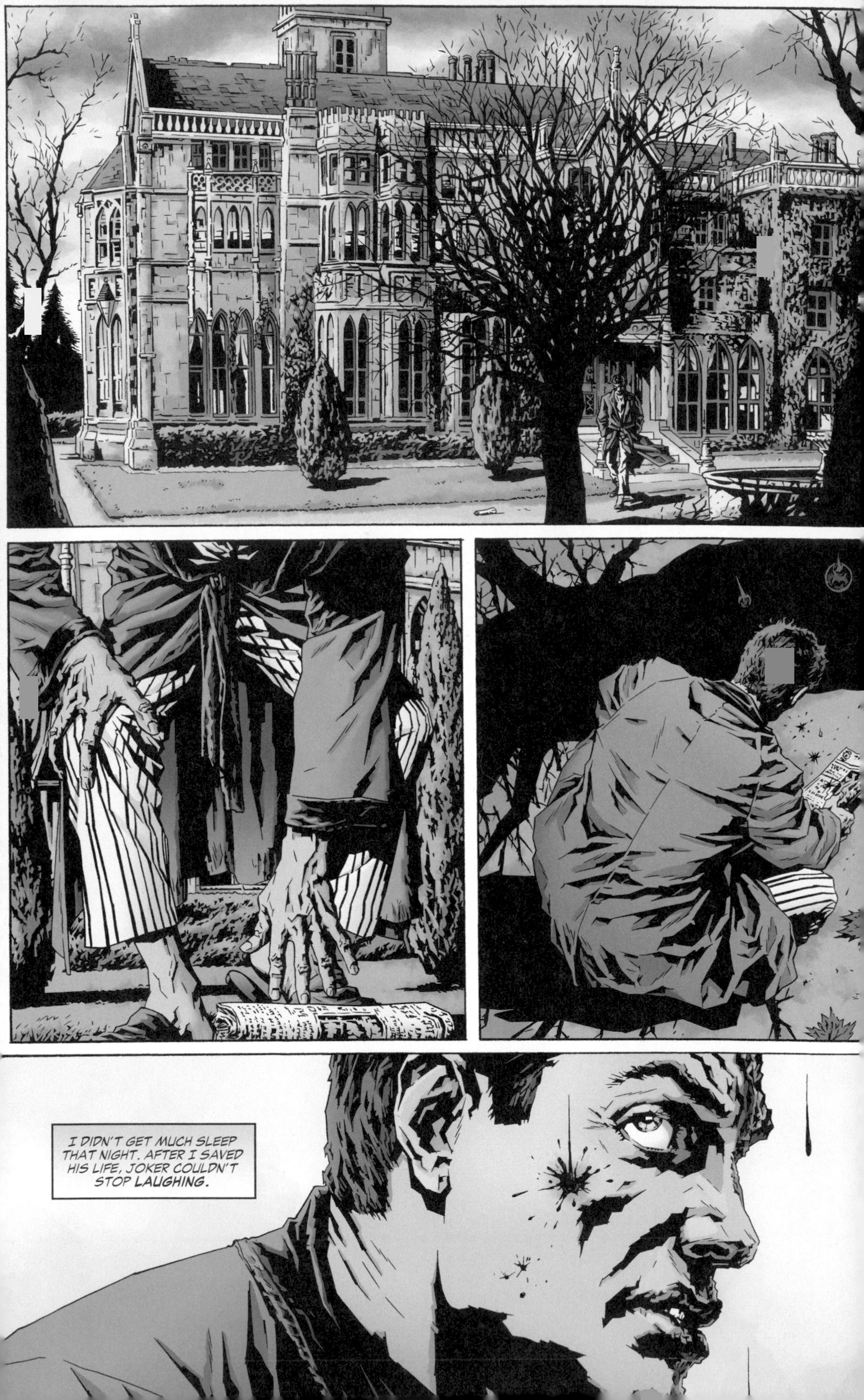
I DIDN'T GET MUCH SLEEP THAT NIGHT. AFTER I SAVED HIS LIFE, JOKER COULDN'T STOP LAUGHING.

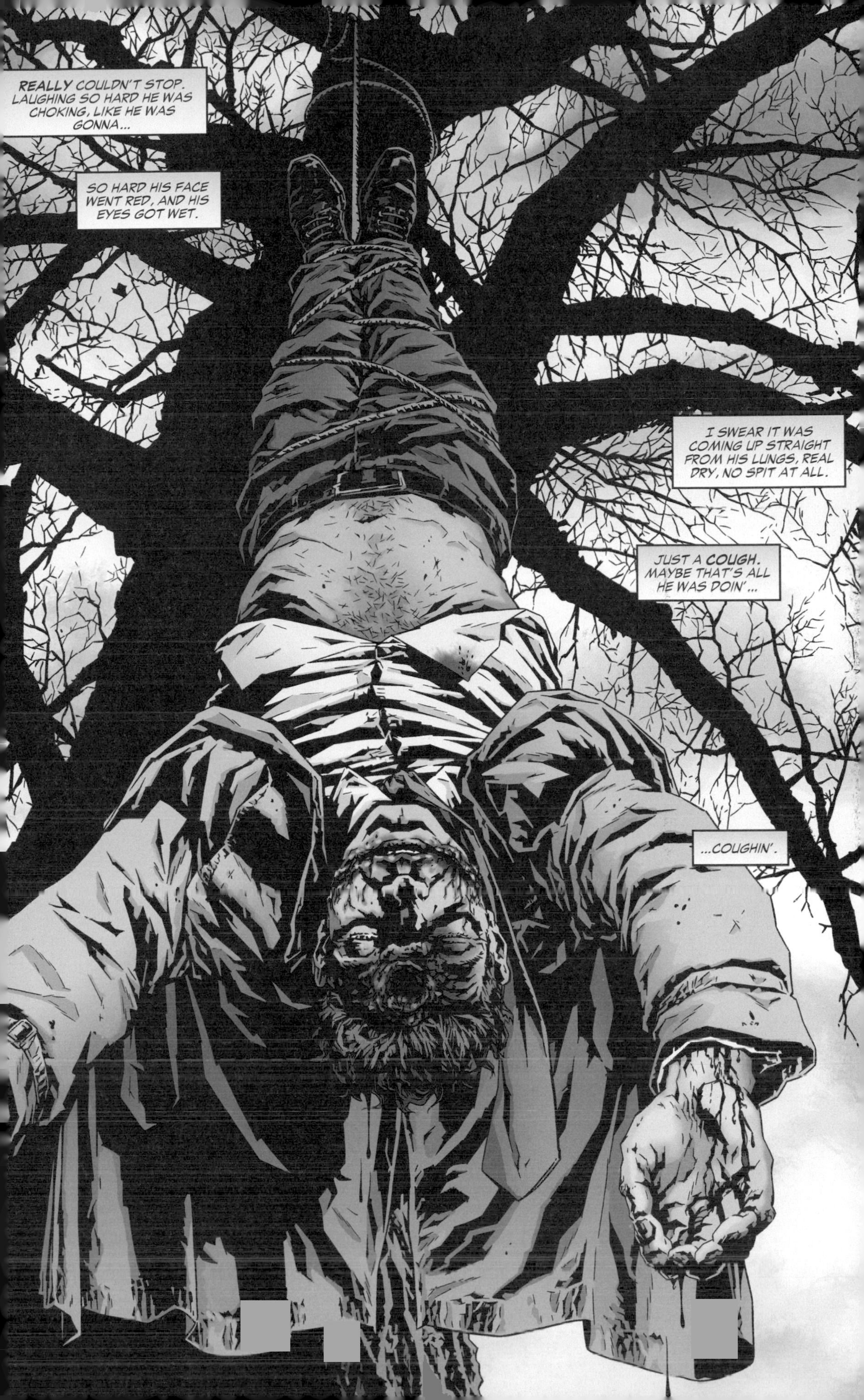
REALLY COULDN'T STOP. LAUGHING SO HARD HE WAS CHOKING, LIKE HE WAS GONNA...
SO HARD HIS FACE WENT RED, AND HIS EYES GOT WET.
I SWEAR IT WAS COMING UP STRAIGHT FROM HIS LUNGS, REAL DRY, NO SPIT AT ALL.
JUST A COUGH. MAYBE THAT'S ALL HE WAS DOIN'...
...COUGHIN'.

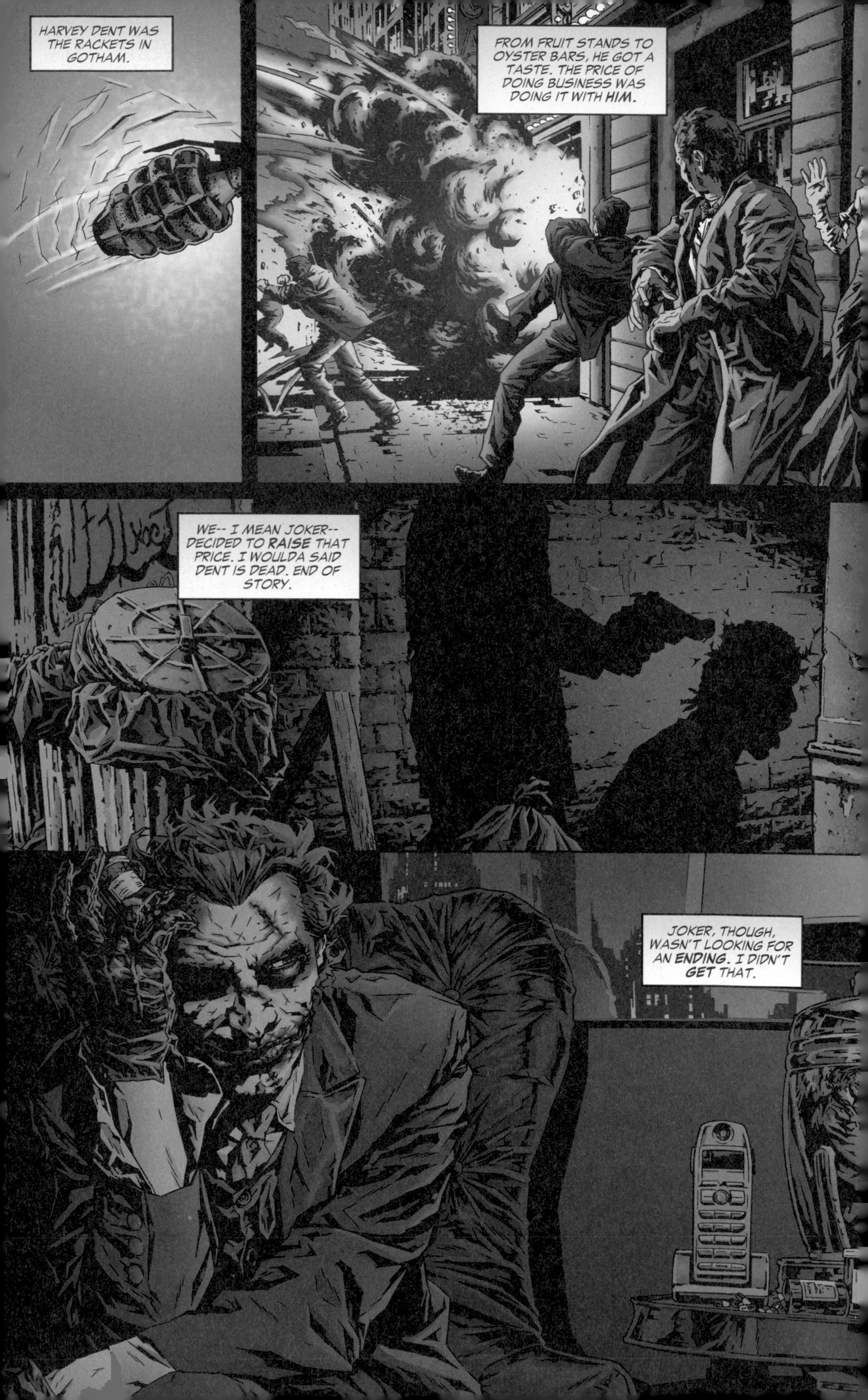
HARVEY DENT WAS THE RACKETS IN GOTHAM.
FROM FRUIT STANDS TO OYSTER BARS, HE GOT A TASTE. THE PRICE OF DOING BUSINESS WAS DOING IT WITH HIM.
WE-- I MEAN JOKER-- DECIDED TO RAISE THAT PRICE. I WOULDA SAID DENT IS DEAD. END OF STORY.
JOKER, THOUGH, WASN'T LOOKING FOR AN ENDING. I DIDN'T GET THAT.

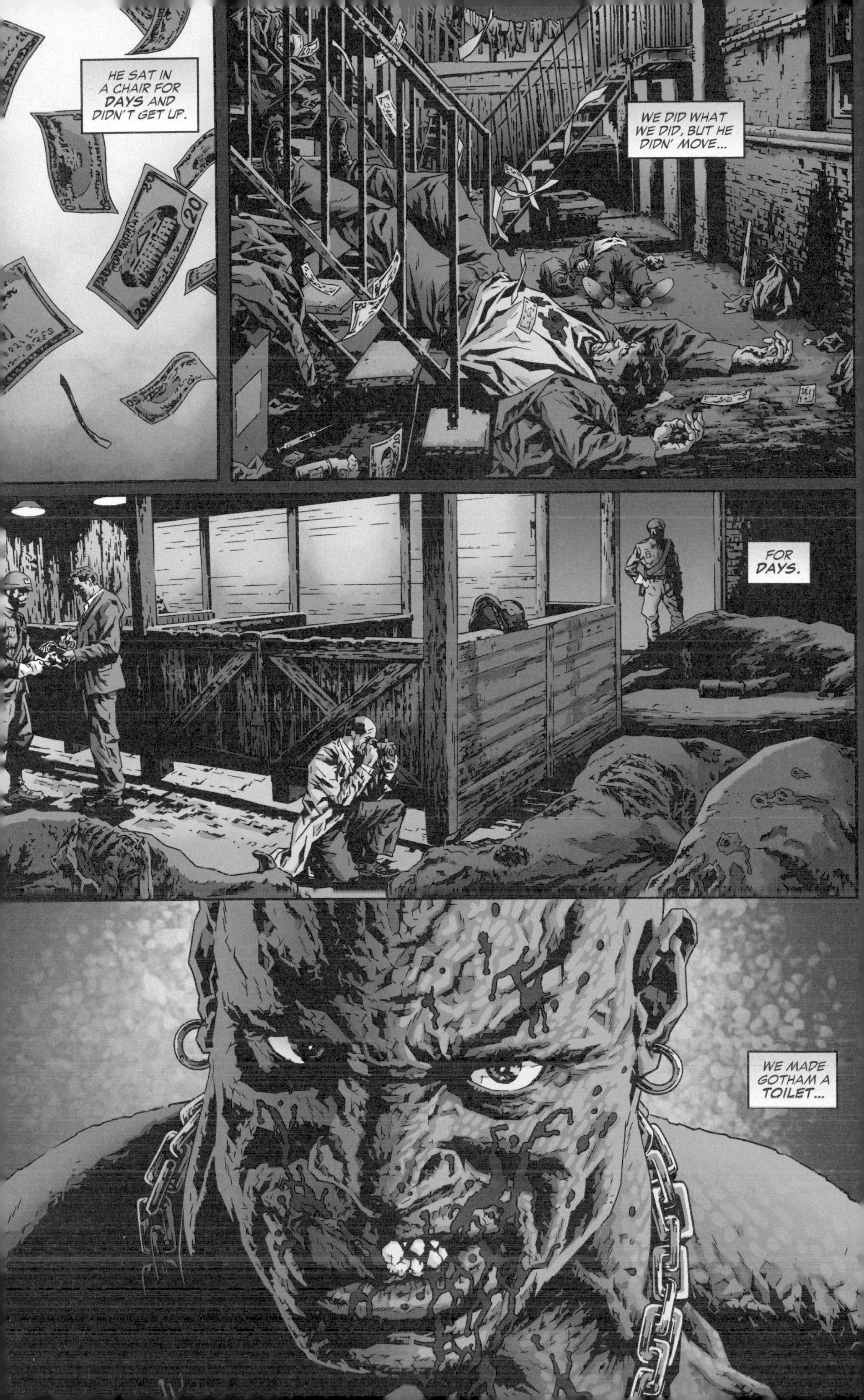
HE SAT IN A CHAIR FOR DAYS AND DIDN'T GET UP.
WE DID WHAT WE DID, BUT HE DIDN' MOVE...
FOR DAYS.
WE MADE GOTHAM A TOILET...

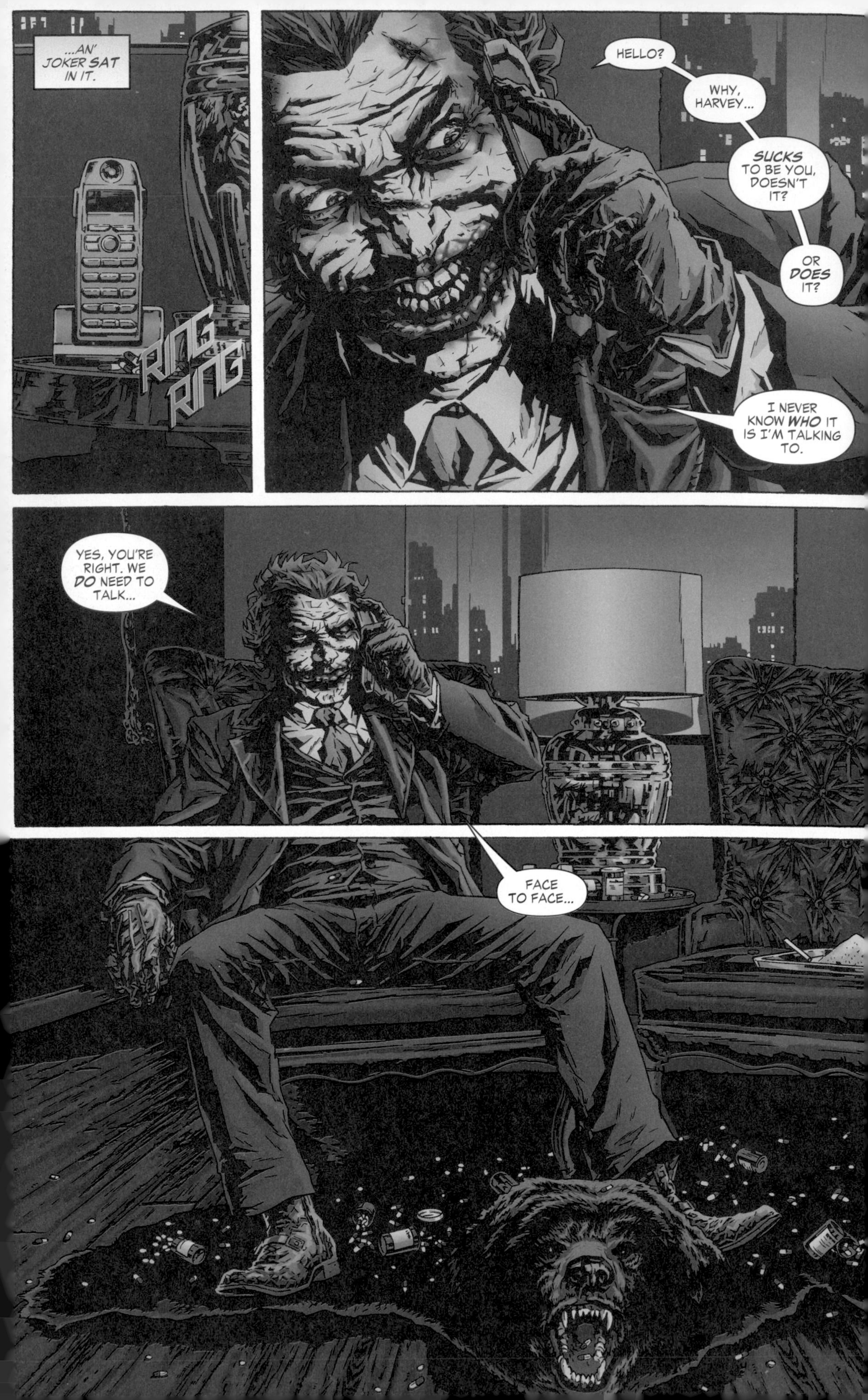
...AN' JOKER SAT IN IT.
RING RING
HELLO?
WHY, HARVEY...
SUCKS TO BE YOU, DOESN'T IT?
OR DOES IT?
I NEVER KNOW WHO IT IS I'M TALKING TO.
YES, YOU'RE RIGHT. WE DO NEED TO TALK...
FACE TO FACE...

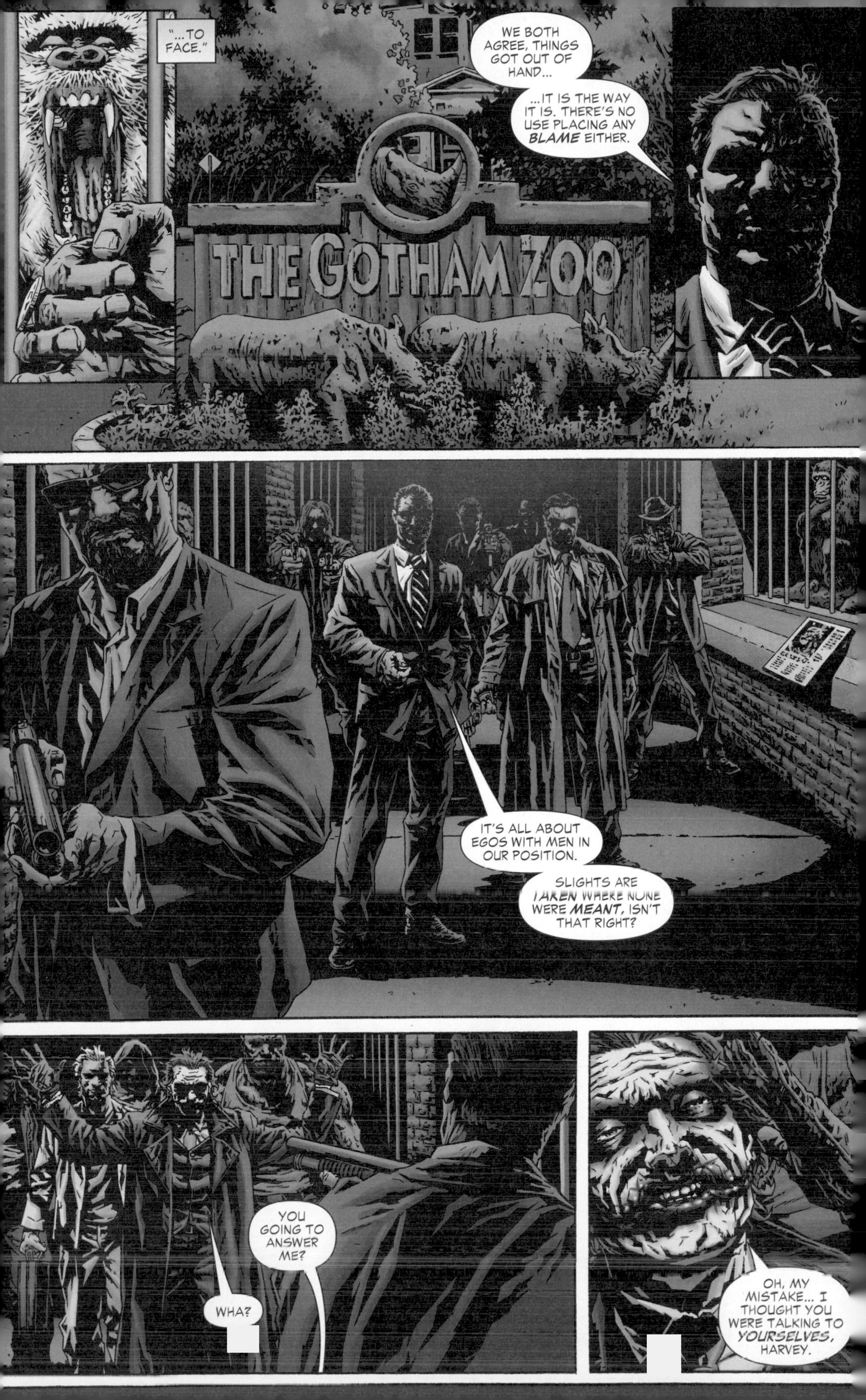
"...TO FACE."
WE BOTH AGREE, THINGS GOT OUT OF HAND...
...IT IS THE WAY IT IS. THERE'S NO USE PLACING ANY *BLAME* EITHER.
THE GOTHAM ZOO
IT'S ALL ABOUT EGOS WITH MEN IN OUR POSITION.
SLIGHTS ARE *TAKEN* WHERE NONE WERE *MEANT*, ISN'T THAT RIGHT?
YOU GOING TO ANSWER ME?
WHA?
OH, MY MISTAKE... I THOUGHT YOU WERE TALKING TO *YOURSELVES*, HARVEY.

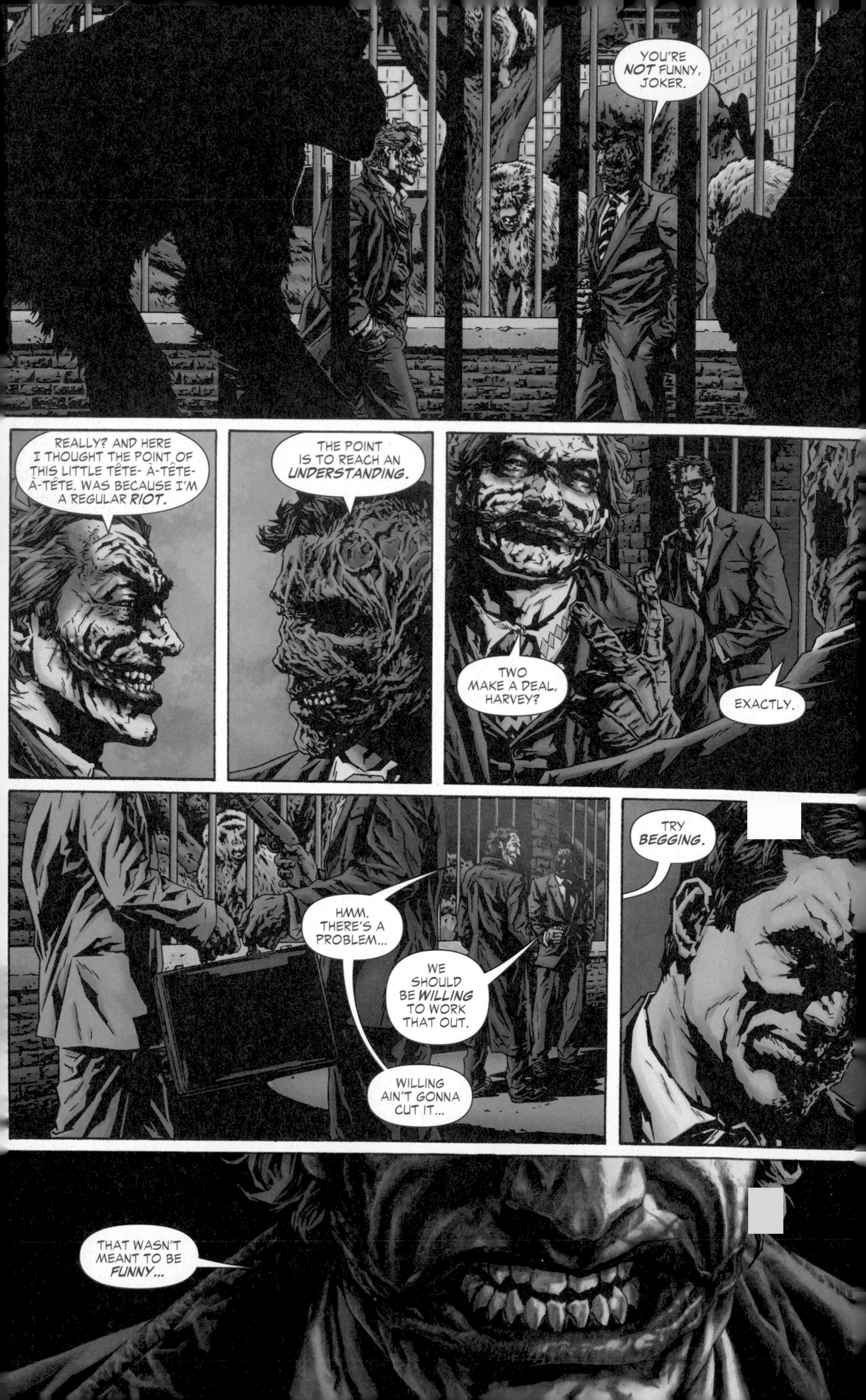
YOU'RE NOT FUNNY, JOKER.
REALLY? AND HERE I THOUGHT THE POINT OF THIS LITTLE TÊTE- À-TÊTE- À-TÊTE. WAS BECAUSE I'M A REGULAR RIOT.
THE POINT IS TO REACH AN UNDERSTANDING.
TWO MAKE A DEAL, HARVEY?
EXACTLY.
HMM. THERE'S A PROBLEM...
WE SHOULD BE WILLING TO WORK THAT OUT.
WILLING AIN'T GONNA CUT IT...
TRY BEGGING.
THAT WASN'T MEANT TO BE FUNNY...

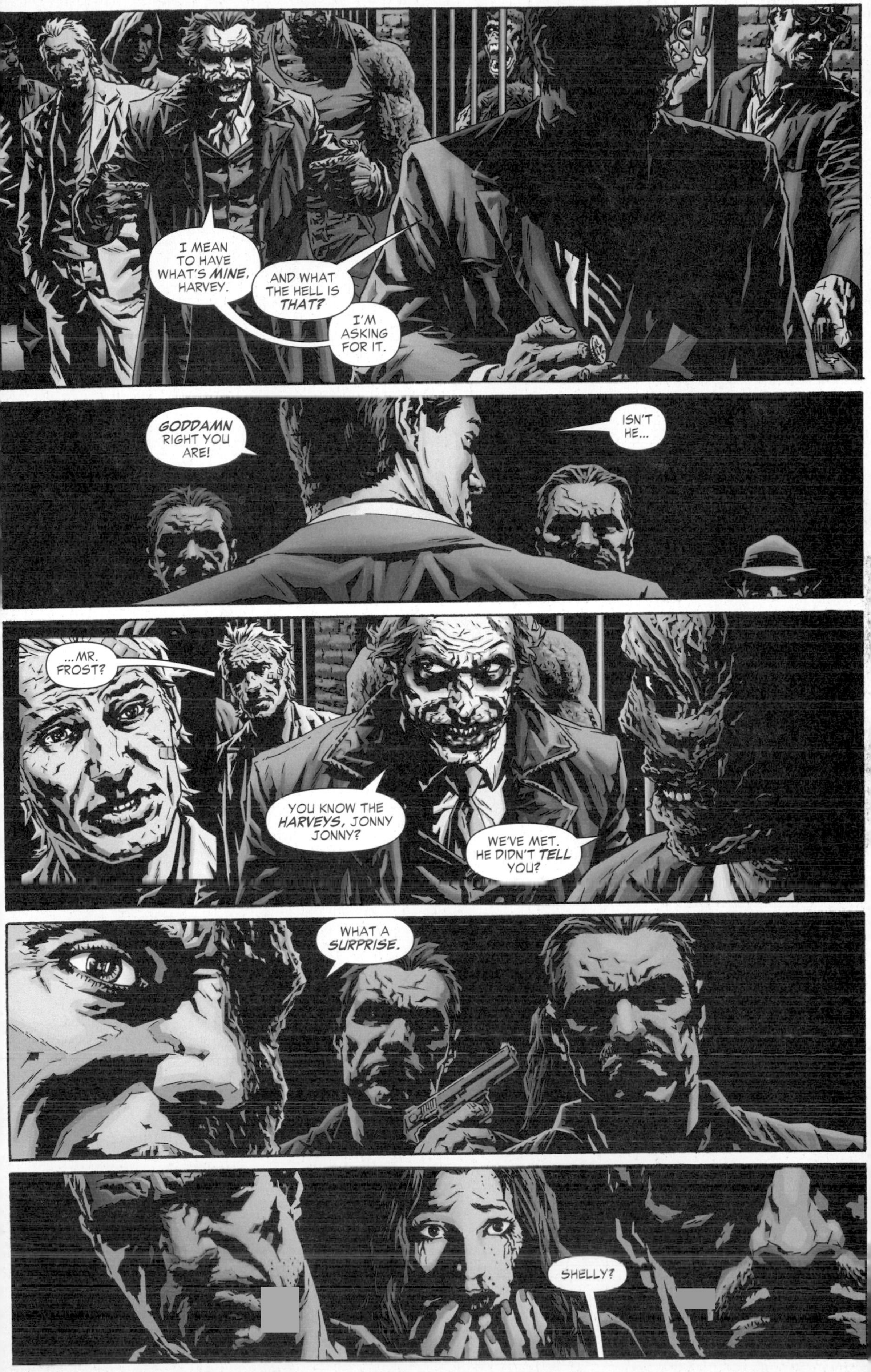
I MEAN TO HAVE WHAT'S *MINE*, HARVEY.
AND WHAT THE HELL IS *THAT?*
I'M ASKING FOR IT.
GODDAMN RIGHT YOU ARE!
ISN'T HE...
...MR. FROST?
YOU KNOW THE *HARVEYS*, JONNY JONNY?
WE'VE MET. HE DIDN'T *TELL* YOU?
WHAT A *SURPRISE*.
SHELLY?

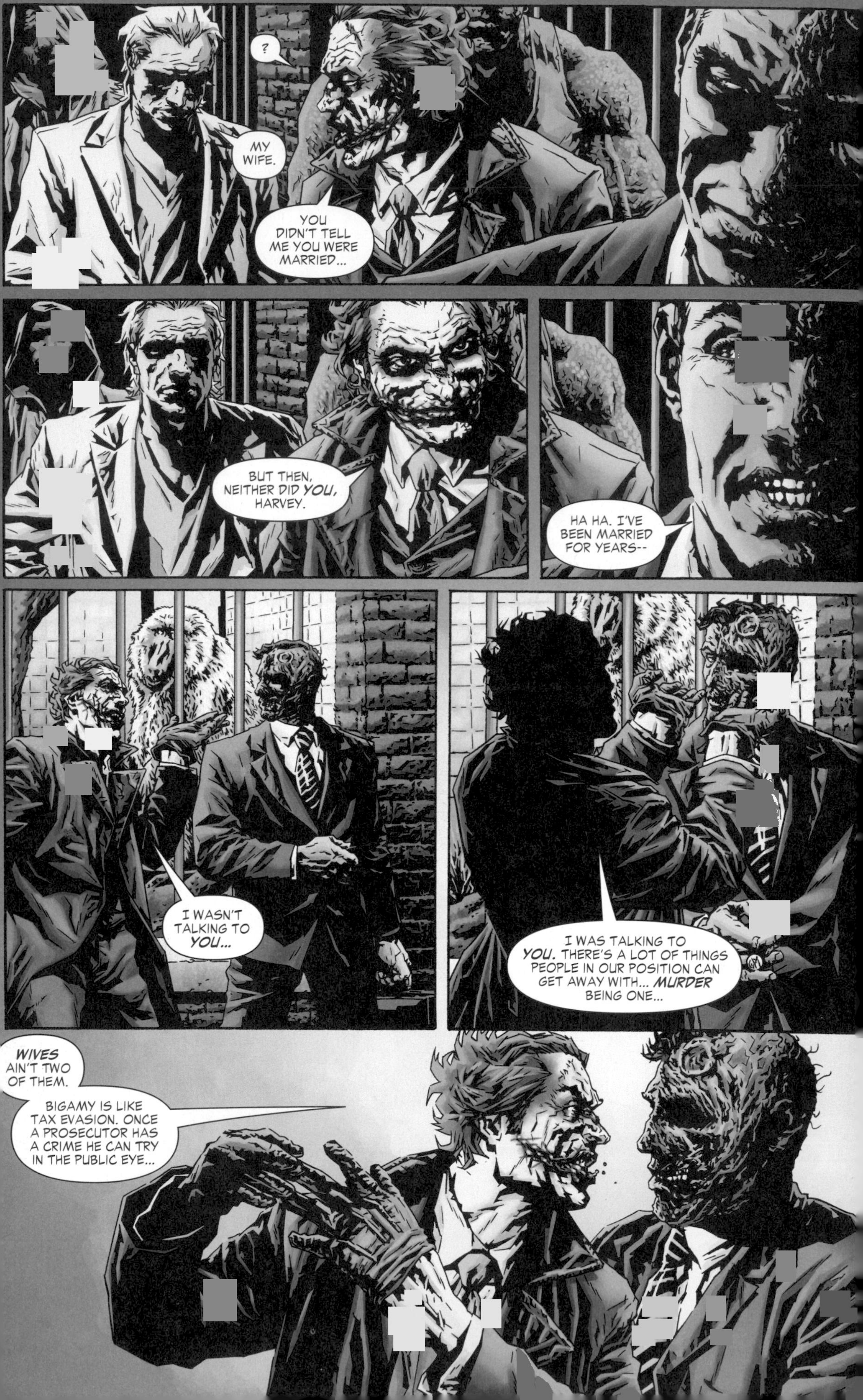
?
MY WIFE.
YOU DIDN'T TELL ME YOU WERE MARRIED...
BUT THEN, NEITHER DID YOU, HARVEY.
HA HA. I'VE BEEN MARRIED FOR YEARS--
I WASN'T TALKING TO YOU...
I WAS TALKING TO YOU. THERE'S A LOT OF THINGS PEOPLE IN OUR POSITION CAN GET AWAY WITH... MURDER BEING ONE...
WIVES AIN'T TWO OF THEM.
BIGAMY IS LIKE TAX EVASION. ONCE A PROSECUTOR HAS A CRIME HE CAN TRY IN THE PUBLIC EYE...

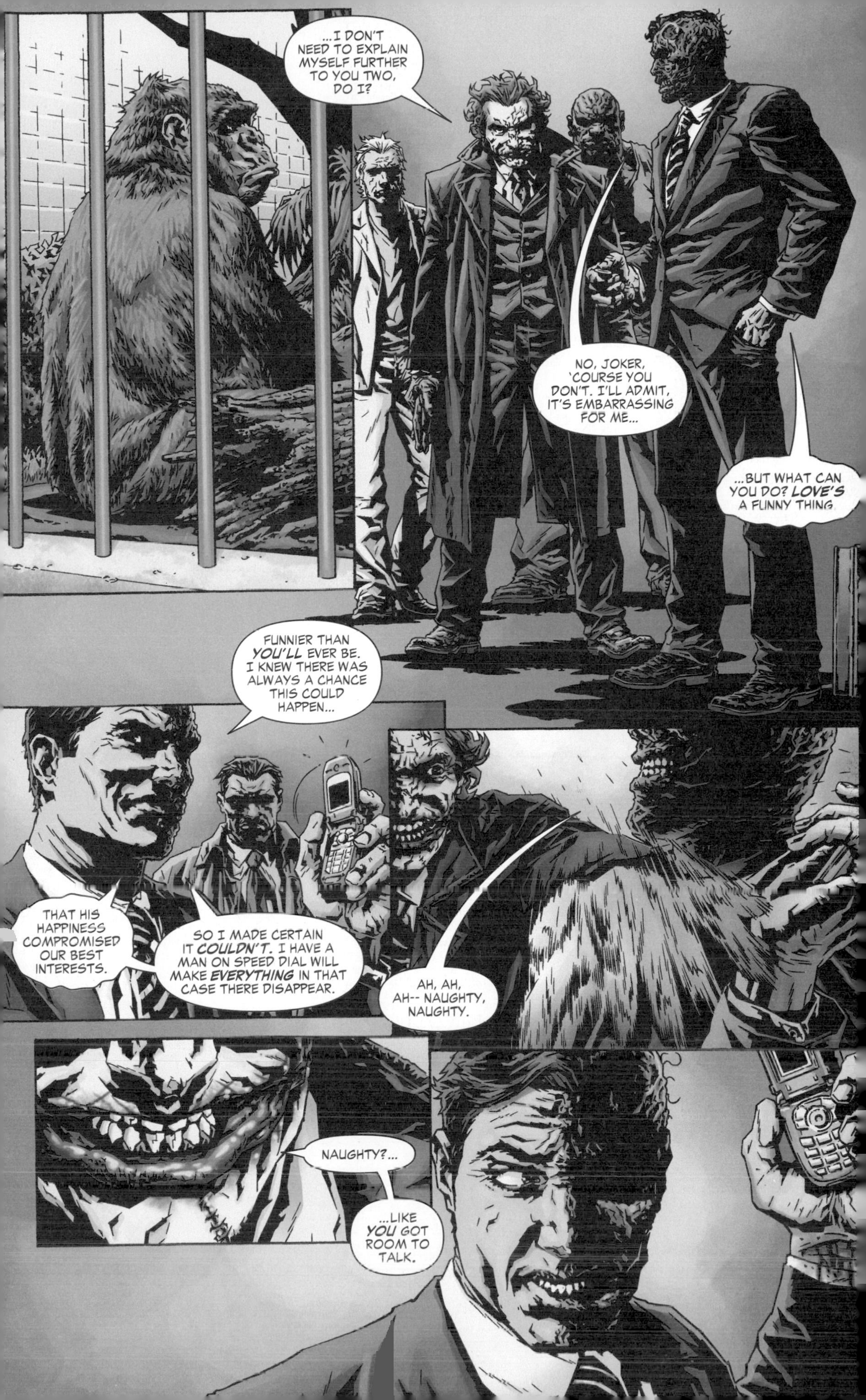
...I DON'T NEED TO EXPLAIN MYSELF FURTHER TO YOU TWO, DO I?
NO, JOKER, 'COURSE YOU DON'T. I'LL ADMIT, IT'S EMBARRASSING FOR ME...
...BUT WHAT CAN YOU DO? LOVE'S A FUNNY THING.
FUNNIER THAN YOU'LL EVER BE. I KNEW THERE WAS ALWAYS A CHANCE THIS COULD HAPPEN...
THAT HIS HAPPINESS COMPROMISED OUR BEST INTERESTS.
SO I MADE CERTAIN IT COULDN'T. I HAVE A MAN ON SPEED DIAL WILL MAKE EVERYTHING IN THAT CASE THERE DISAPPEAR.
AH, AH, AH-- NAUGHTY, NAUGHTY.
NAUGHTY?...
...LIKE YOU GOT ROOM TO TALK.

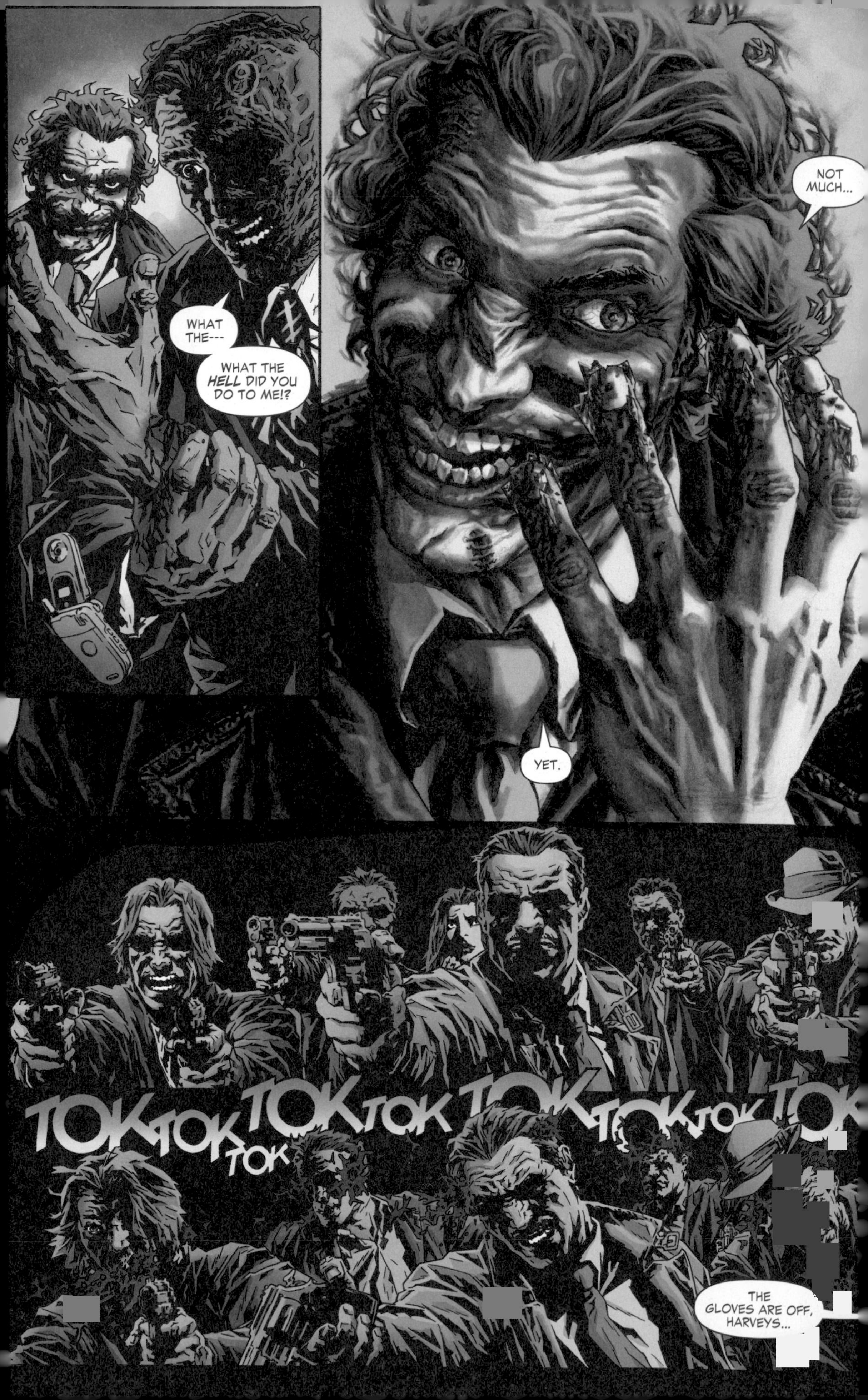
WHAT THE---
WHAT THE HELL DID YOU DO TO ME!?
NOT MUCH...
YET.
TOK TOK TOK TOK TOK TOK TOK TOK TOK TOK
THE GLOVES ARE OFF, HARVEYS...

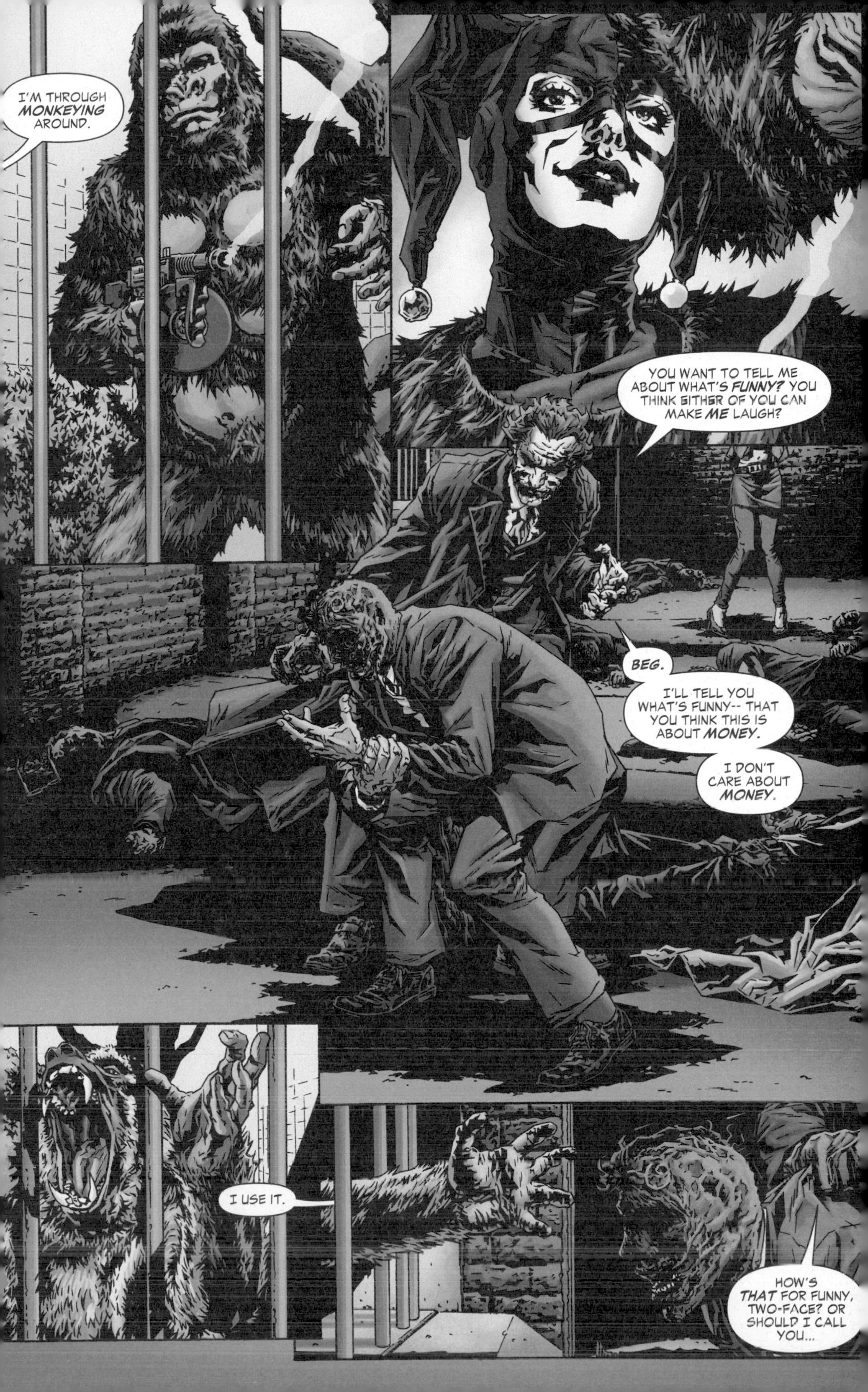

I'M THROUGH MONKEYING AROUND.
YOU WANT TO TELL ME ABOUT WHAT'S FUNNY? YOU THINK EITHER OF YOU CAN MAKE ME LAUGH?
BEG.
I'LL TELL YOU WHAT'S FUNNY-- THAT YOU THINK THIS IS ABOUT MONEY.
I DON'T CARE ABOUT MONEY.
I USE IT.
HOW'S THAT FOR FUNNY, TWO-FACE? OR SHOULD I CALL YOU...

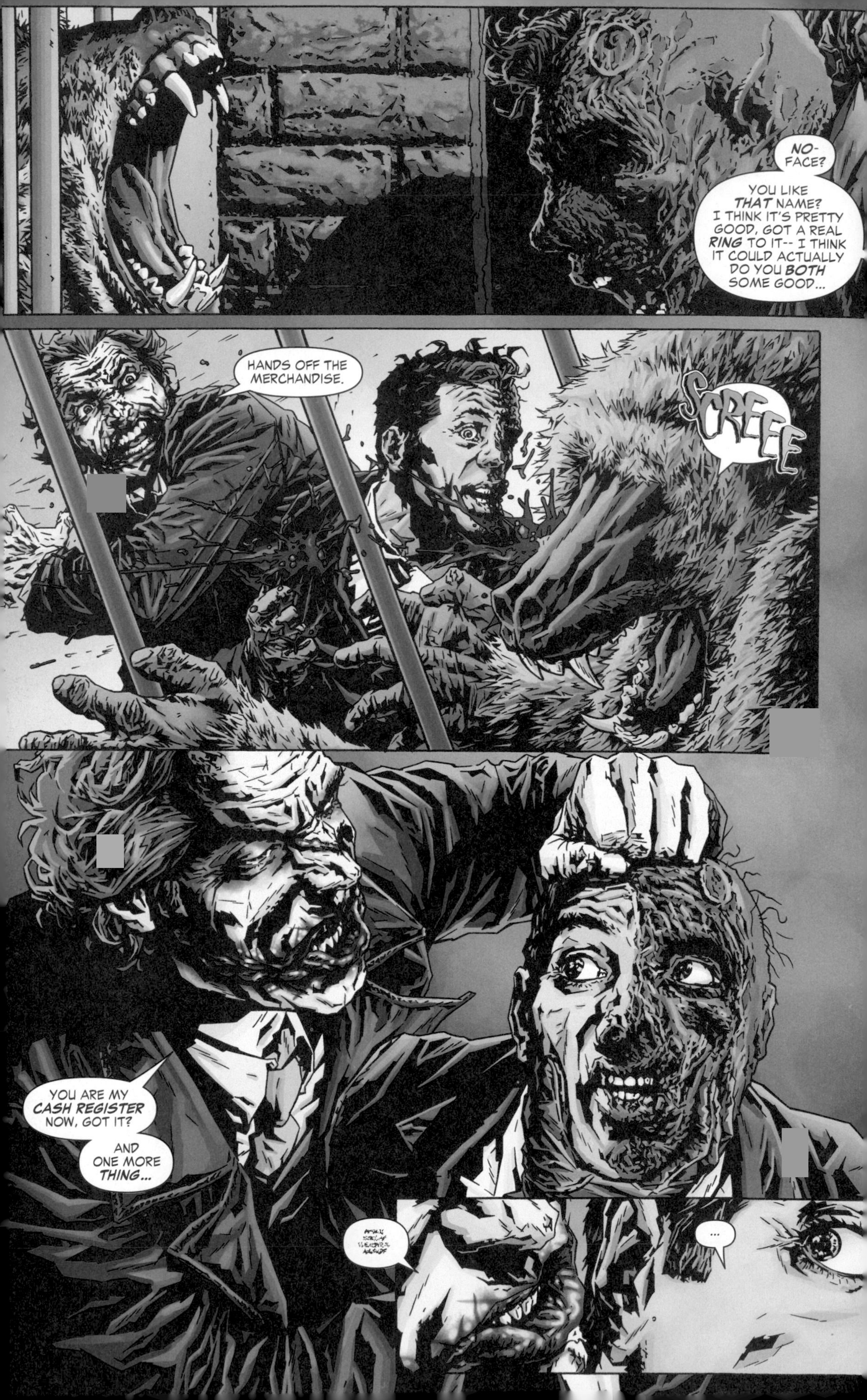
NO-FACE?
YOU LIKE THAT NAME? I THINK IT'S PRETTY GOOD, GOT A REAL RING TO IT-- I THINK IT COULD ACTUALLY DO YOU BOTH SOME GOOD...
HANDS OFF THE MERCHANDISE.
SCREEE
YOU ARE MY CASH REGISTER NOW, GOT IT?
AND ONE MORE THING...
...

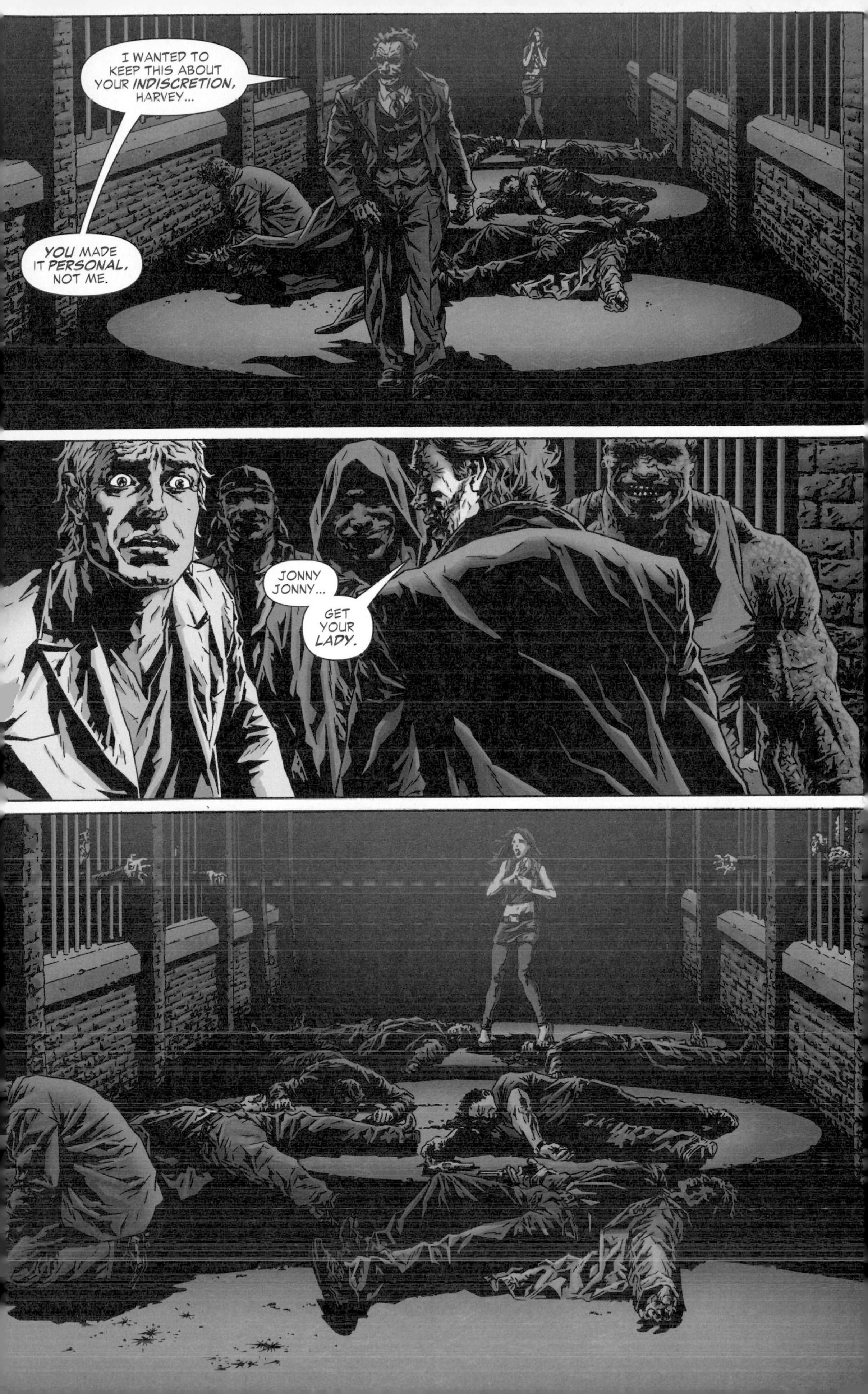
I WANTED TO KEEP THIS ABOUT YOUR INDISCRETION, HARVEY...
YOU MADE IT PERSONAL, NOT ME.
JONNY JONNY...
GET YOUR LADY.

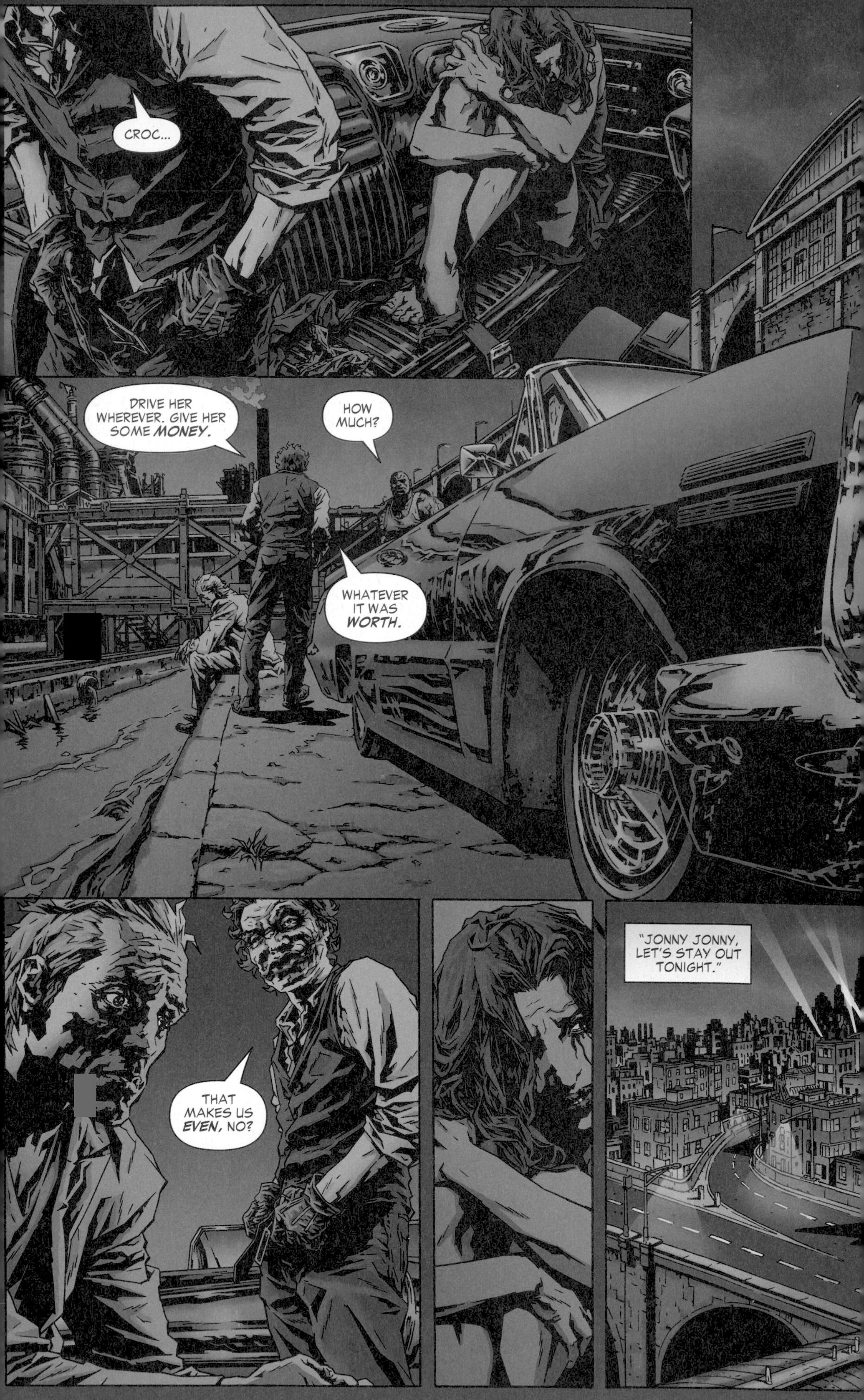
CROC...
DRIVE HER WHEREVER. GIVE HER SOME MONEY.
HOW MUCH?
WHATEVER IT WAS WORTH.
THAT MAKES US EVEN, NO?
"JONNY JONNY, LET'S STAY OUT TONIGHT."

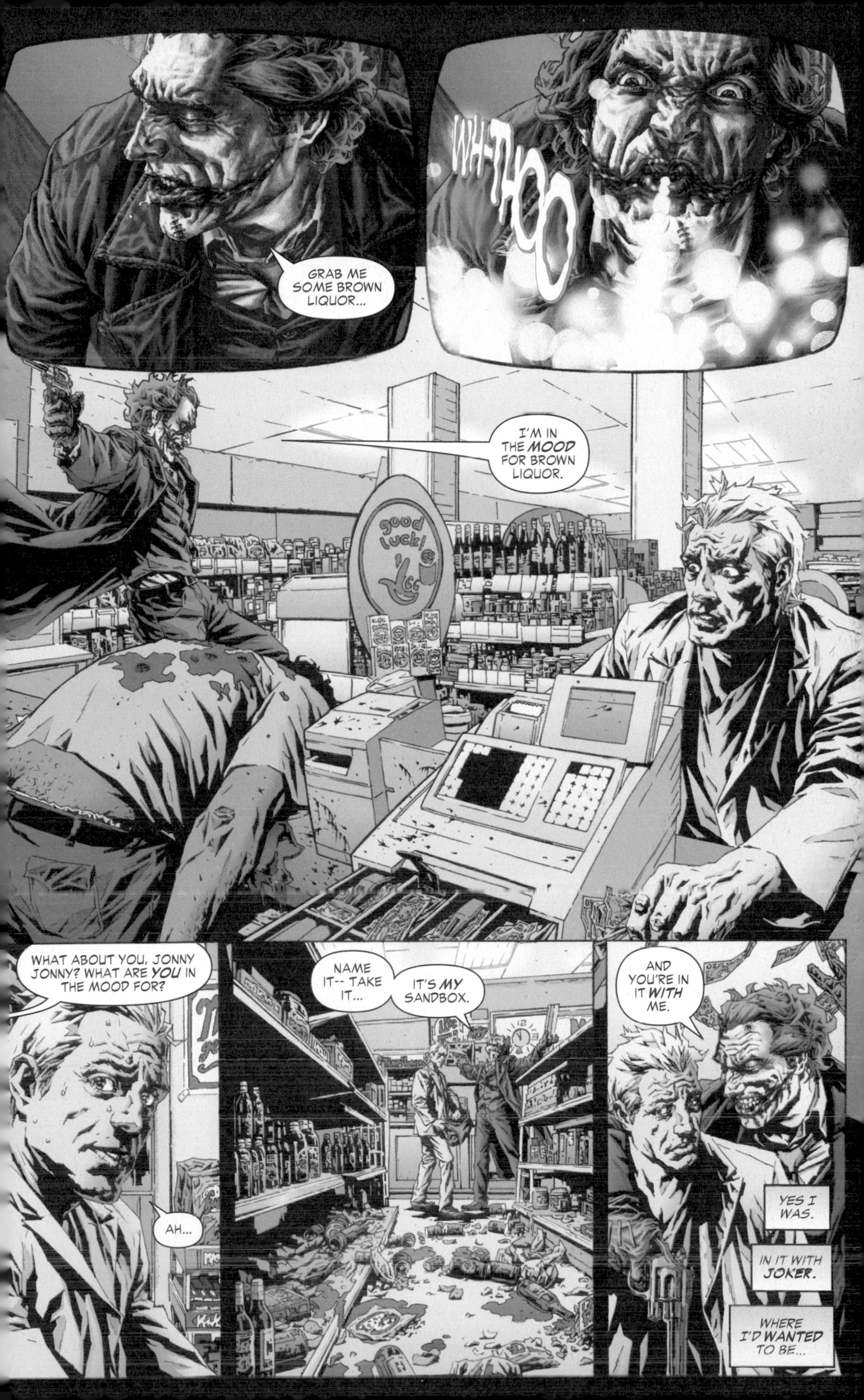
GRAB ME SOME BROWN LIQUOR...
WH-THOO
I'M IN THE MOOD FOR BROWN LIQUOR.
good luck!
WHAT ABOUT YOU, JONNY JONNY? WHAT ARE YOU IN THE MOOD FOR?
AH...
NAME IT-- TAKE IT...
IT'S MY SANDBOX.
AND YOU'RE IN IT WITH ME.
YES I WAS.
IN IT WITH JOKER.
WHERE I'D WANTED TO BE...

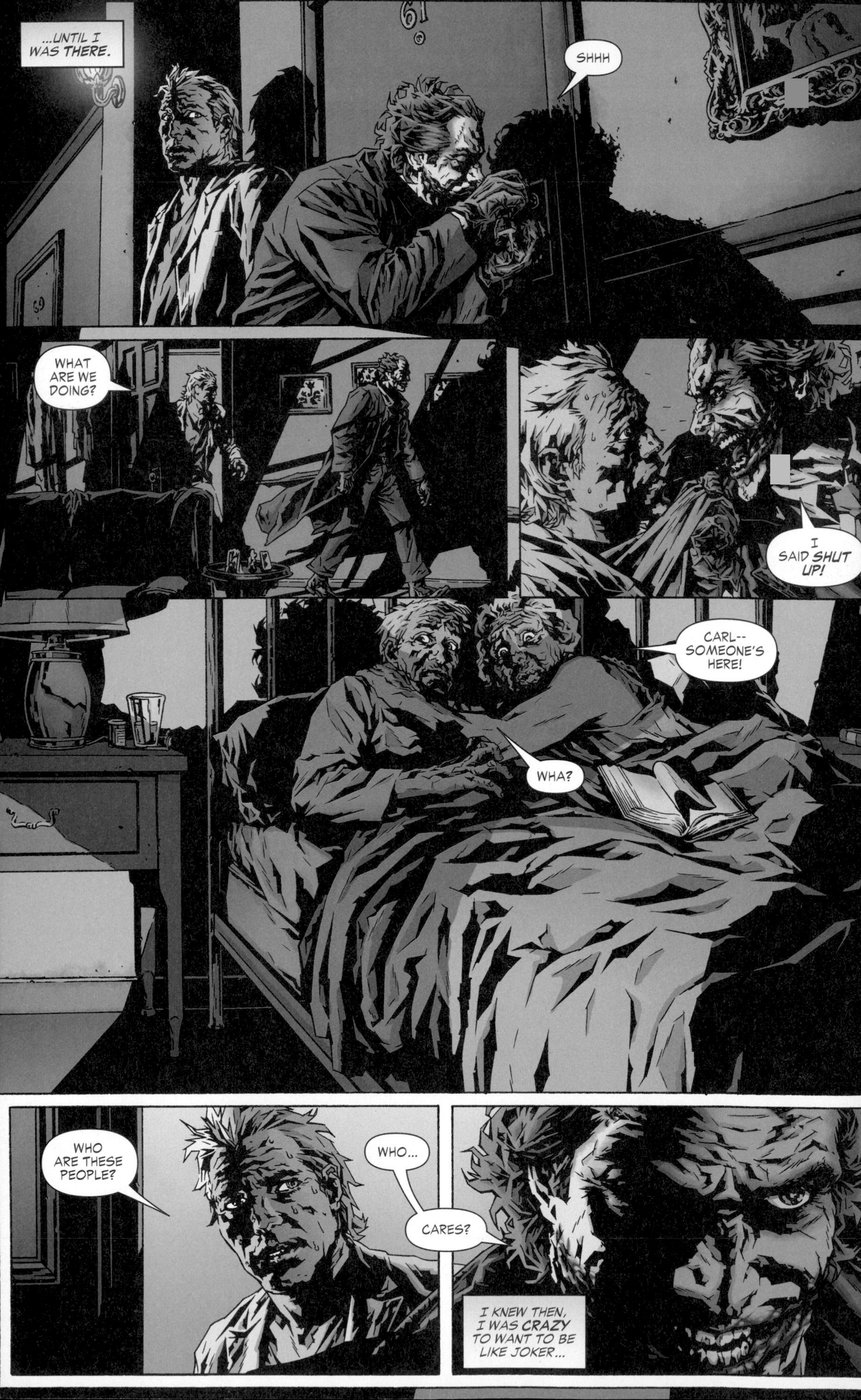
...UNTIL I WAS THERE.
SHHH
WHAT ARE WE DOING?
I SAID SHUT UP!
CARL-- SOMEONE'S HERE!
WHA?
WHO ARE THESE PEOPLE?
WHO...
CARES?
I KNEW THEN, I WAS CRAZY TO WANT TO BE LIKE JOKER...

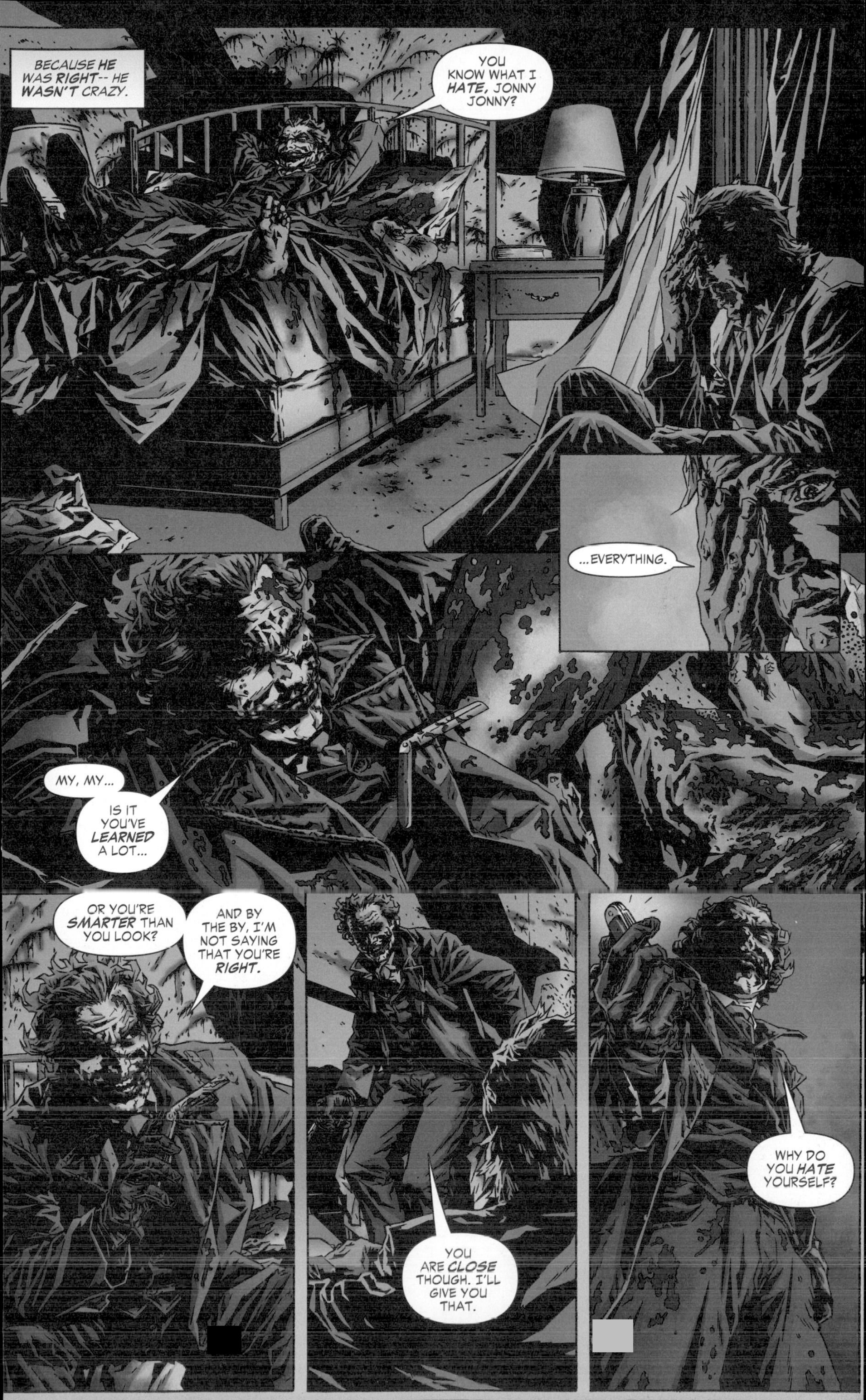
BECAUSE HE WAS RIGHT-- HE WASN'T CRAZY.
YOU KNOW WHAT I HATE, JONNY JONNY?
...EVERYTHING.
MY, MY...
IS IT YOU'VE LEARNED A LOT...
OR YOU'RE SMARTER THAN YOU LOOK?
AND BY THE BY, I'M NOT SAYING THAT YOU'RE RIGHT.
YOU ARE CLOSE THOUGH. I'LL GIVE YOU THAT.
WHY DO YOU HATE YOURSELF?

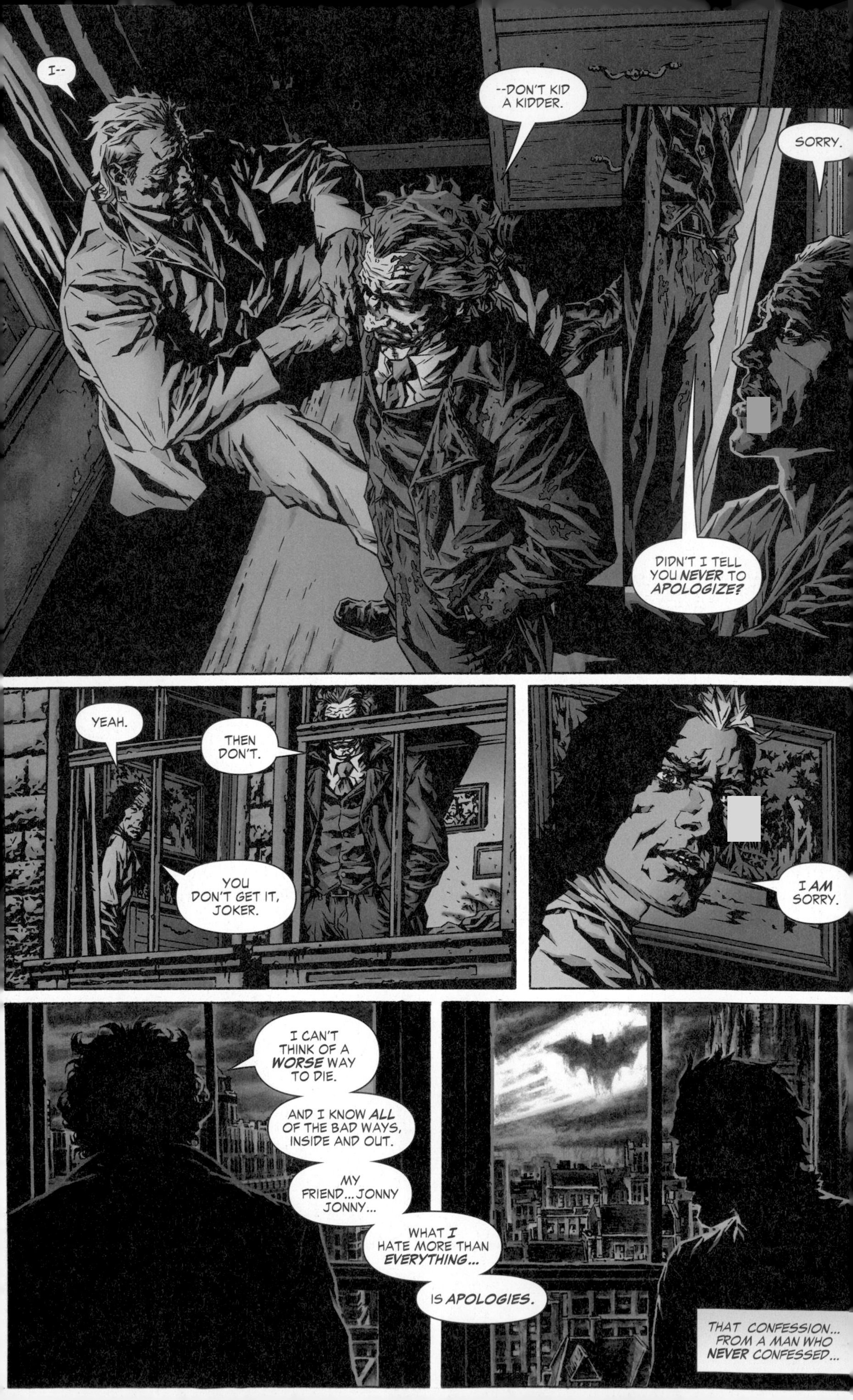
I--
--DON'T KID A KIDDER.
SORRY.
DIDN'T I TELL YOU NEVER TO APOLOGIZE?
YEAH.
THEN DON'T.
YOU DON'T GET IT, JOKER.
I AM SORRY.
I CAN'T THINK OF A WORSE WAY TO DIE.
AND I KNOW ALL OF THE BAD WAYS, INSIDE AND OUT.
MY FRIEND... JONNY JONNY...
WHAT I HATE MORE THAN EVERYTHING...
IS APOLOGIES.
THAT CONFESSION... FROM A MAN WHO NEVER CONFESSED...

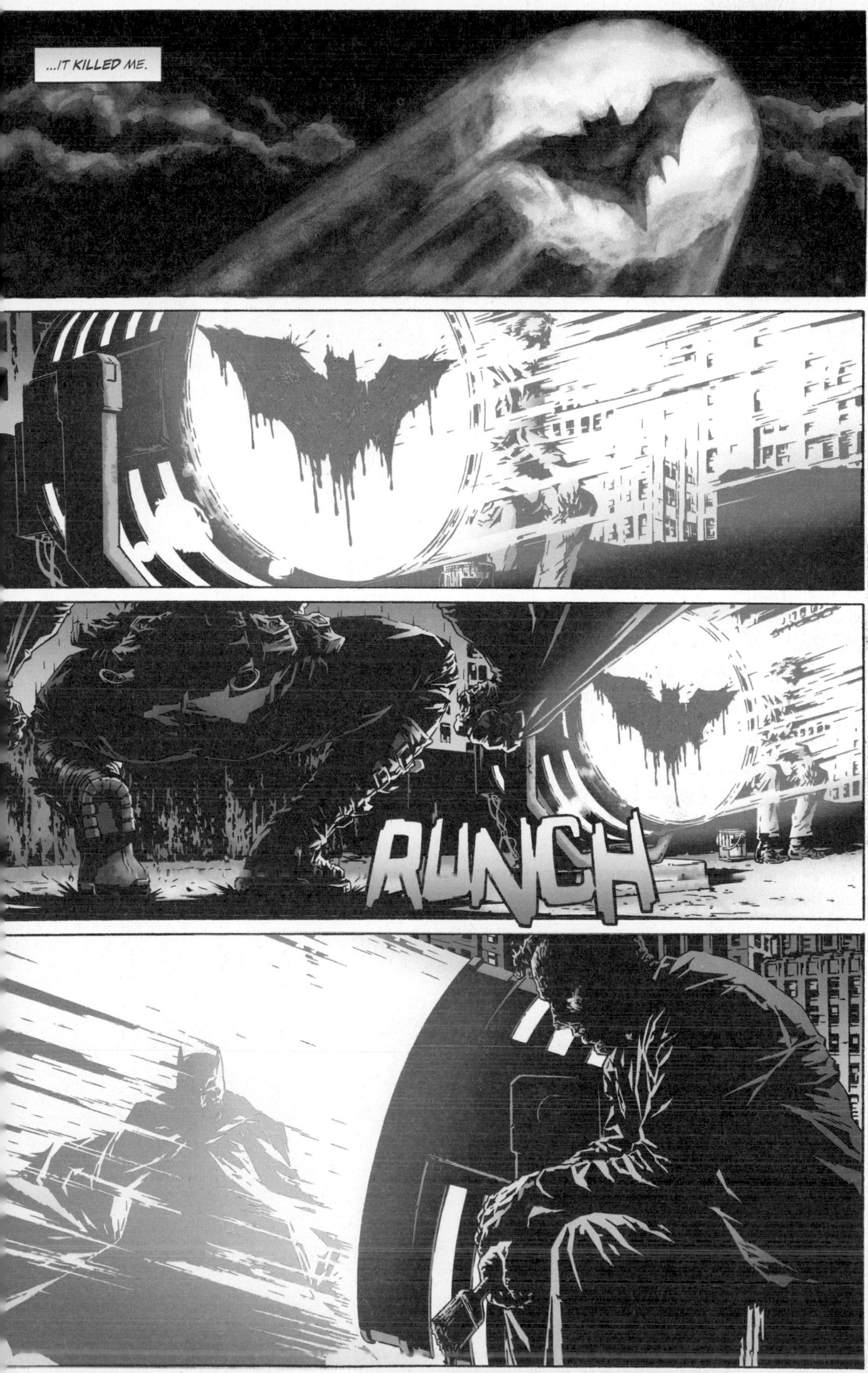
...IT KILLED ME.
RUNCH

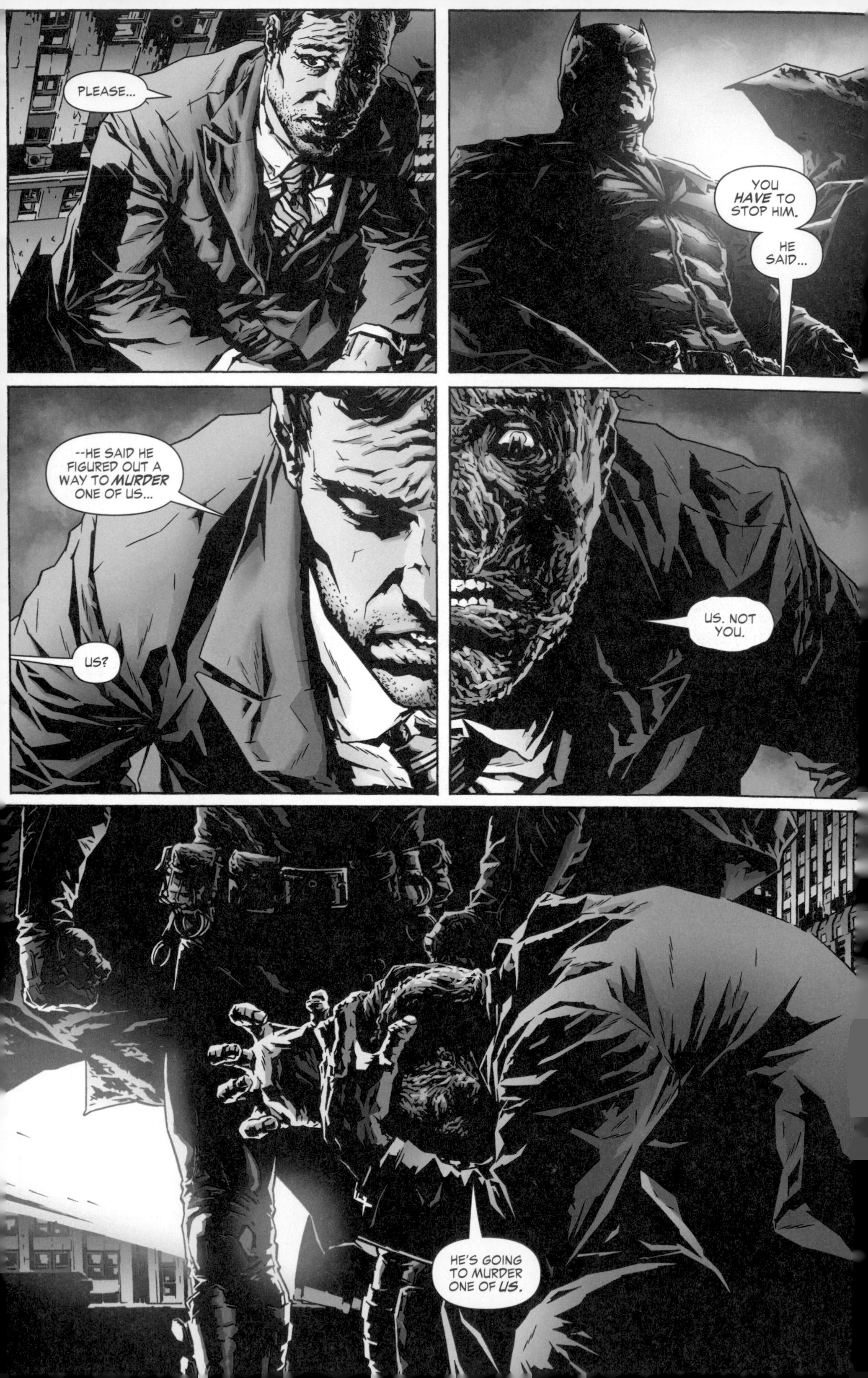
PLEASE...
YOU HAVE TO STOP HIM.
HE SAID...
--HE SAID HE FIGURED OUT A WAY TO MURDER ONE OF US...
US?
US. NOT YOU.
HE'S GOING TO MURDER ONE OF US.

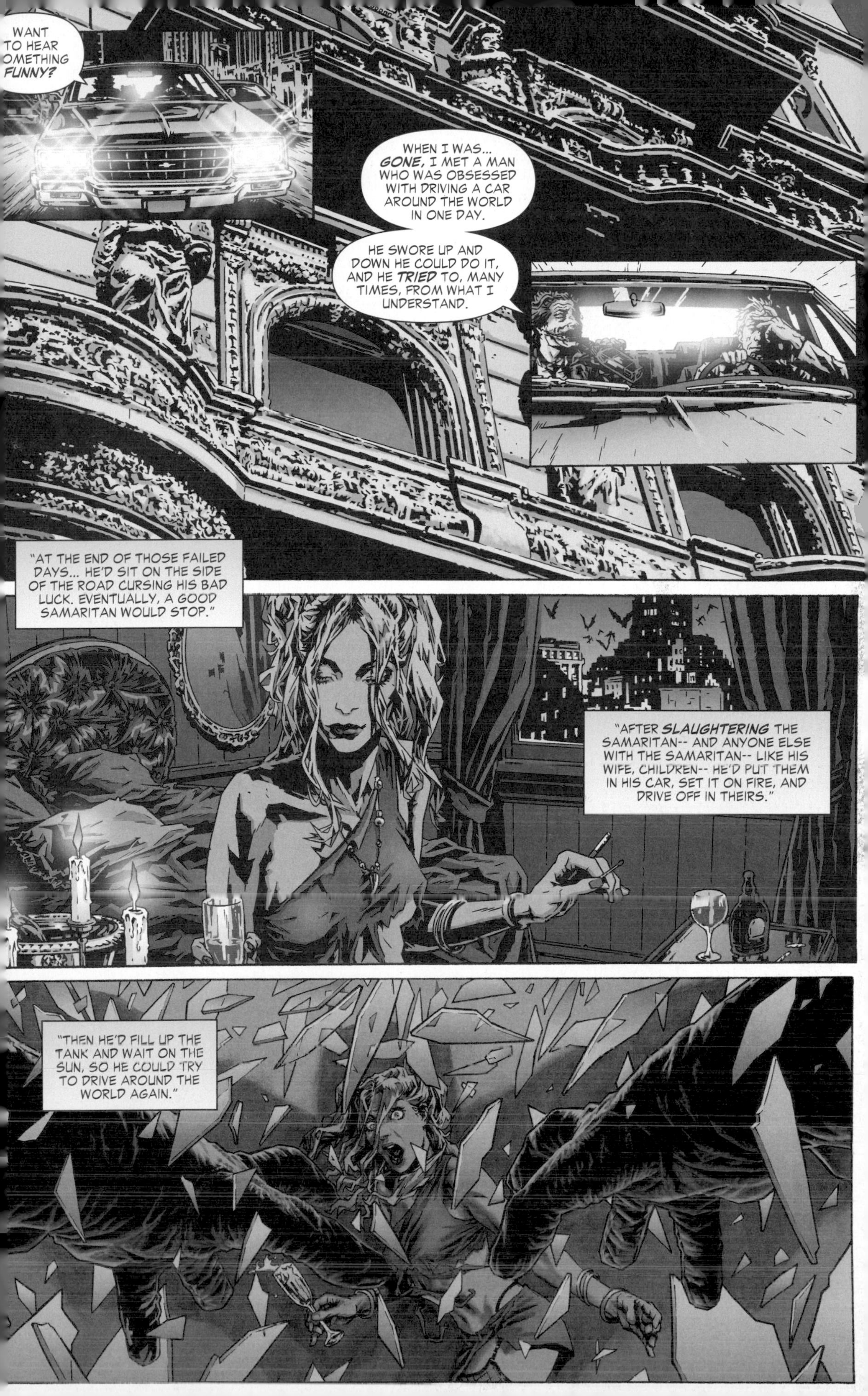
WANT TO HEAR OMETHING FUNNY?
WHEN I WAS... GONE, I MET A MAN WHO WAS OBSESSED WITH DRIVING A CAR AROUND THE WORLD IN ONE DAY.
HE SWORE UP AND DOWN HE COULD DO IT, AND HE TRIED TO, MANY TIMES, FROM WHAT I UNDERSTAND.
"AT THE END OF THOSE FAILED DAYS... HE'D SIT ON THE SIDE OF THE ROAD CURSING HIS BAD LUCK. EVENTUALLY, A GOOD SAMARITAN WOULD STOP."
"AFTER SLAUGHTERING THE SAMARITAN-- AND ANYONE ELSE WITH THE SAMARITAN-- LIKE HIS WIFE, CHILDREN-- HE'D PUT THEM IN HIS CAR, SET IT ON FIRE, AND DRIVE OFF IN THEIRS."
"THEN HE'D FILL UP THE TANK AND WAIT ON THE SUN, SO HE COULD TRY TO DRIVE AROUND THE WORLD AGAIN."

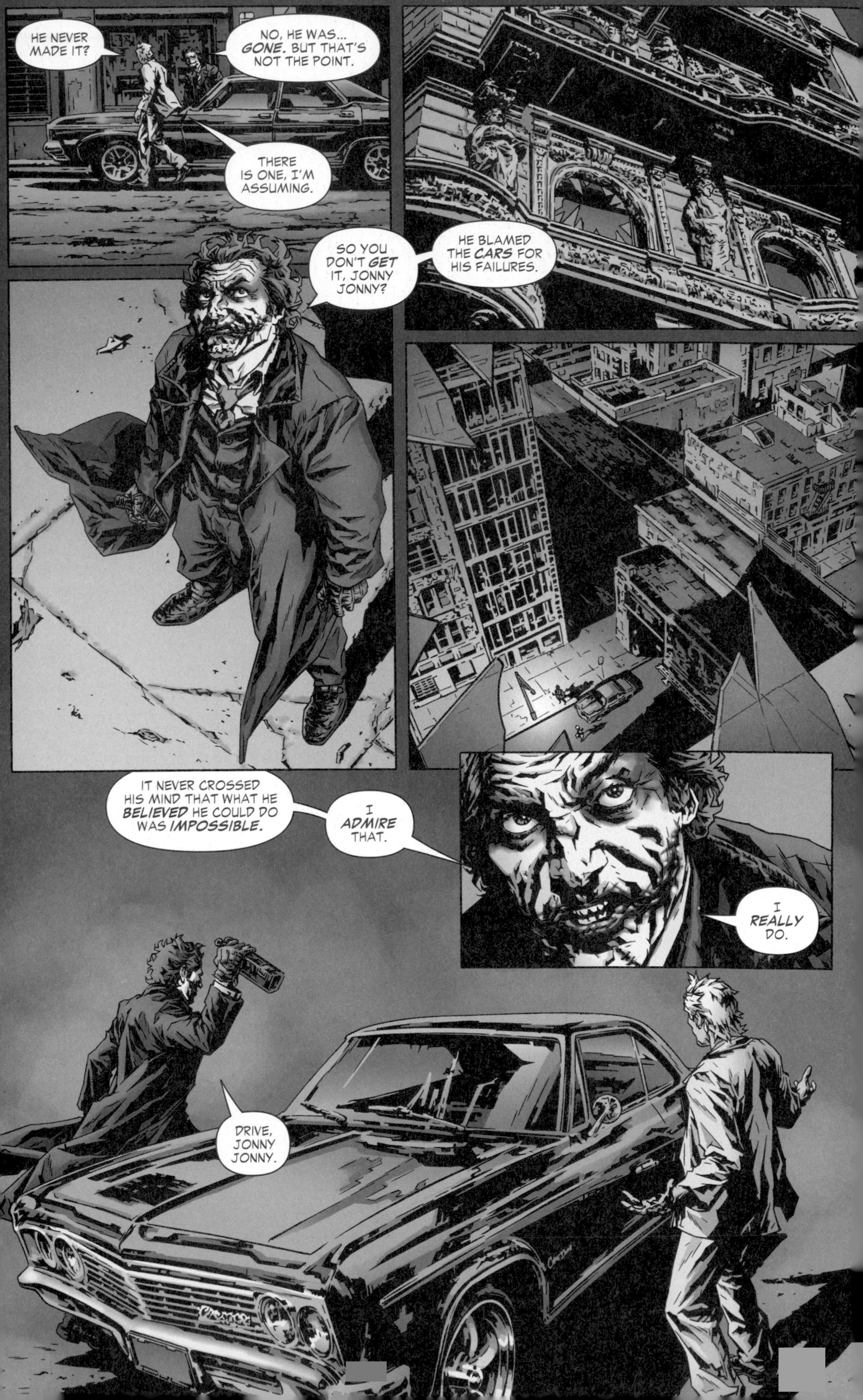
HE NEVER MADE IT?
NO, HE WAS... GONE. BUT THAT'S NOT THE POINT.
THERE IS ONE, I'M ASSUMING.
SO YOU DON'T GET IT, JONNY JONNY?
HE BLAMED THE CARS FOR HIS FAILURES.
IT NEVER CROSSED HIS MIND THAT WHAT HE BELIEVED HE COULD DO WAS IMPOSSIBLE.
I ADMIRE THAT.
I REALLY DO.
DRIVE, JONNY JONNY.

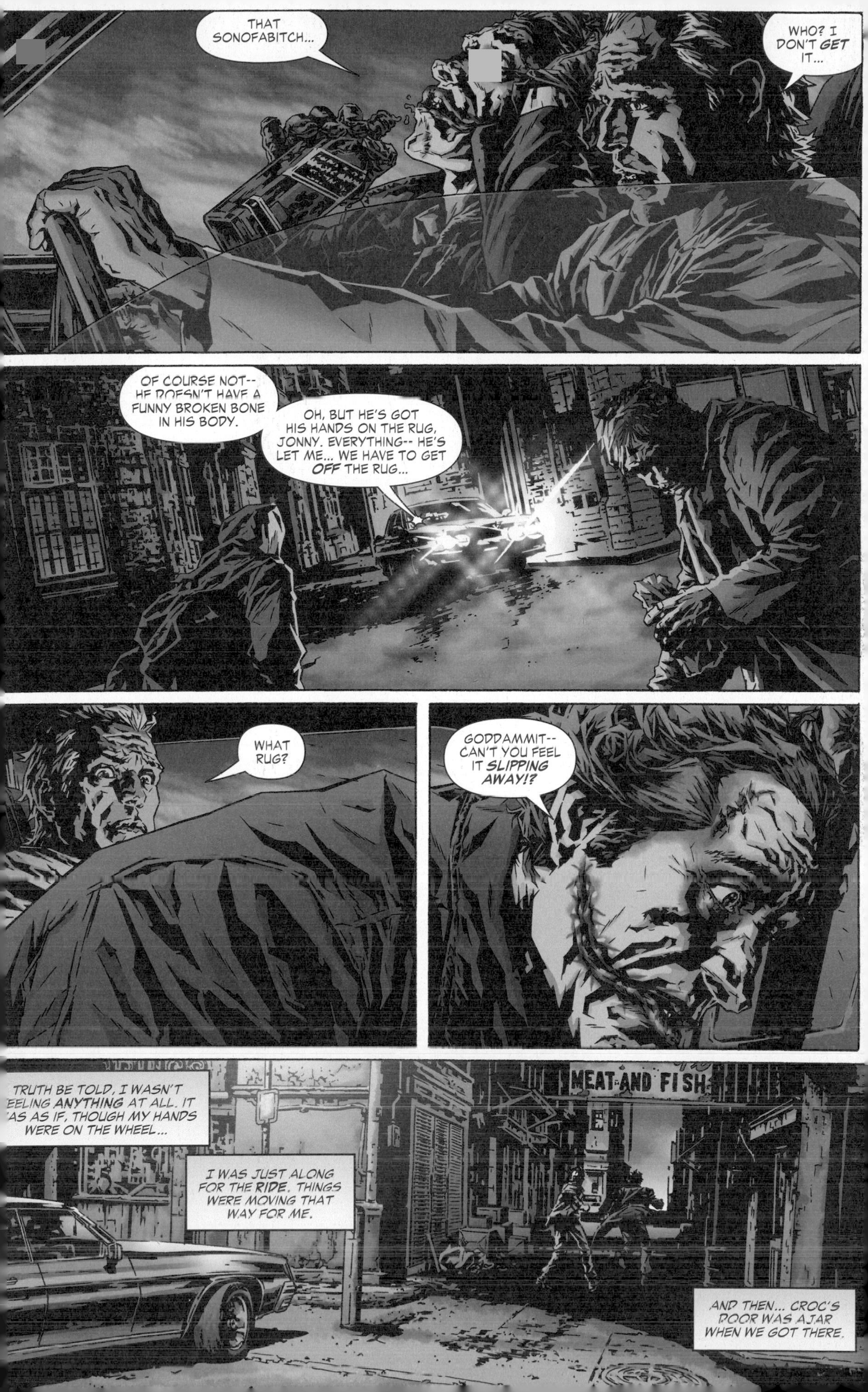
THAT SONOFABITCH...
WHO? I DON'T GET IT...
OF COURSE NOT-- HF DOFSN'T HAVF A FUNNY BROKEN BONE IN HIS BODY.
OH, BUT HE'S GOT HIS HANDS ON THE RUG, JONNY. EVERYTHING-- HE'S LET ME... WE HAVE TO GET OFF THE RUG...
WHAT RUG?
GODDAMMIT-- CAN'T YOU FEEL IT SLIPPING AWAY!?
TRUTH BE TOLD, I WASN'T EELING ANYTHING AT ALL. IT AS AS IF, THOUGH MY HANDS WERE ON THE WHEEL...
MEAT AND FISH
I WAS JUST ALONG FOR THE RIDE. THINGS WERE MOVING THAT WAY FOR ME.
AND THEN... CROC'S DOOR WAS AJAR WHEN WE GOT THERE.

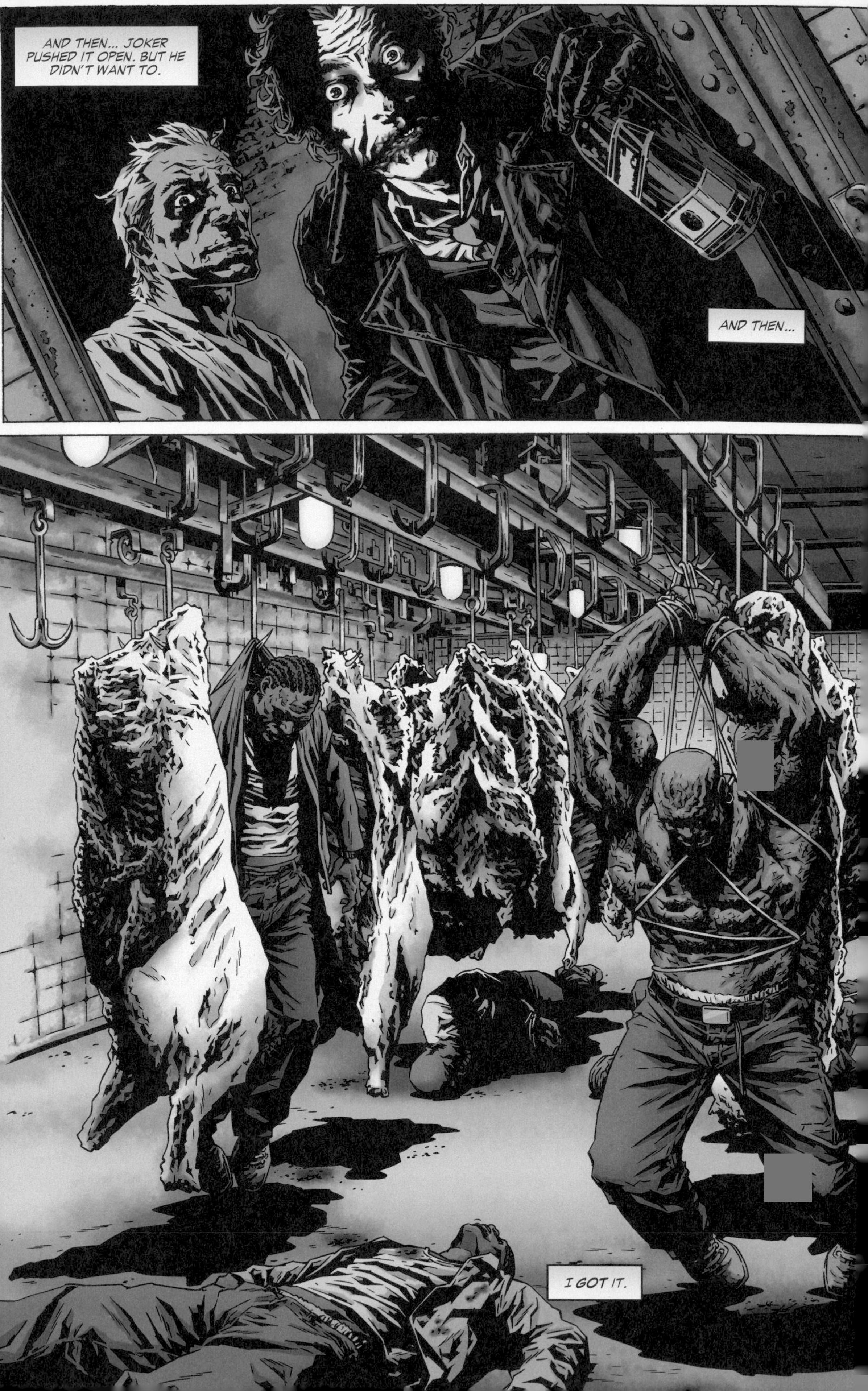
AND THEN... JOKER PUSHED IT OPEN. BUT HE DIDN'T WANT TO.
AND THEN...
I GOT IT.

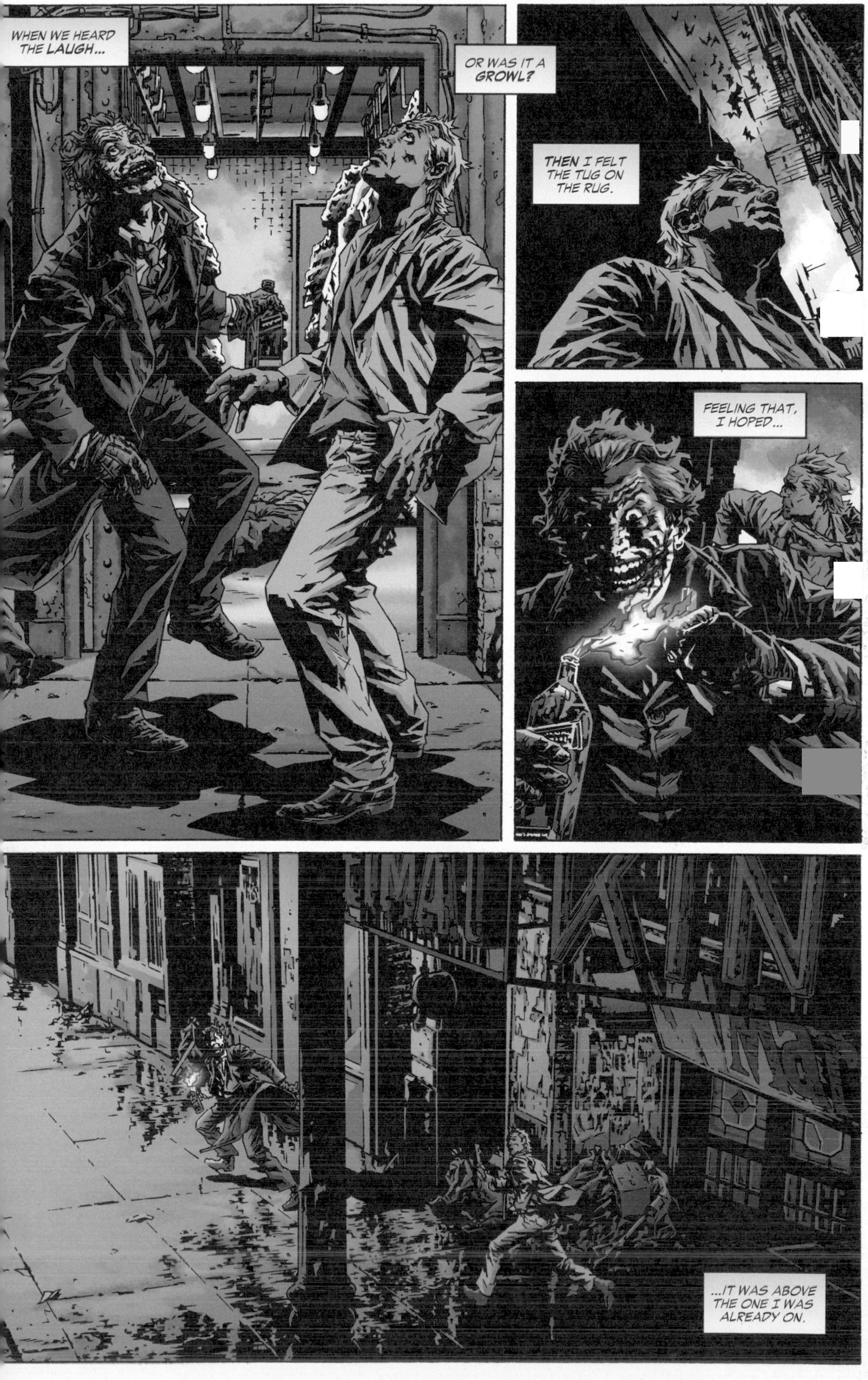
WHEN WE HEARD THE LAUGH...
OR WAS IT A GROWL?
THEN I FELT THE TUG ON THE RUG.
FEELING THAT, I HOPED...
...IT WAS ABOVE THE ONE I WAS ALREADY ON.

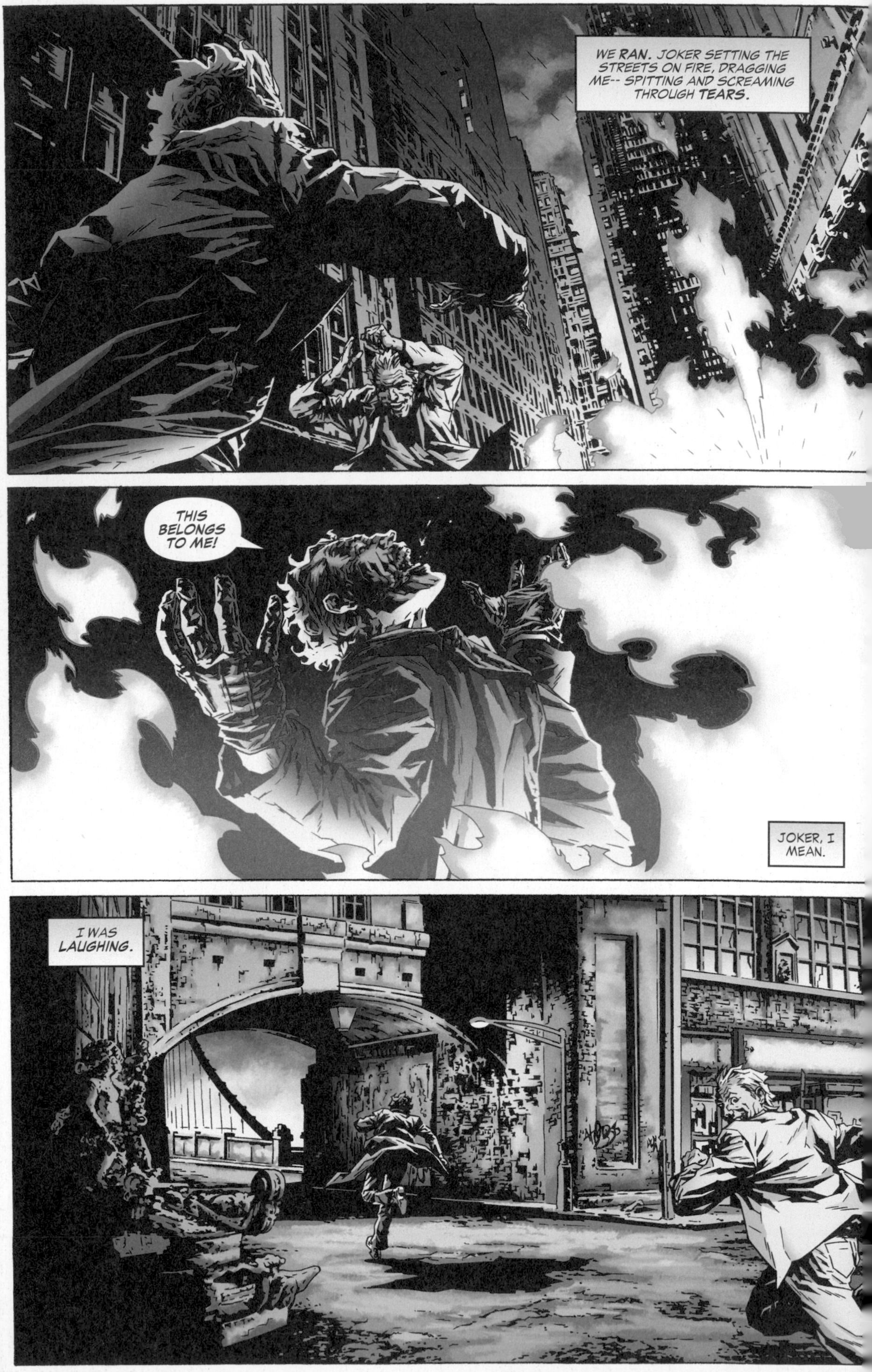
WE RAN. JOKER SETTING THE STREETS ON FIRE, DRAGGING ME-- SPITTING AND SCREAMING THROUGH TEARS.
THIS BELONGS TO ME!
JOKER, I MEAN.
I WAS LAUGHING.

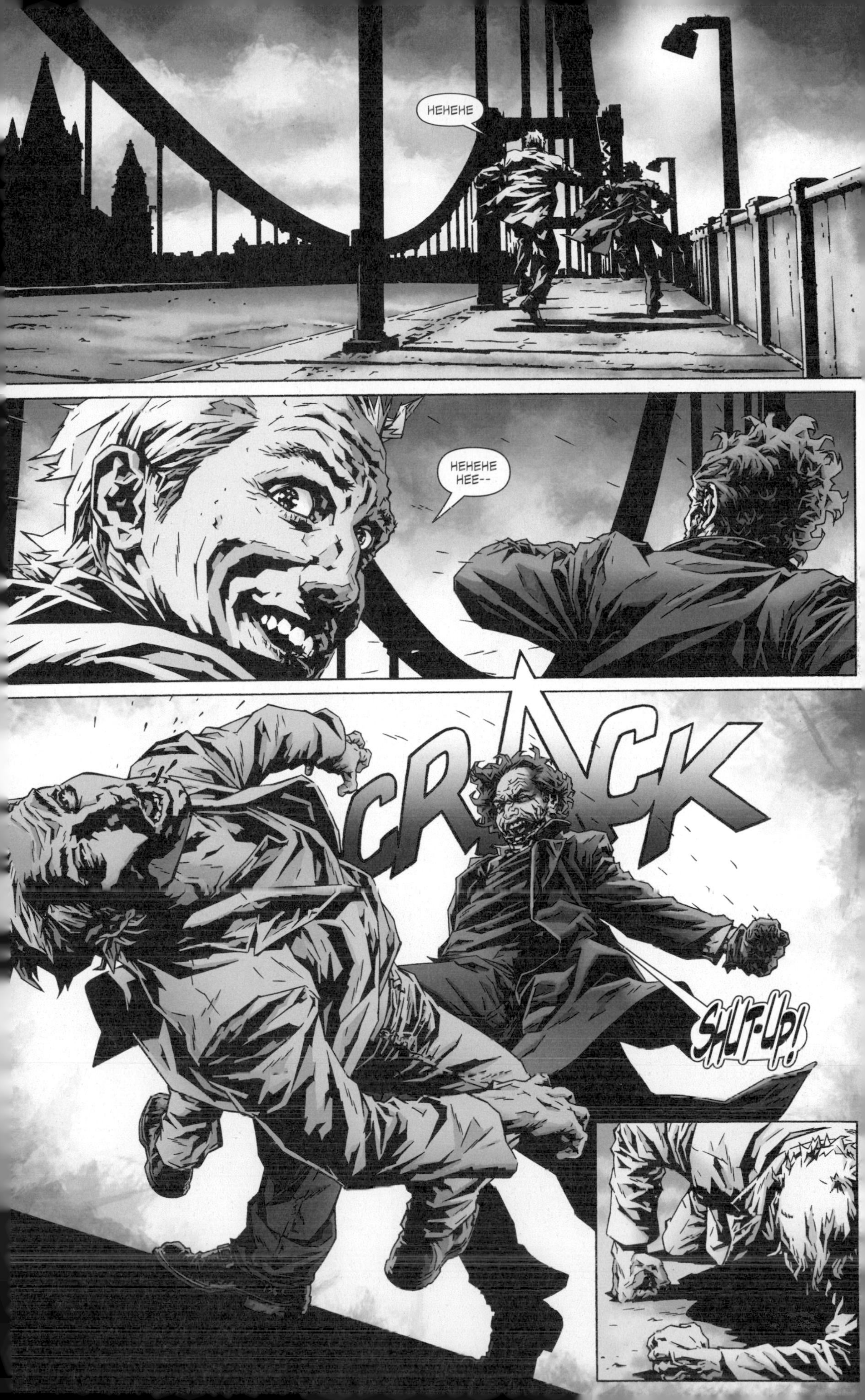
HEHEHE
HEHEHE HEE--
CRACK
SHUT-UP!

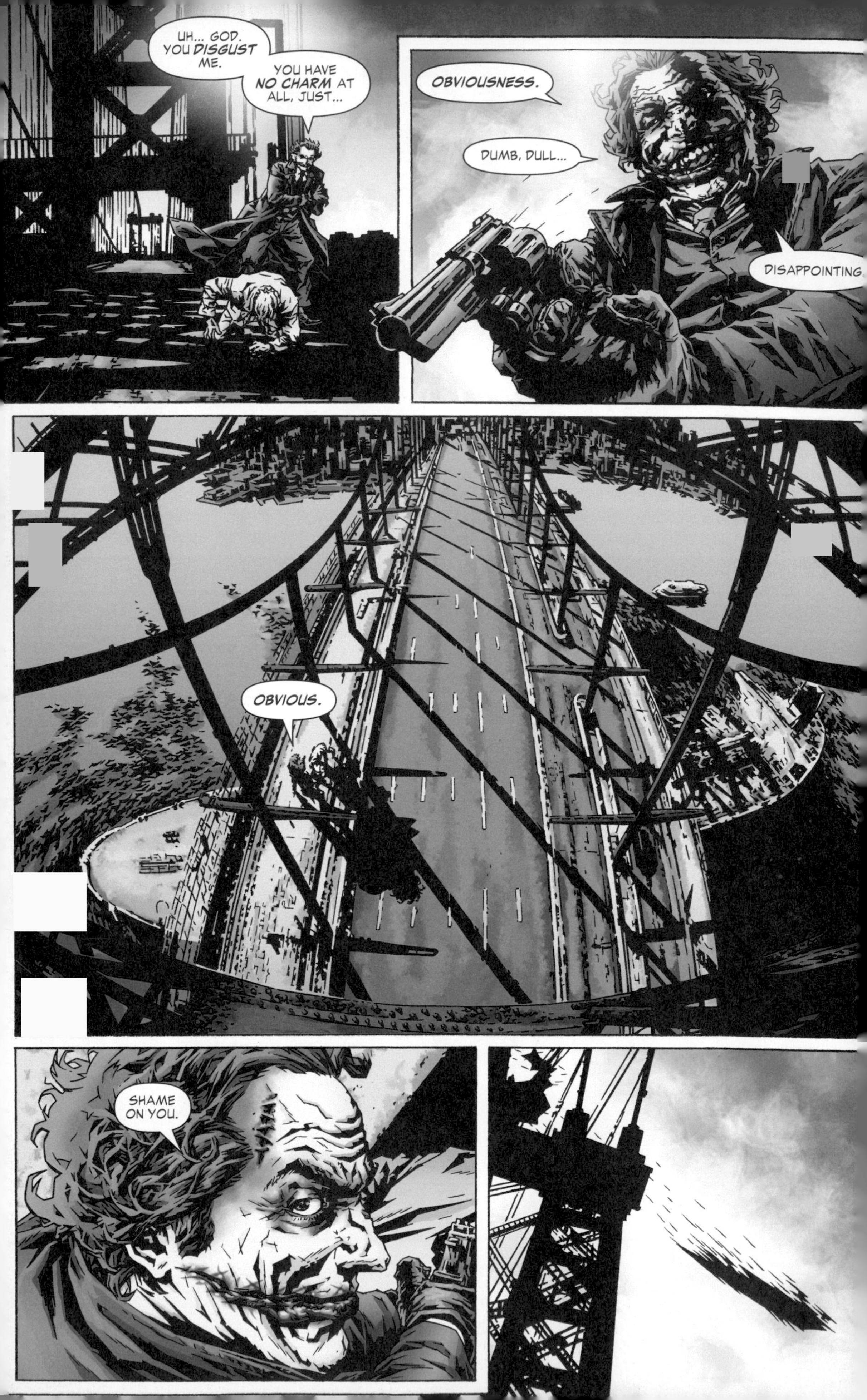
UH... GOD. YOU DISGUST ME.
YOU HAVE NO CHARM AT ALL, JUST...
OBVIOUSNESS.
DUMB, DULL...
DISAPPOINTING.
OBVIOUS.
SHAME ON YOU.

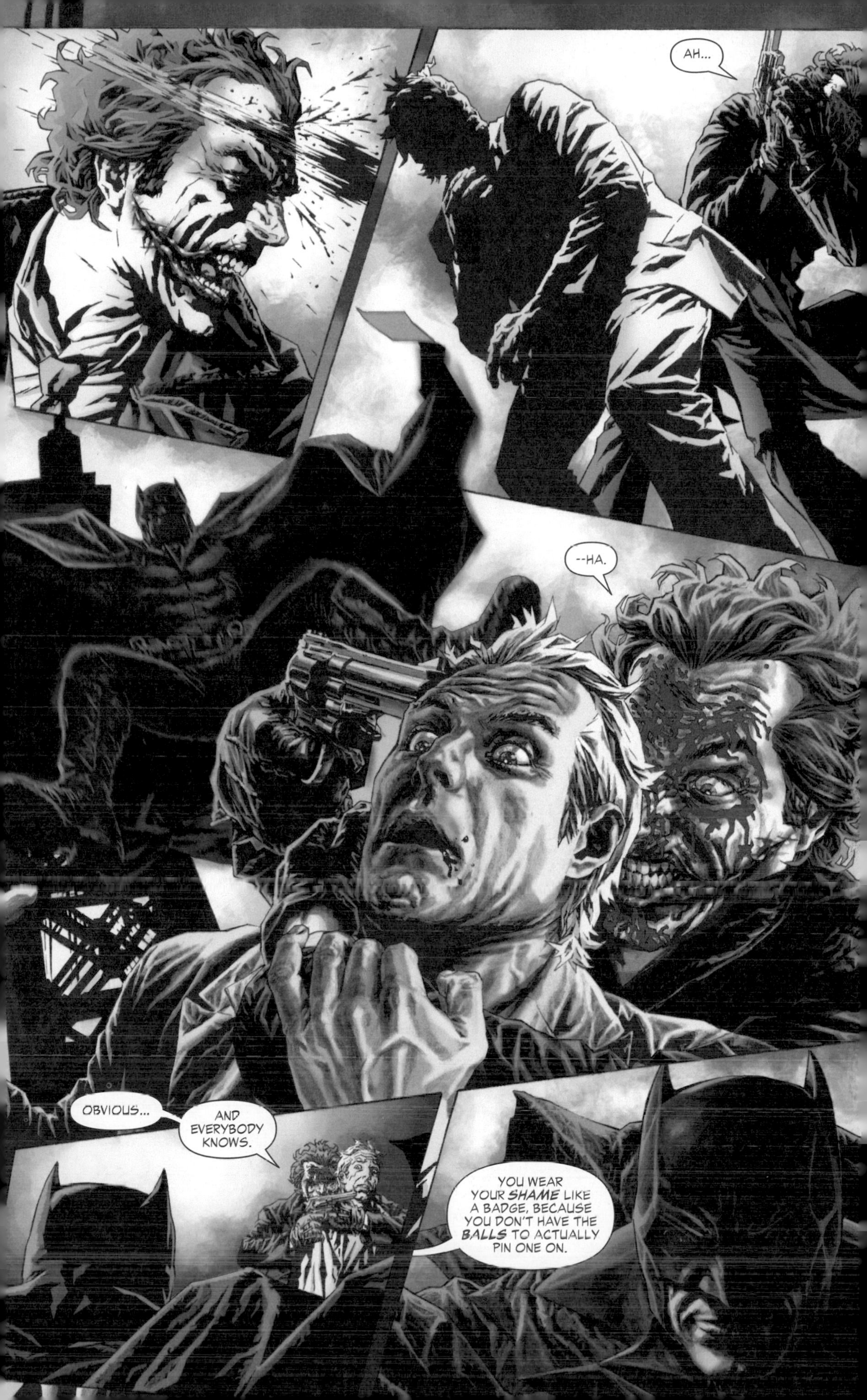
AH...
--HA.
OBVIOUS...
AND EVERYBODY KNOWS.
YOU WEAR YOUR SHAME LIKE A BADGE, BECAUSE YOU DON'T HAVE THE BALLS TO ACTUALLY PIN ONE ON.

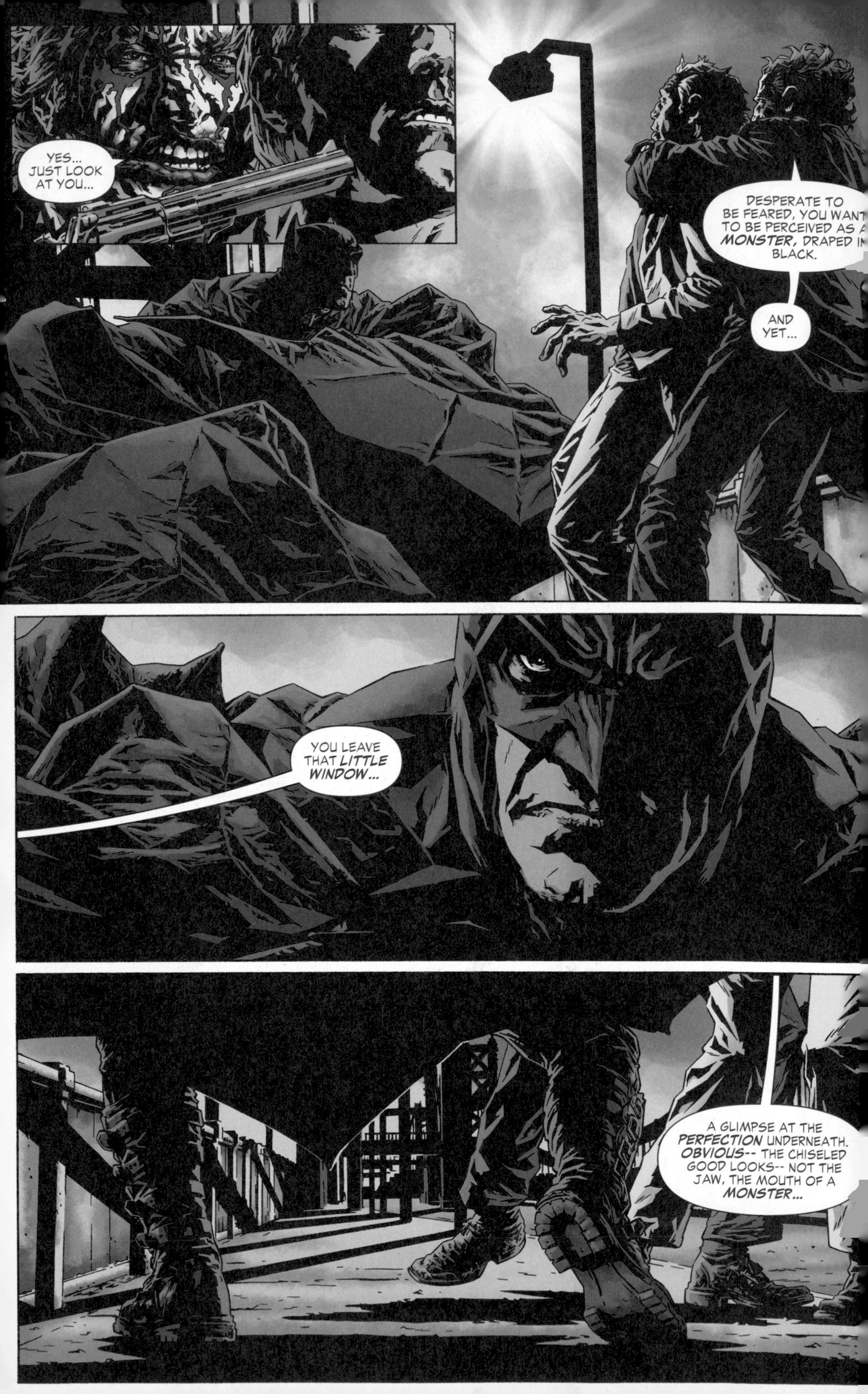
YES... JUST LOOK AT YOU...
DESPERATE TO BE FEARED, YOU WANT TO BE PERCEIVED AS A MONSTER, DRAPED IN BLACK.
AND YET...
YOU LEAVE THAT LITTLE WINDOW...
A GLIMPSE AT THE PERFECTION UNDERNEATH. OBVIOUS-- THE CHISELED GOOD LOOKS-- NOT THE JAW, THE MOUTH OF A MONSTER...

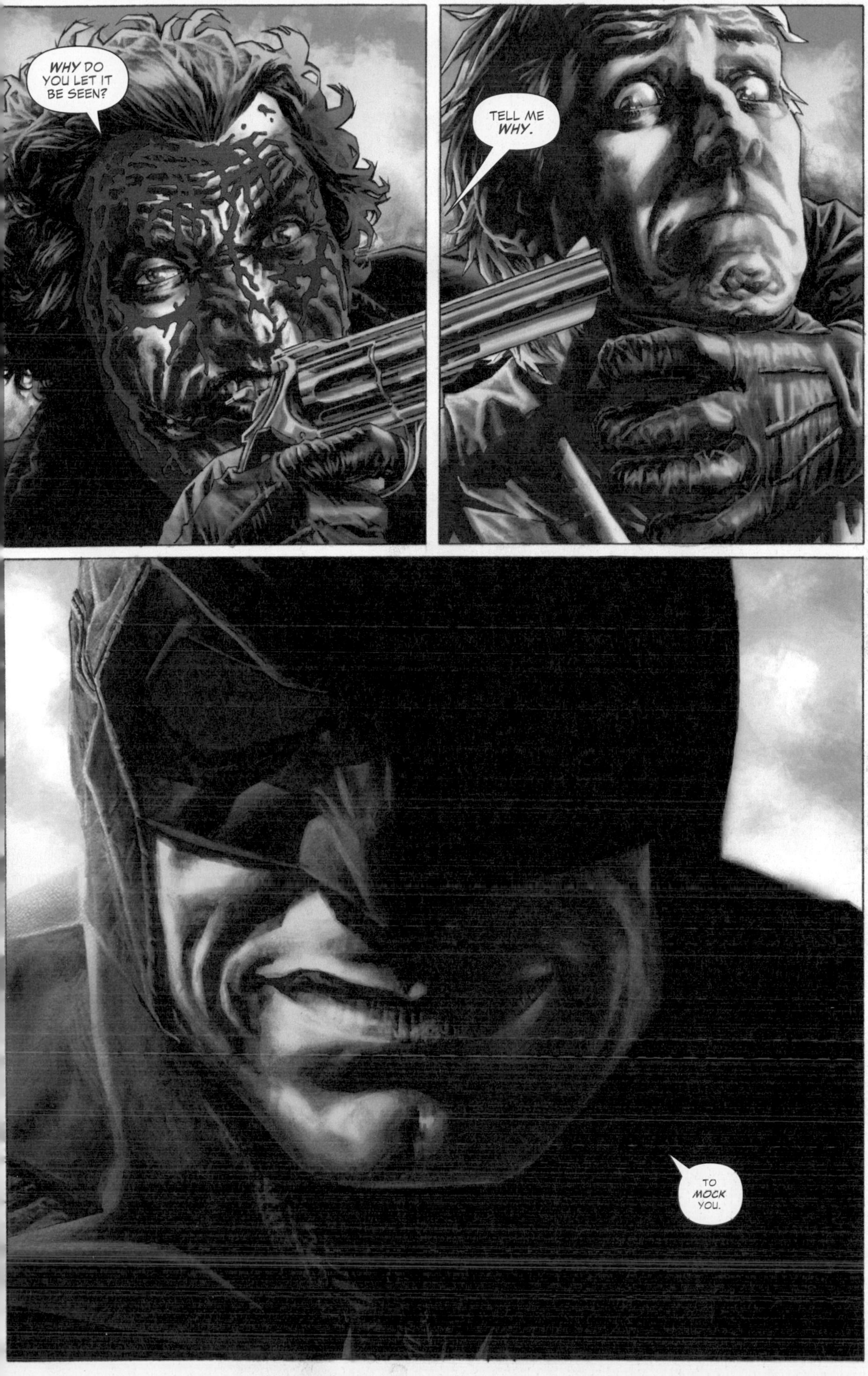
WHY DO YOU LET IT BE SEEN?
TELL ME WHY.
TO MOCK YOU.

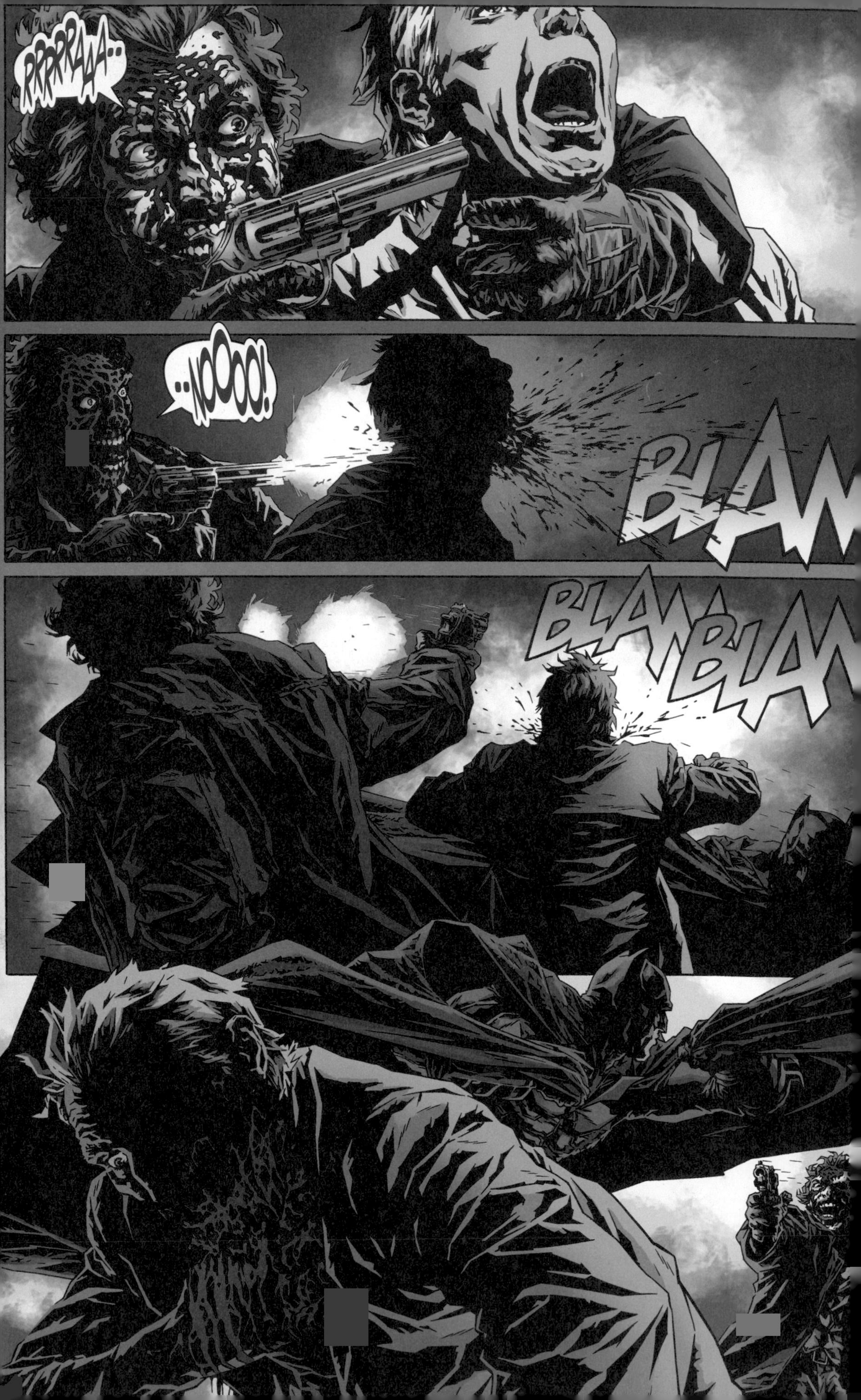
RRRRRAAA..
..NOOOO!
BLAM
BLAM BLAM

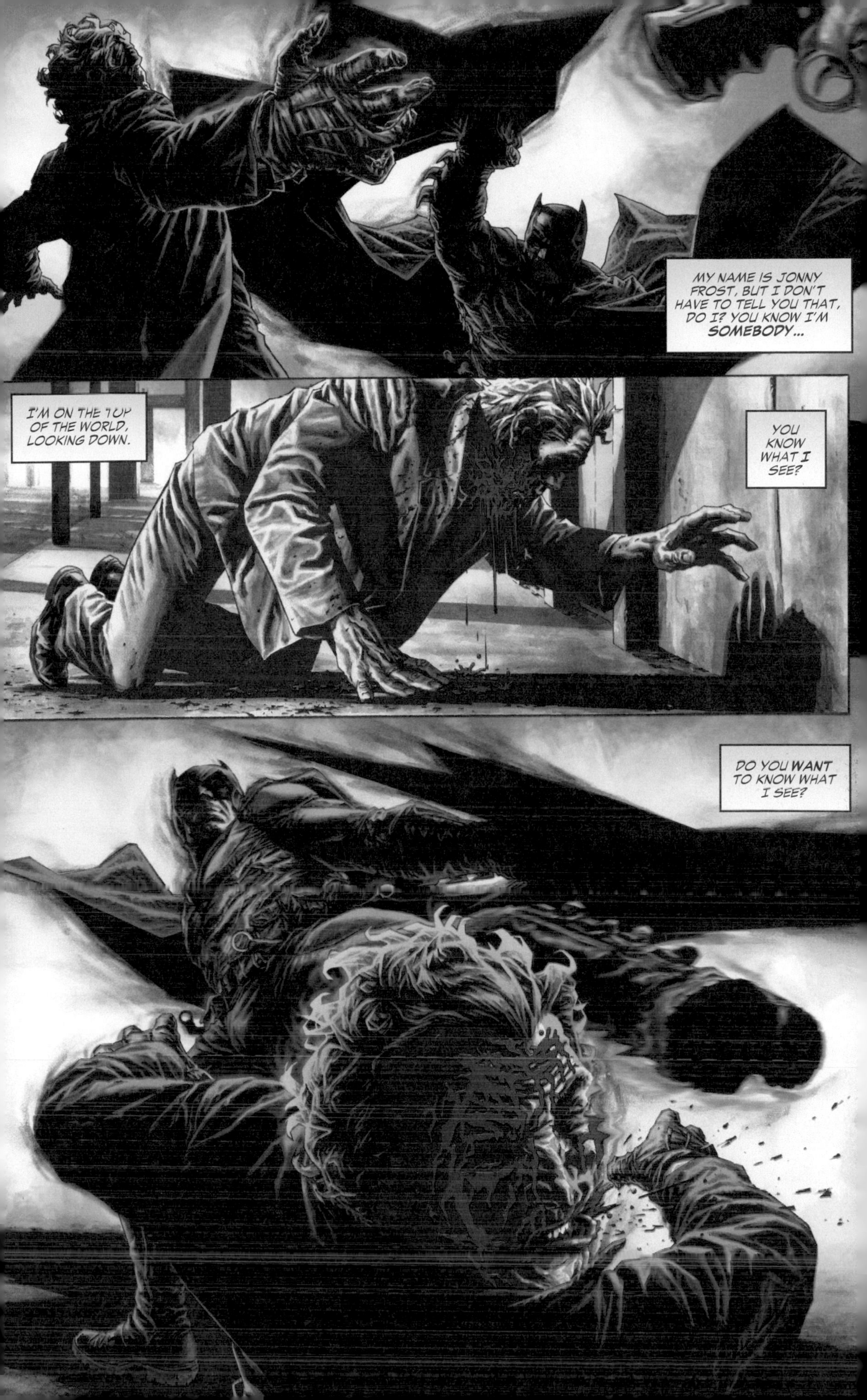
MY NAME IS JONNY FROST, BUT I DON'T HAVE TO TELL YOU THAT, DO I? YOU KNOW I'M SOMEBODY...
I'M ON THE TOP OF THE WORLD, LOOKING DOWN.
YOU KNOW WHAT I SEE?
DO YOU WANT TO KNOW WHAT I SEE?

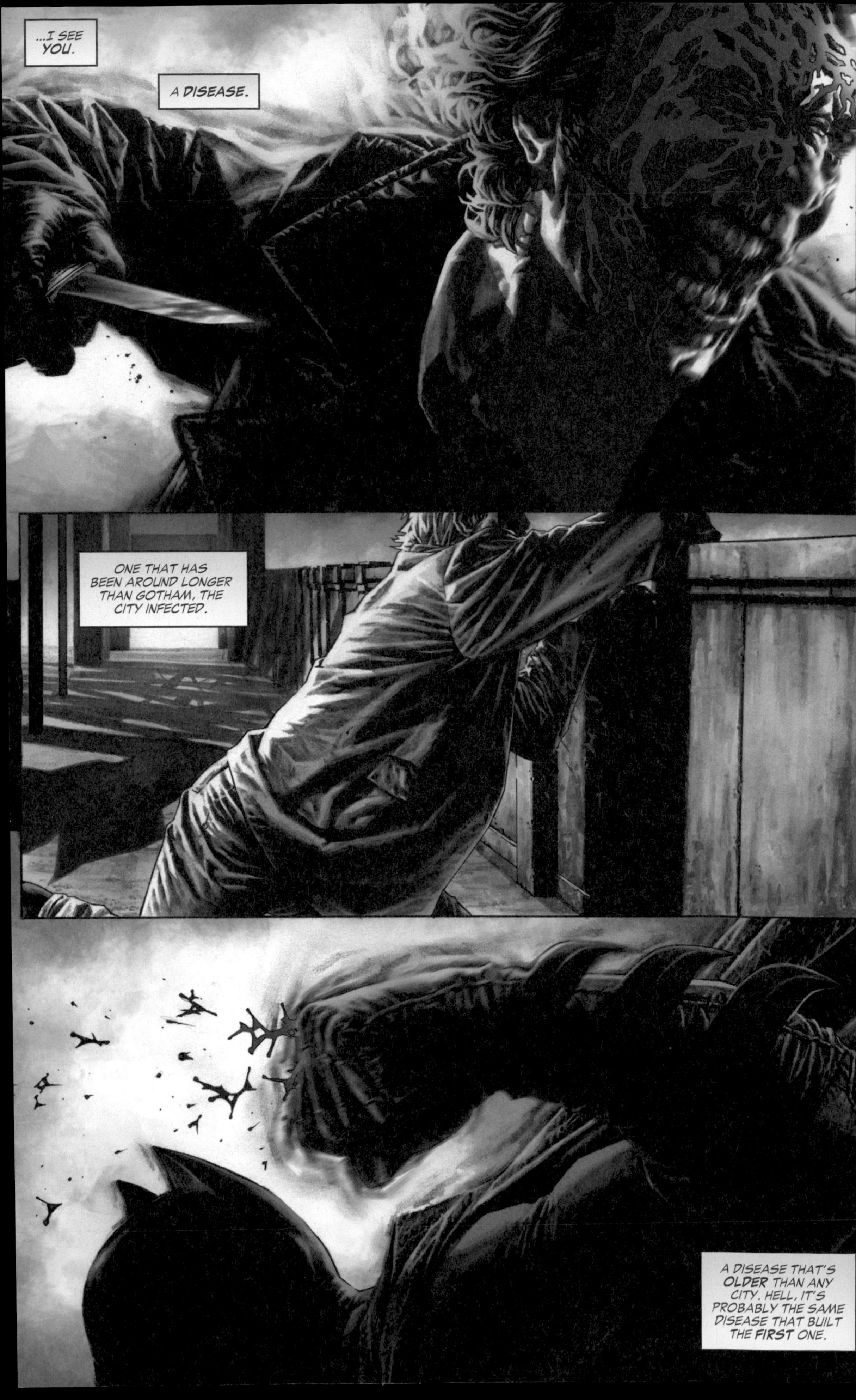
...I SEE YOU.
A DISEASE.
ONE THAT HAS BEEN AROUND LONGER THAN GOTHAM, THE CITY INFECTED.
A DISEASE THAT'S OLDER THAN ANY CITY. HELL, IT'S PROBABLY THE SAME DISEASE THAT BUILT THE FIRST ONE.

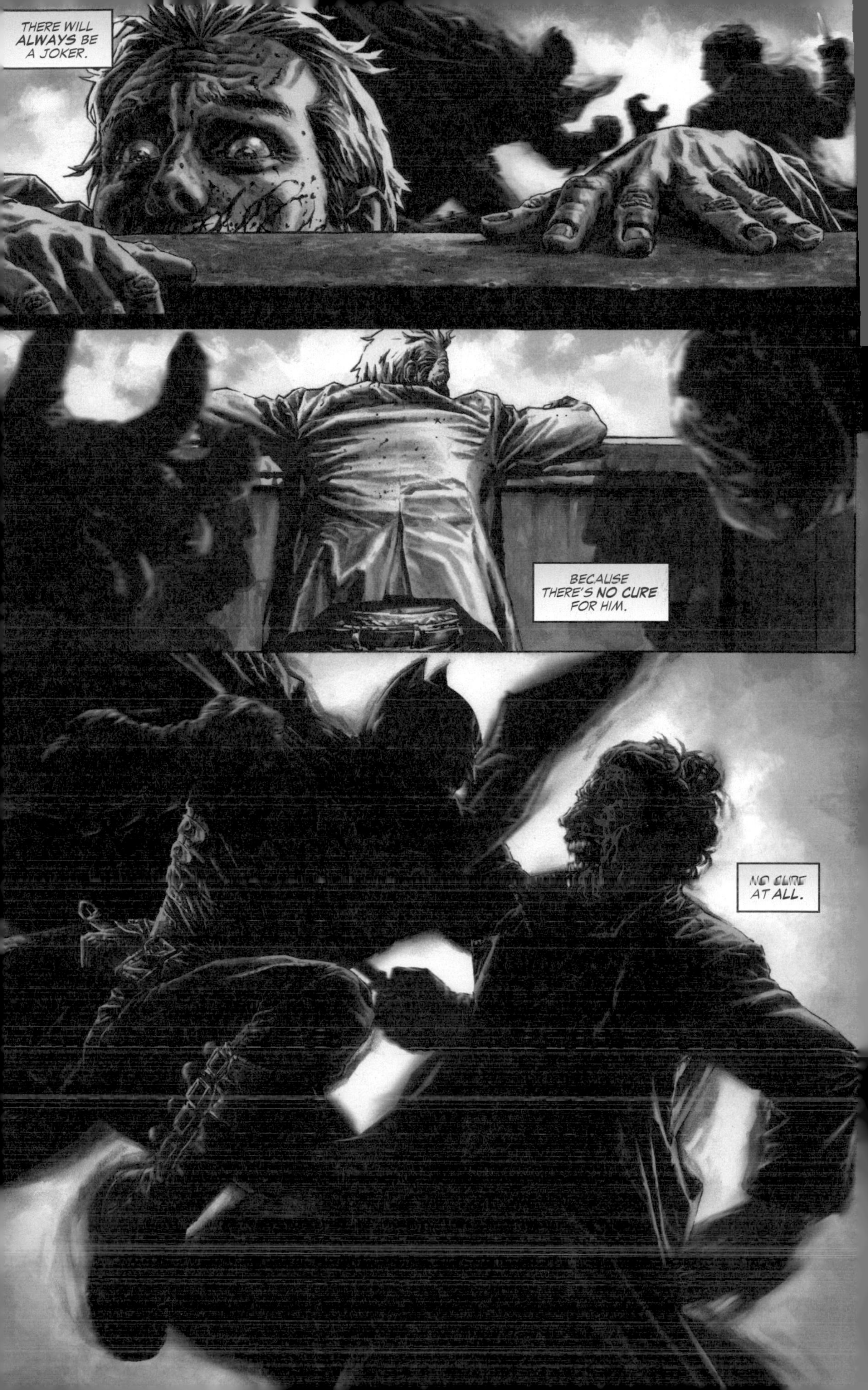
THERE WILL ALWAYS BE A JOKER.
BECAUSE THERE'S NO CURE FOR HIM.
NO CURE AT ALL.

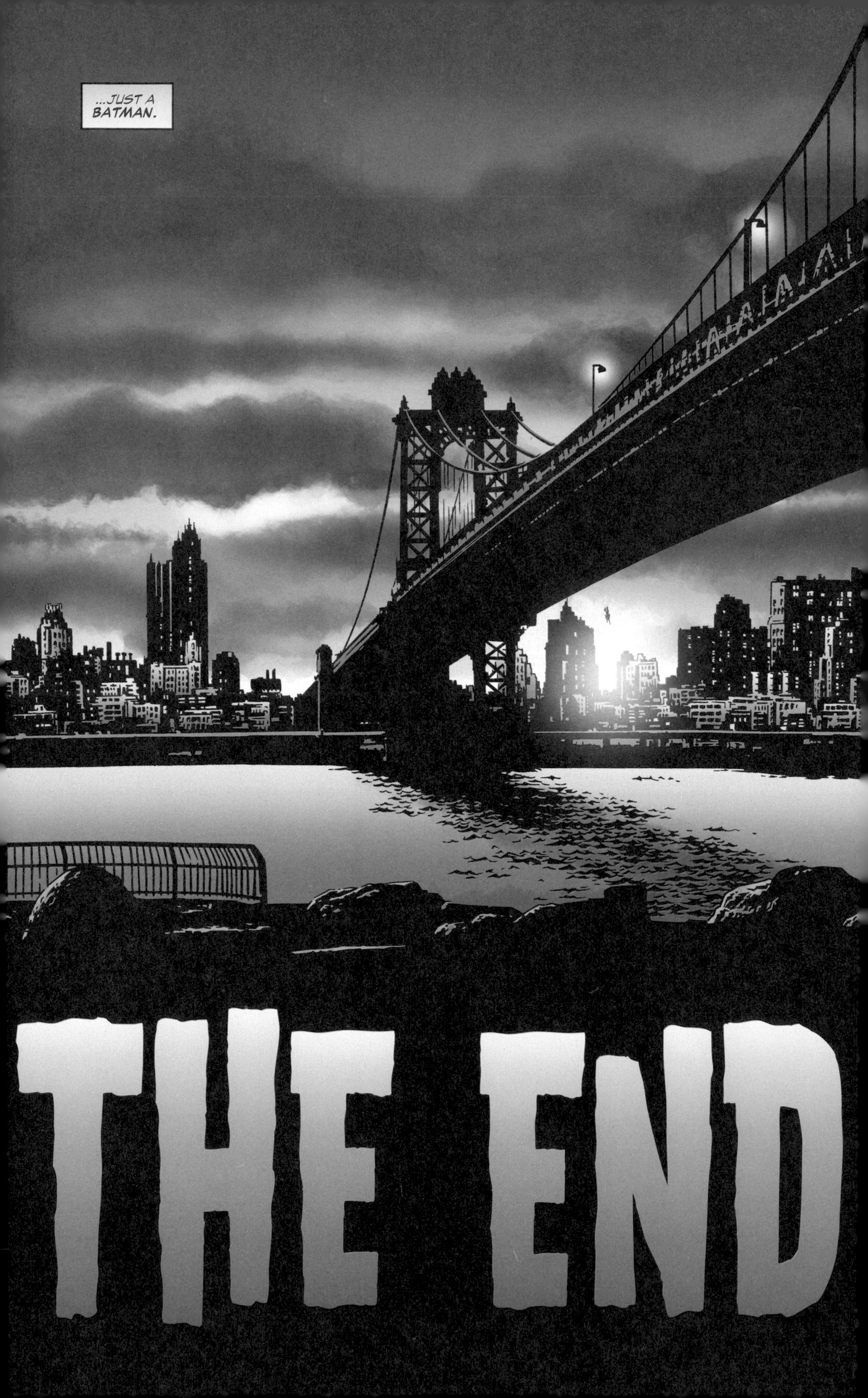
...JUST A
BATMAN.
THE END

HELD FOR OBSERVATION
EVALUATIONS FROM BRIAN AZZARELLO AND LEE BERMEJO

Promotional art created in 2008 for the Las Vegas premiere of the film The Dark Knight *at the Palms Casino Resort.*

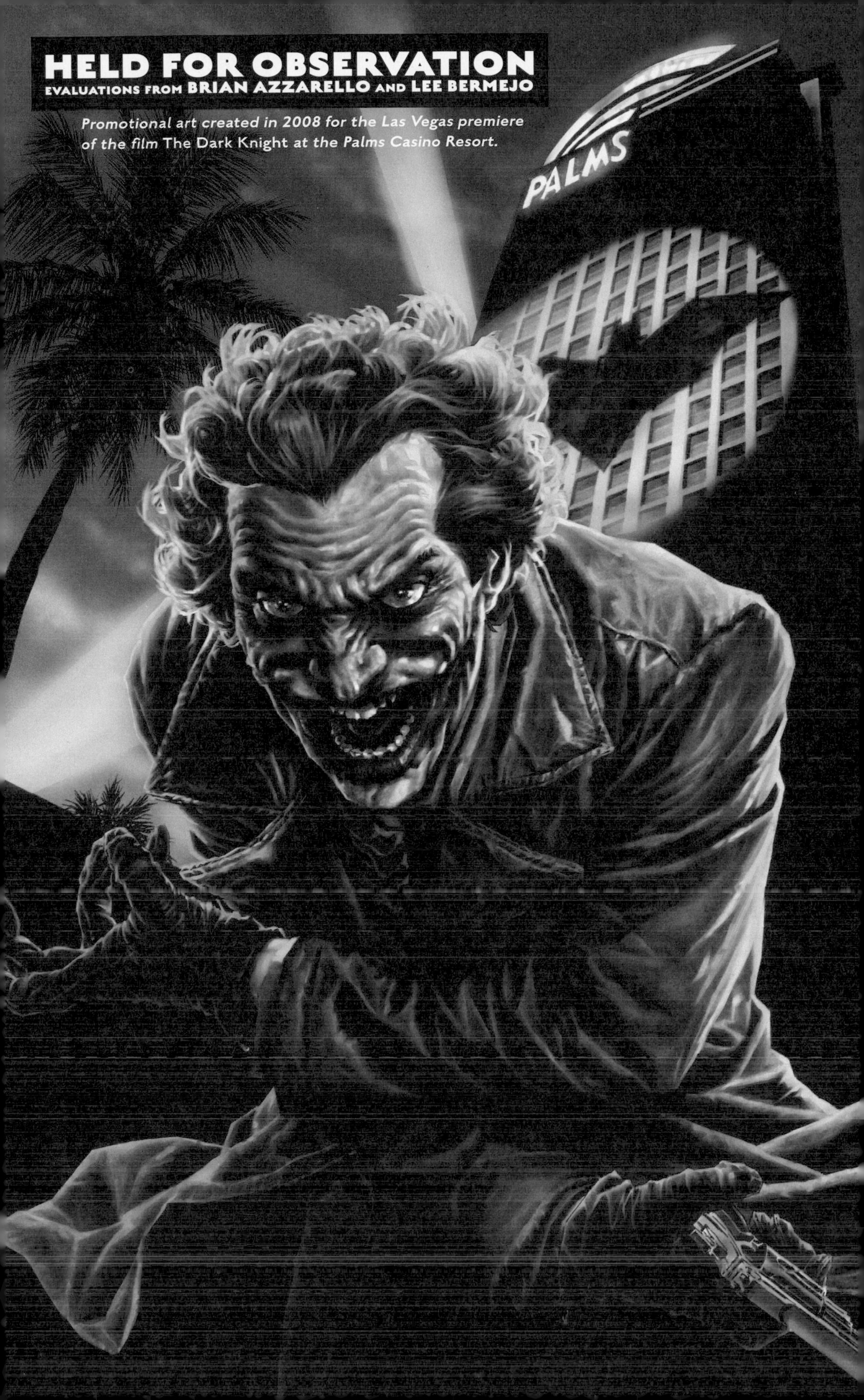
PALMS

JOKER: DARK NIGHT

Proposal by Brian Azzarello & Lee Bermejo

"The news spread through the back alleys to the penthouses; from rooms where everything you'd ever want was for sale, to the confessionals where it was all paid for. It spread like wildfire — or more aptly put — a disease. Because that's what he is, I guess; a disease that's infected Gotham City that there is no cure for. A disease that somehow, with the help of god or the devil — pick your poison — had convinced his doctors he himself wasn't diseased anymore. The news spread. Joker was being released from Arkham Asylum."

— Johnny Frost

So begins JOKER: DARK NIGHT, a story that pits a newly freed Joker against Gotham's underworld as he seeks to reestablish his stranglehold on it. Being Gotham, it means he'll go up against the likes of Riddler, Penguin, Scarface, and Two-Face; all powerful ganglords in their own right. And the turf they've managed to grab while Joker was locked up is not something they're willing to hand over without a fight. But, as this series will illustrate, while they may be scared of Batman, they're absolutely terrified of the Joker.

We look at this as a bookend to our LEX LUTHOR: MAN OF STEEL. But unlike LL: MOS, Joker won't be our narrator. We feel this would not only be a mistake, but a disservice to the character; he is insane (which is really important), and his power is derived from absolutely no one knowing anything about what he is thinking.

To this end, our guide into Joker's psyche will be Johnny Frost, a low-level hood who insinuates himself into Joker's gang. Like Joker, Johnny is also newly back on the streets, and he sees Joker as a way to establish himself. Johnny's not stupid, but he is a criminal, so t he allure of easy money and power blinds him to the fact that he's working for a madman. We'll see things through Johnny's eyes: Joker's terrible mood swings, his grand brutality, uncharacteristic moments of kindness, glimpses of clarity, and ultimately why he's obsessed with Batman.

Batman. The shadow that hangs over Gotham, disappearing when anyone looks his way. Batman. He's never there, but he's always around. Batman... Goddamn Batman.

"It was at that moment, the last time I looked into his eyes, that I understood what some people had said was a lie. 'There would be no Joker without Batman.' Bull. There would always be a Joker, because there was no cure for him. No cure at all. Just a Batman."

— Johnny Frost.

The original proposal for the JOKER: DARK NIGHT miniseries, which became the JOKER graphic novel

Cover art for Wizard Magazine #194, featuring three of the DC Universe's greatest villains.

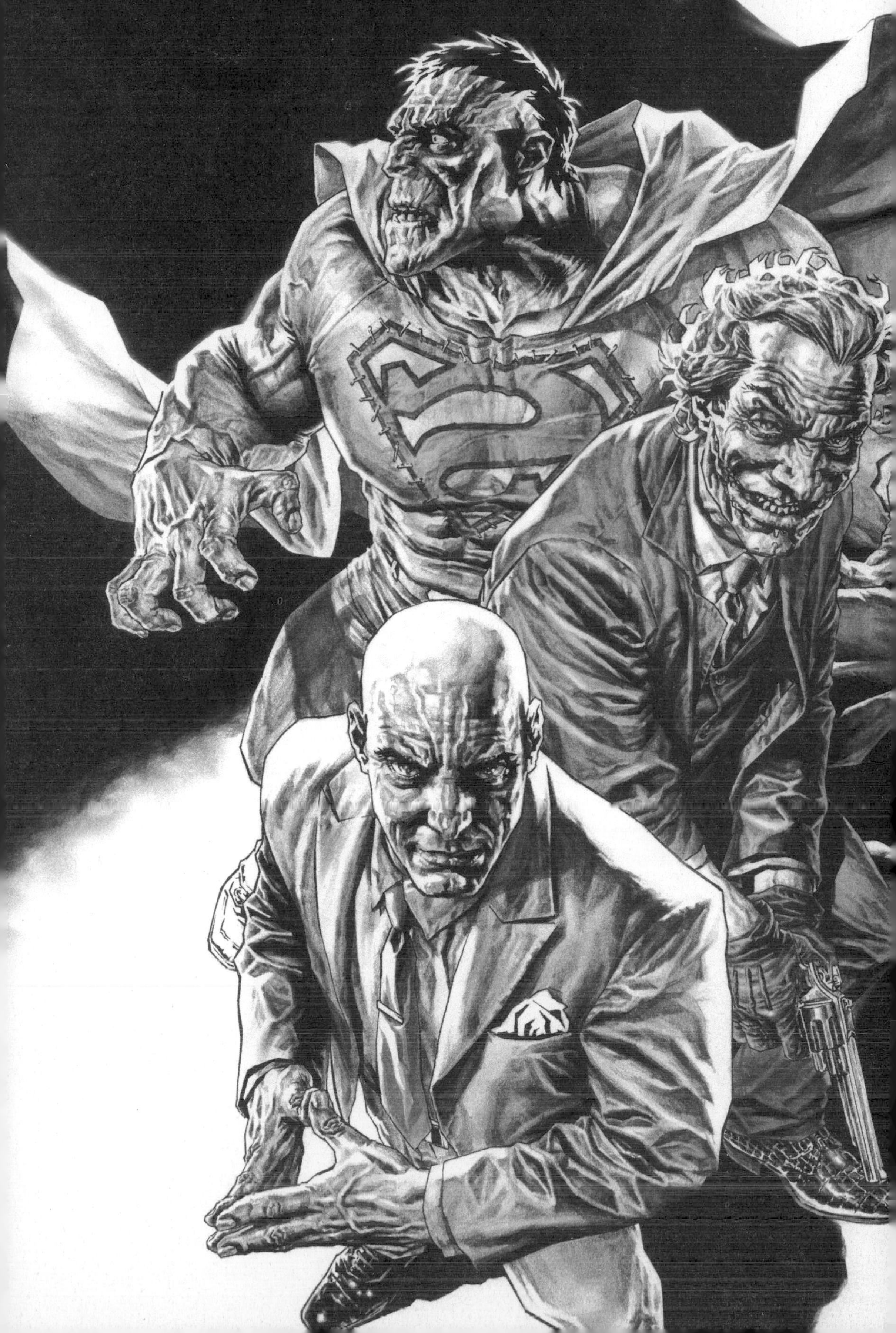

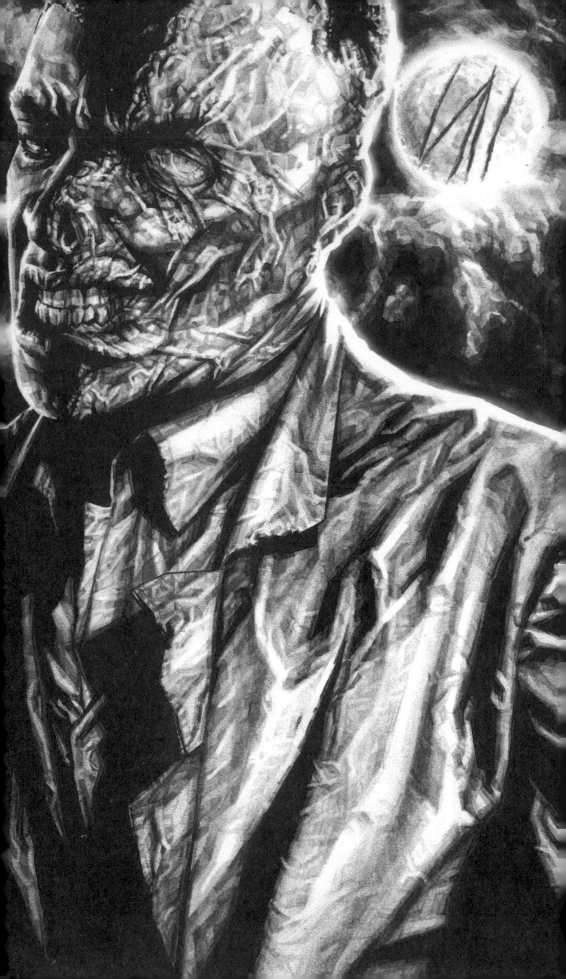

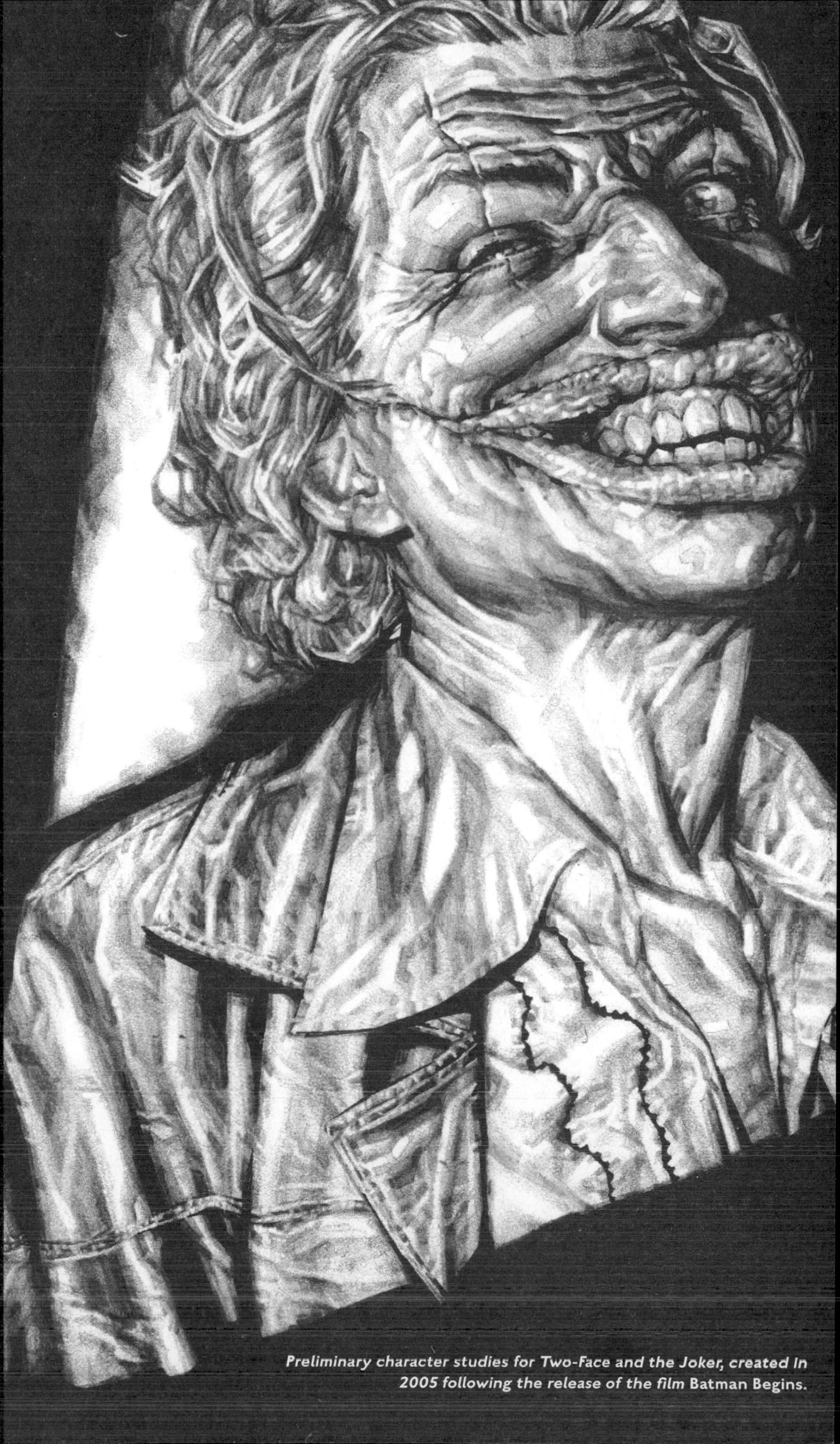

Preliminary character studies for Two-Face and the Joker, created in 2005 following the release of the film Batman Begins.

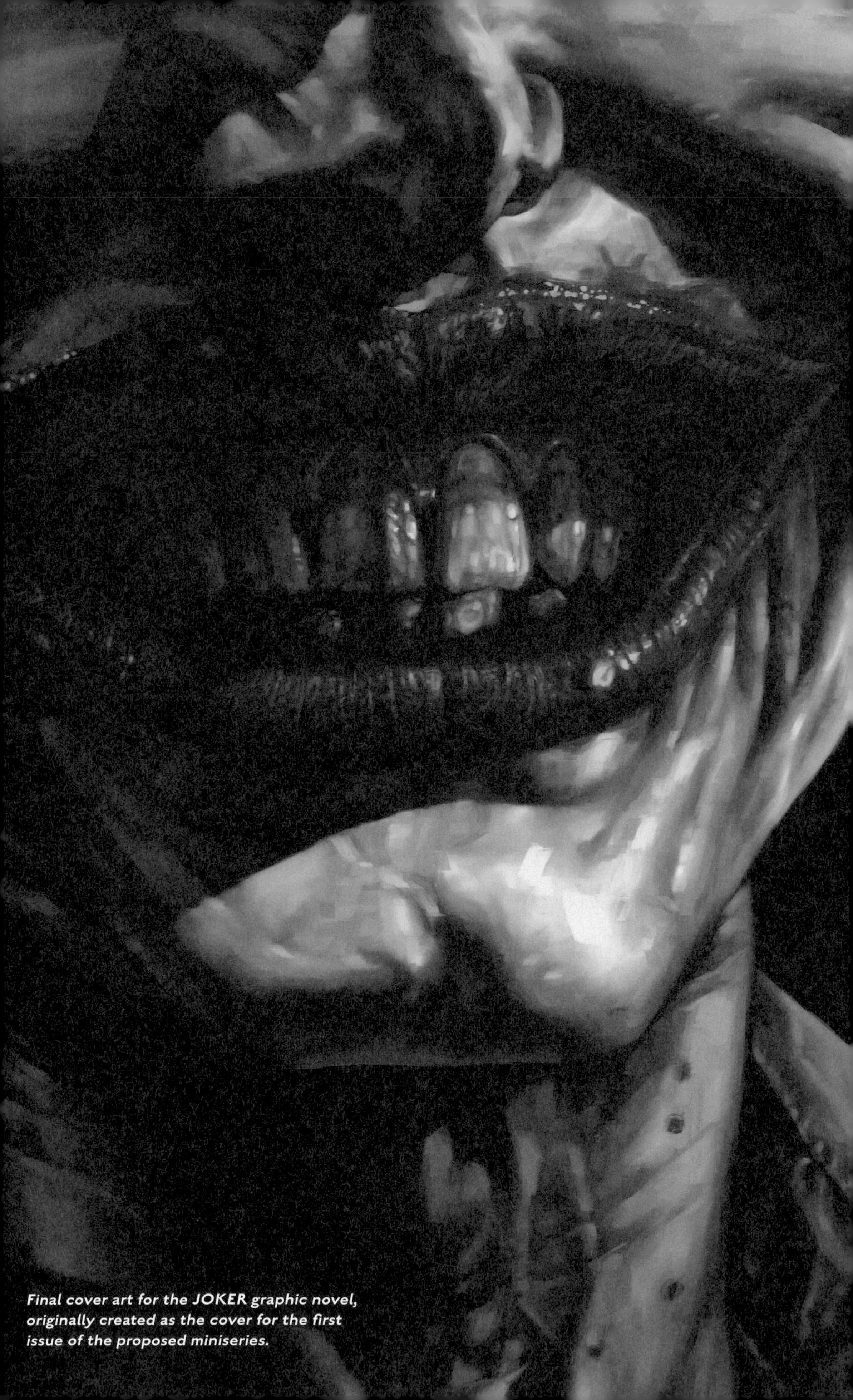

Final cover art for the JOKER graphic novel, originally created as the cover for the first issue of the proposed miniseries.

Unused cover art for the second issue of the proposed miniseries.

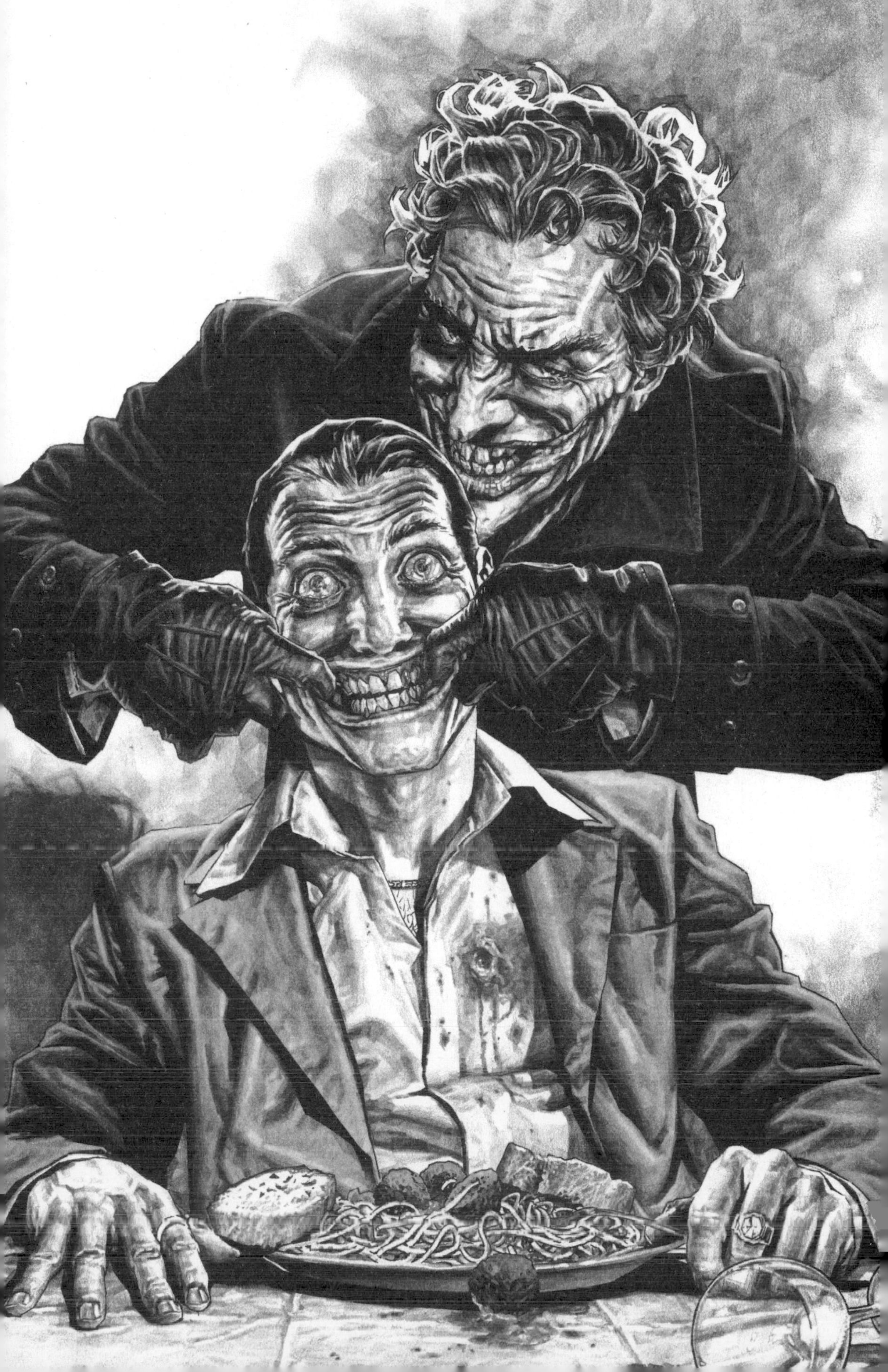

Black-and-white art for page 4.

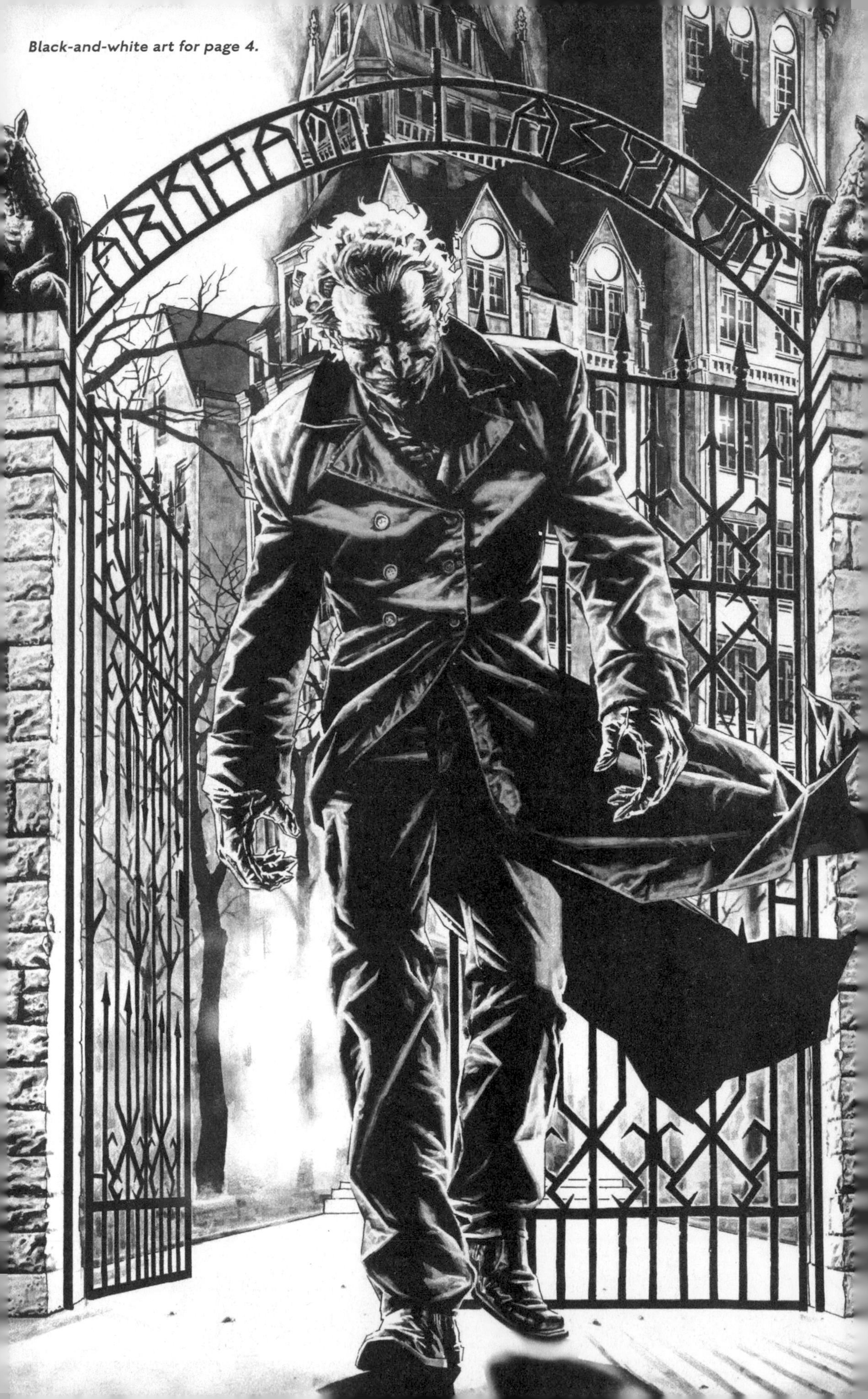
ARKHAM ASYLUM

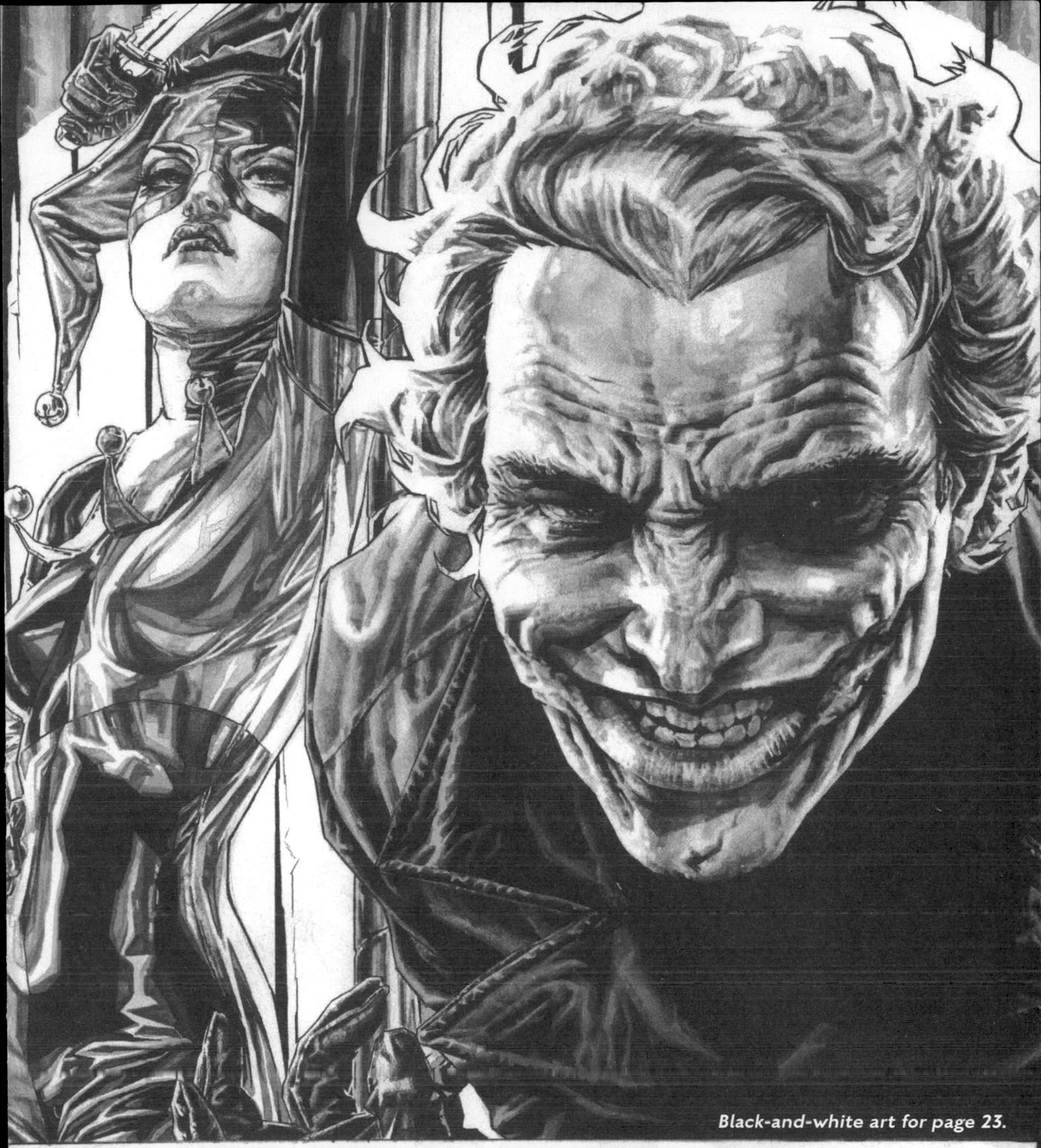

Black-and-white art for page 23.

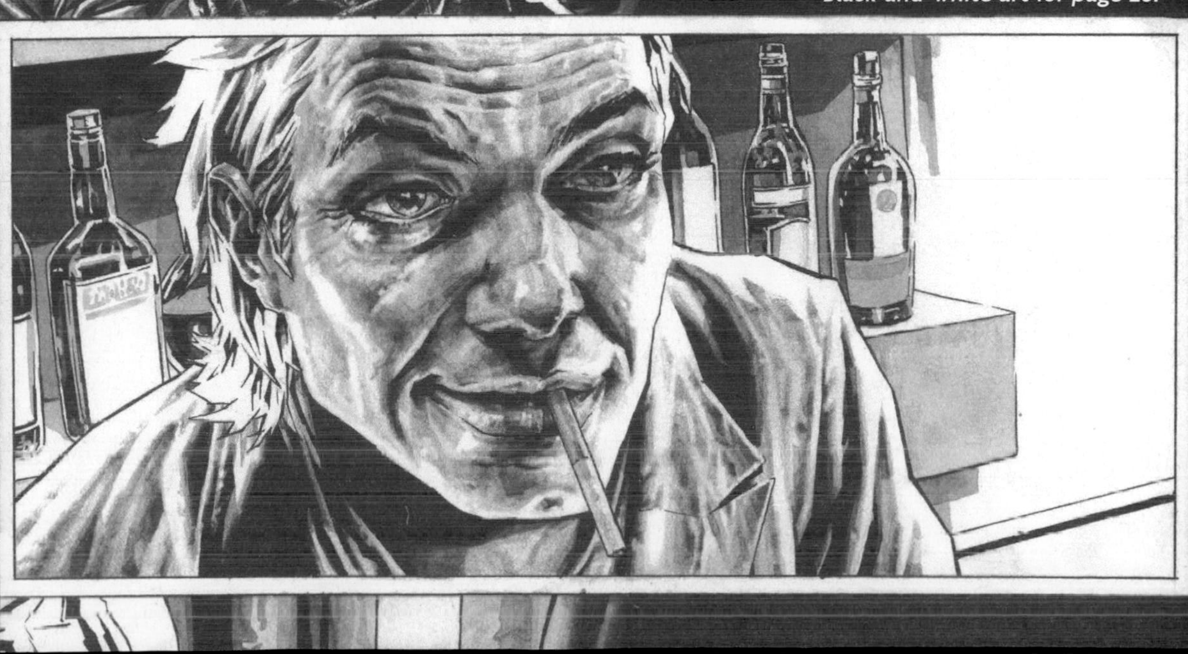

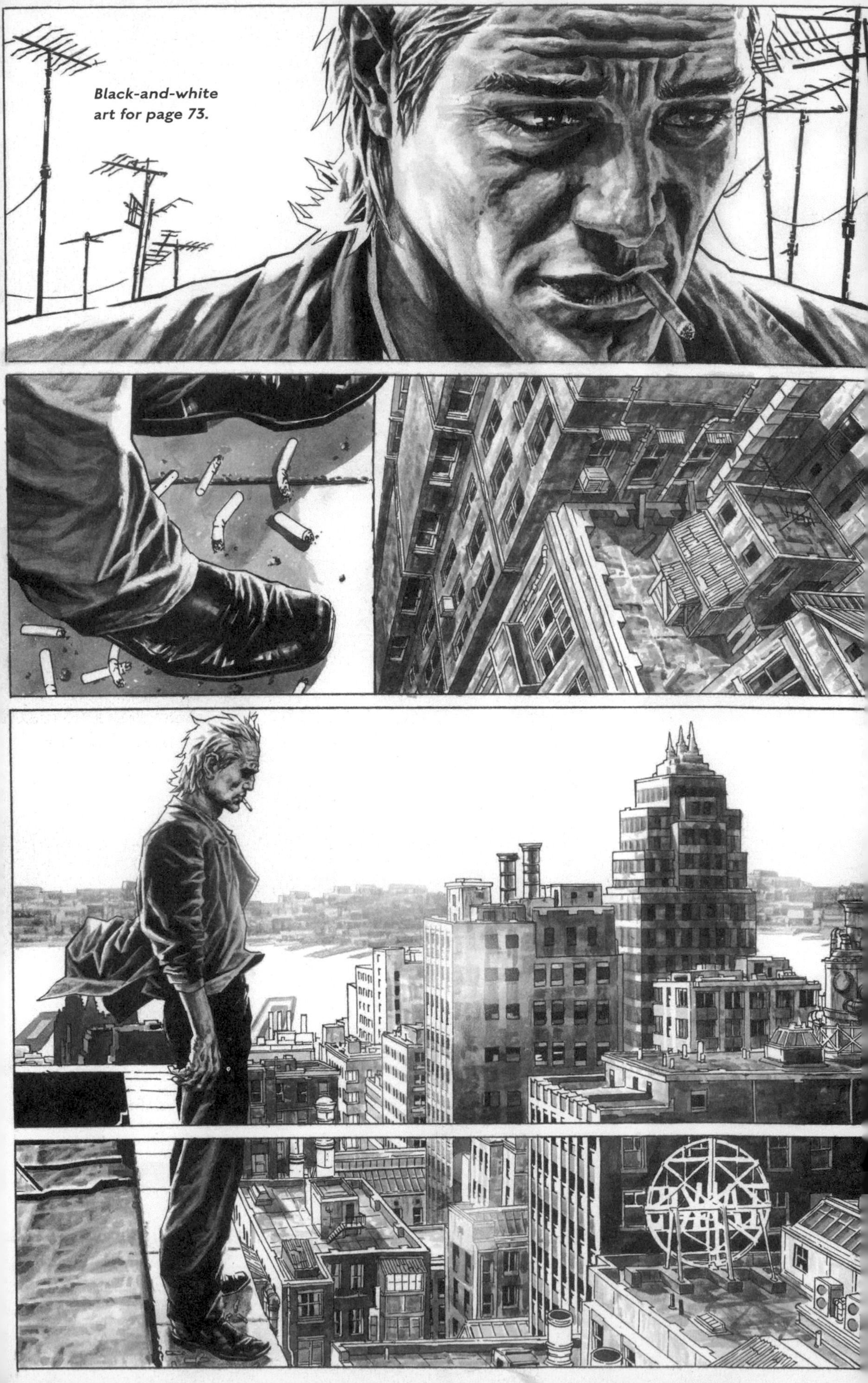

Black-and-white art for page 73.

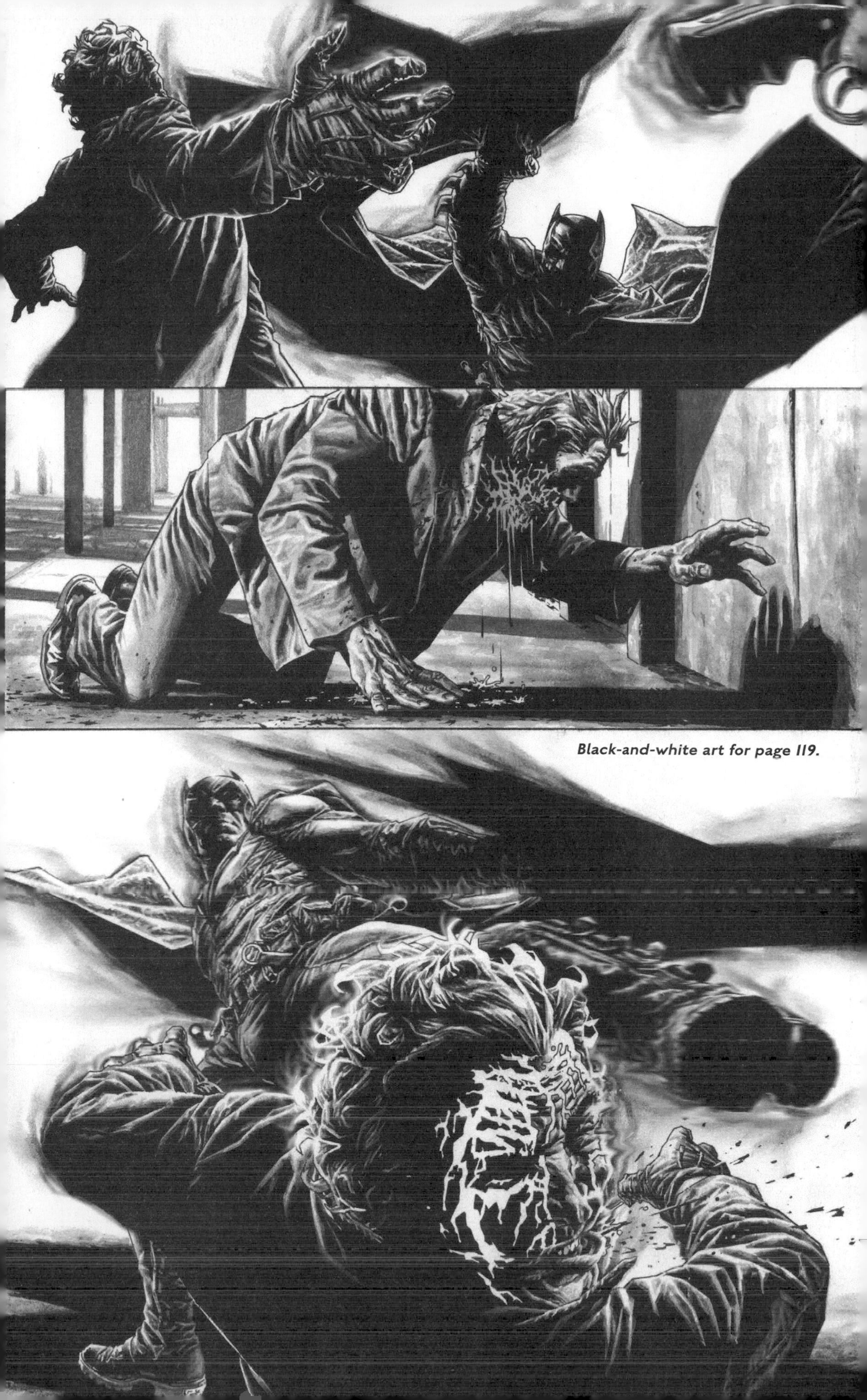

Black-and-white art for page 119.

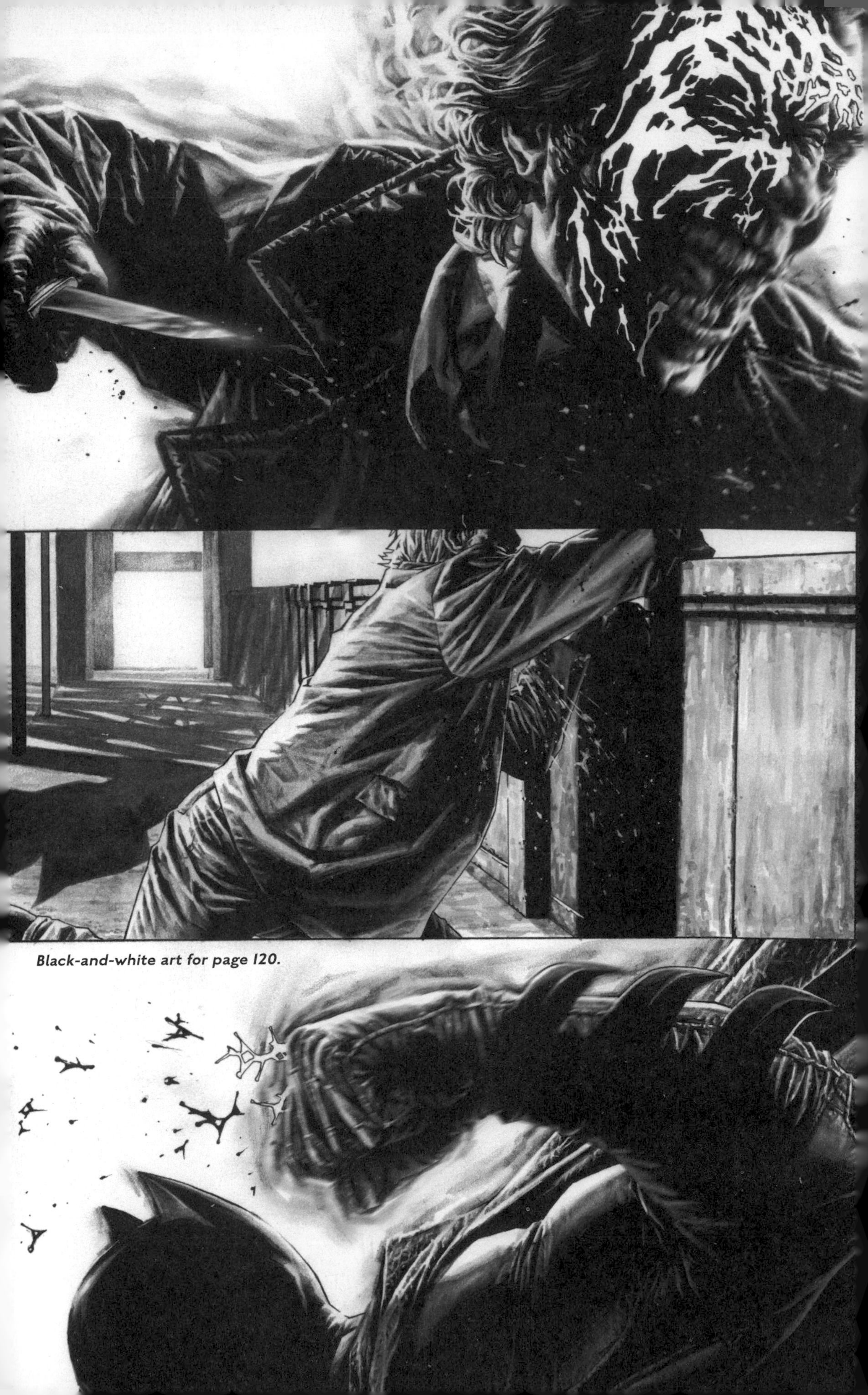

Black-and-white art for page 120.

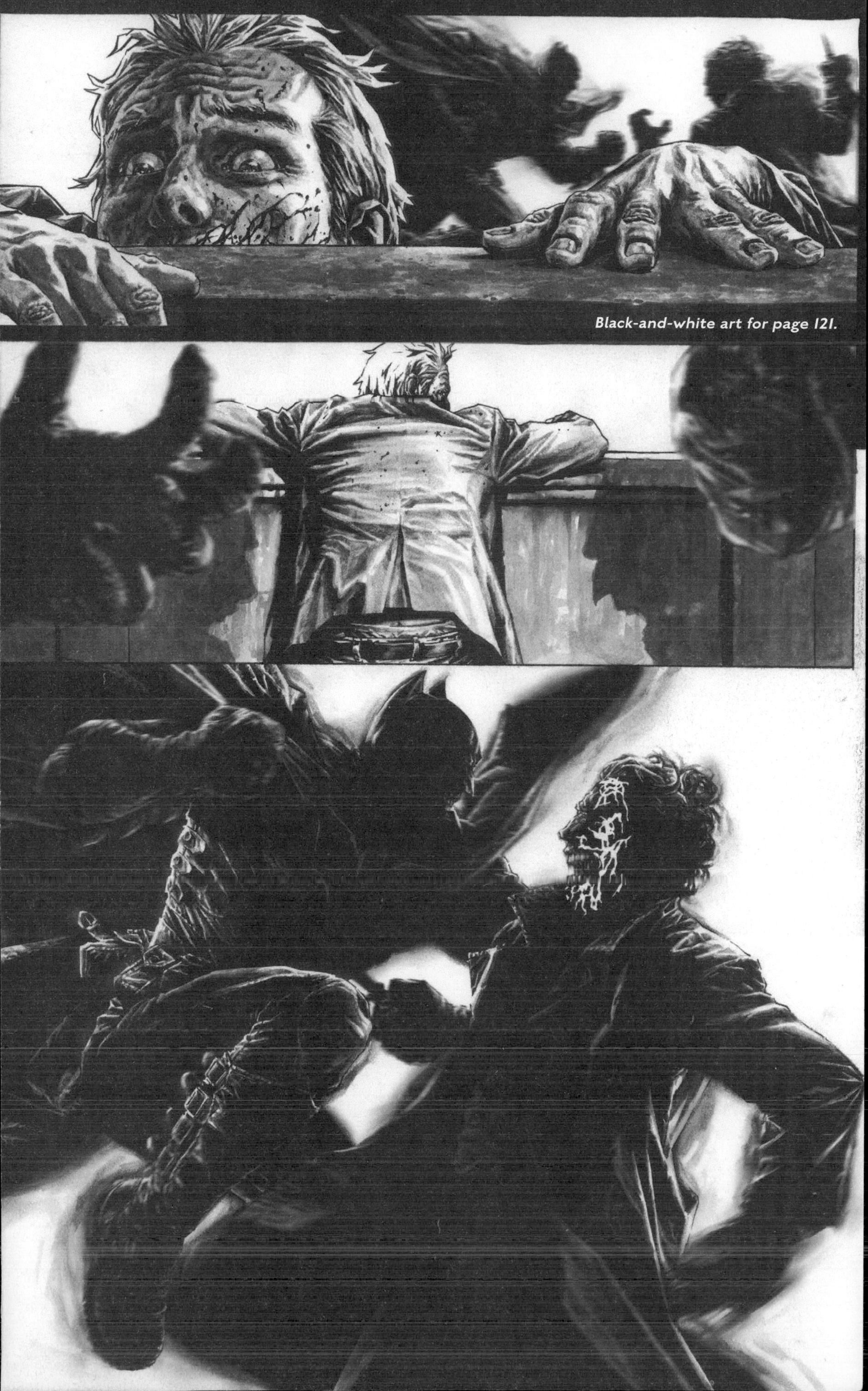

Black-and-white art for page 121.

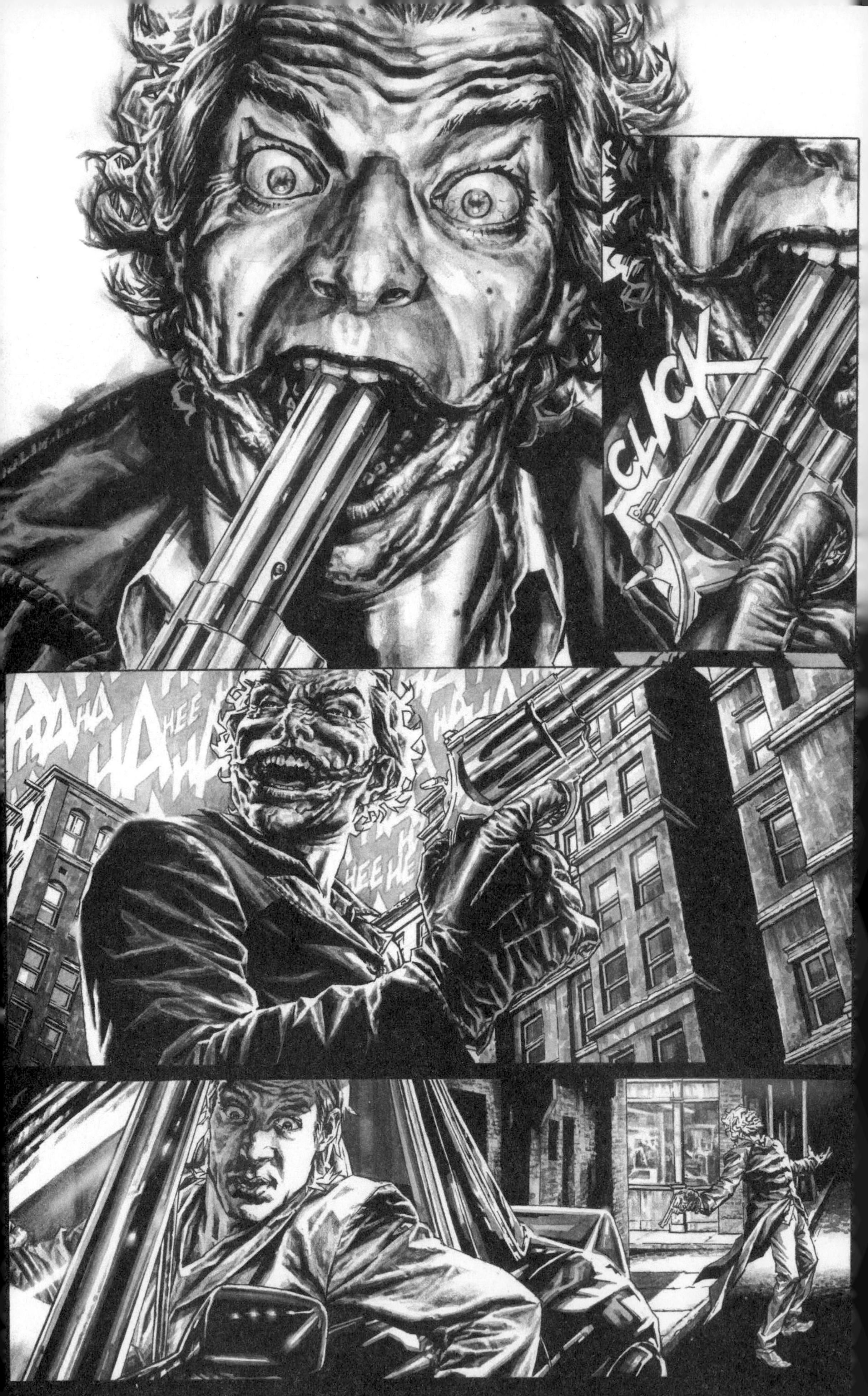
CLICK
HA HA HEE
HEE HEE

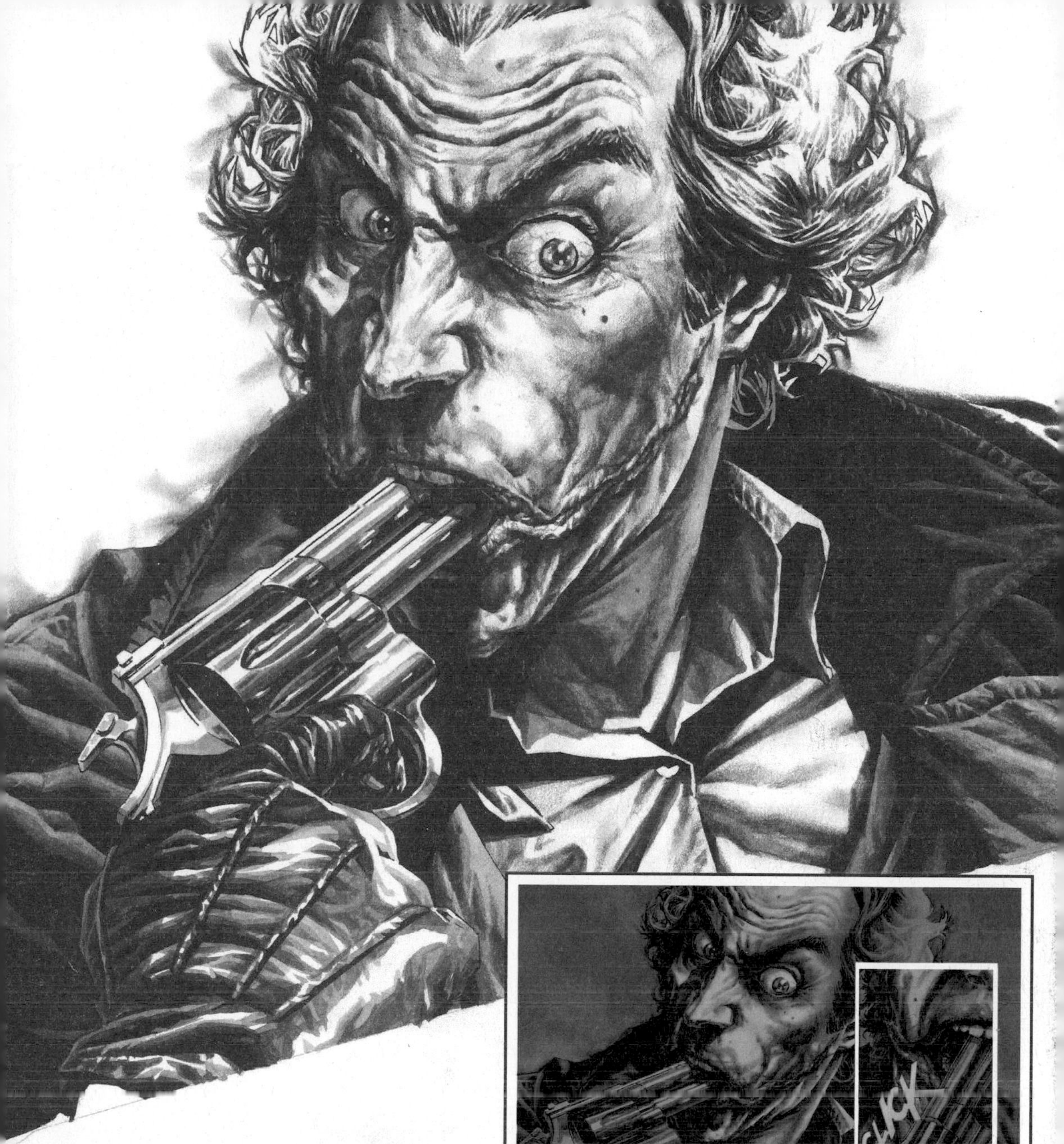

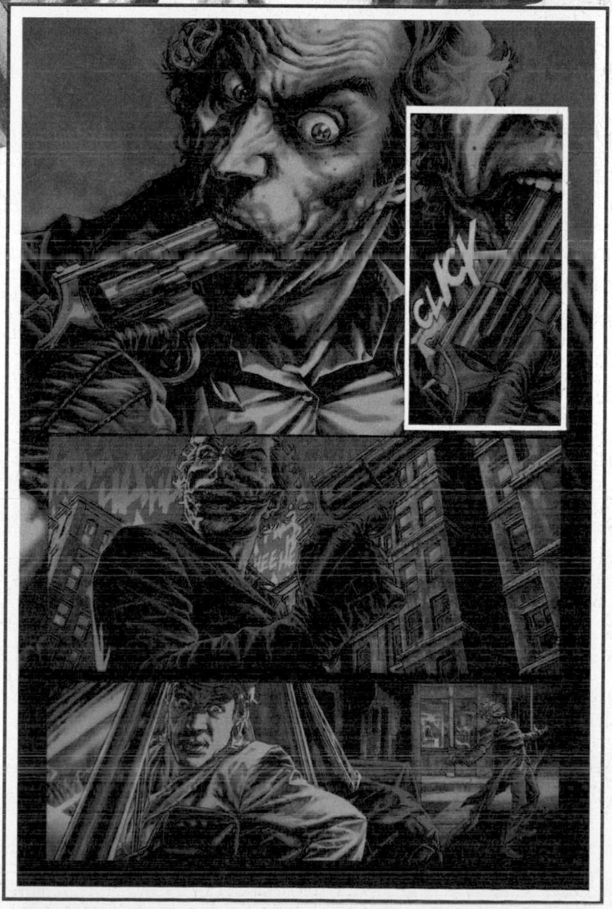
CLICK

Original and reworked art for page 49.

Created in the summer of 2010, this homage to Bill Watterson's classic newspaper strip Calvin and Hobbes ran in the special 60-page SUPERMAN/BATMAN #75.

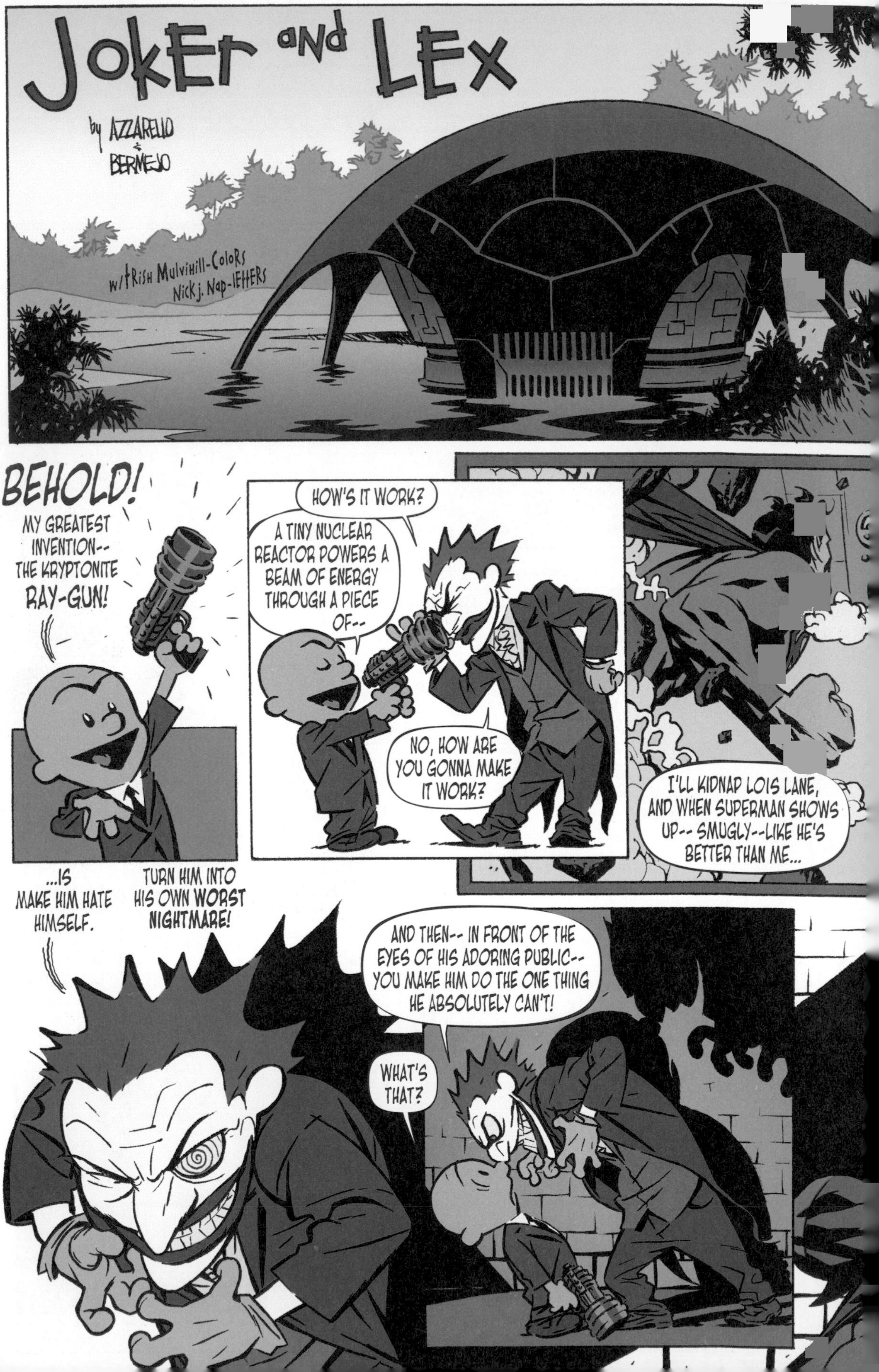
Joker and Lex
by AZZARELLO & BERMEJO
w/Trish Mulvihill-Colors
Nick J. Nap-letters
BEHOLD!
MY GREATEST INVENTION-- THE KRYPTONITE RAY-GUN!
HOW'S IT WORK?
A TINY NUCLEAR REACTOR POWERS A BEAM OF ENERGY THROUGH A PIECE OF--
NO, HOW ARE YOU GONNA MAKE IT WORK?
I'LL KIDNAP LOIS LANE, AND WHEN SUPERMAN SHOWS UP-- SMUGLY--LIKE HE'S BETTER THAN ME...
...IS MAKE HIM HATE HIMSELF.
TURN HIM INTO HIS OWN WORST NIGHTMARE!
AND THEN-- IN FRONT OF THE EYES OF HIS ADORING PUBLIC-- YOU MAKE HIM DO THE ONE THING HE ABSOLUTELY CAN'T!
WHAT'S THAT?

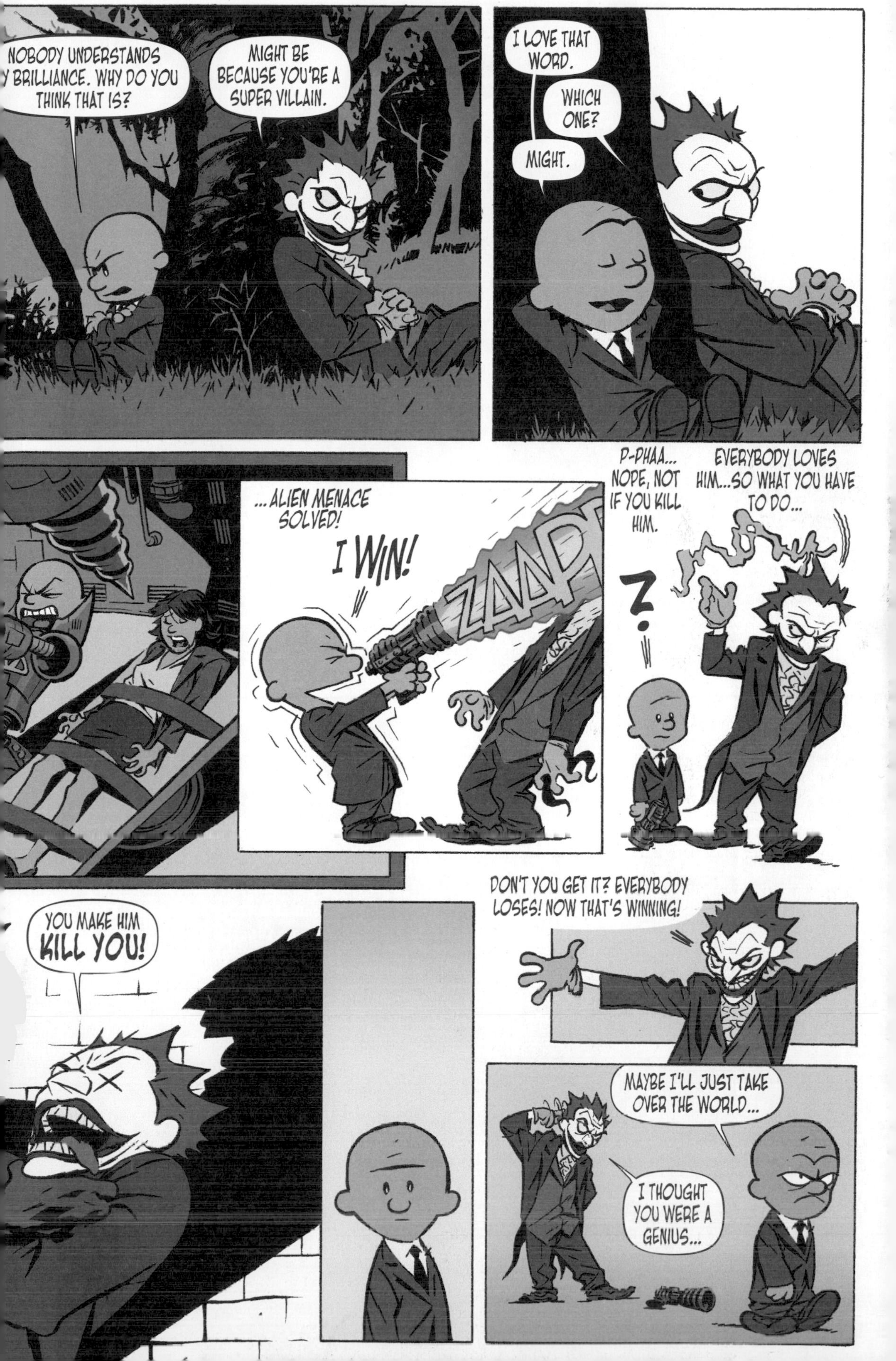
NOBODY UNDERSTANDS Y BRILLIANCE. WHY DO YOU THINK THAT IS?
MIGHT BE BECAUSE YOU'RE A SUPER VILLAIN.
I LOVE THAT WORD.
WHICH ONE?
MIGHT.
...ALIEN MENACE SOLVED!
I WIN!
P-PHAA... NOPE, NOT IF YOU KILL HIM.
EVERYBODY LOVES HIM...SO WHAT YOU HAVE TO DO...
YOU MAKE HIM KILL YOU!
DON'T YOU GET IT? EVERYBODY LOSES! NOW THAT'S WINNING!
MAYBE I'LL JUST TAKE OVER THE WORLD...
I THOUGHT YOU WERE A GENIUS...

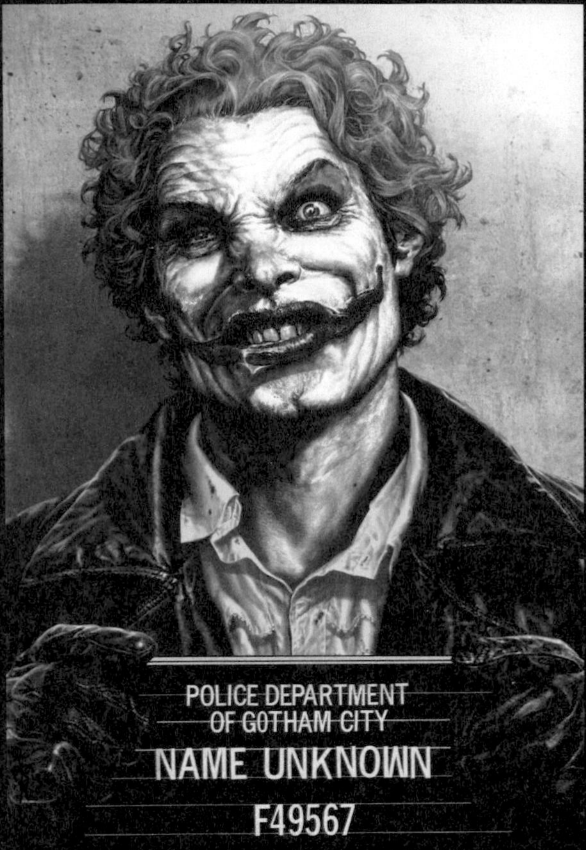

POLICE DEPARTMENT
OF GOTHAM CITY
NAME UNKNOWN
F49567

ABSOLUTE JOKER SLIPCASE cover.

Brian Azzarello has been writing comics professionally since the mid-1990s. He is the *New York Times* best-selling author of BATMAN, JONNY DOUBLE, SPACEMAN, *Moonshine* and the groundbreaking, Harvey and Eisner award-winning series 100 BULLETS, all created in collaboration with artist Eduardo Risso. His other works include HELLBLAZER and LOVELESS (both with Marcelo Frusin), SUPERMAN: FOR TOMORROW (with Jim Lee), JOKER, LUTHOR, BEFORE WATCHMEN and BATMAN: DAMNED (all with Lee Bermejo), a character-defining three-year run on WONDER WOMAN (with Cliff Chiang) as well as DARK KNIGHT III: THE MASTER RACE (with Frank Miller and Andy Kubert). He hails from Chicago.

Award-winning artist **Lee Bermejo** is the illustrator of the graphic novels BATMAN/ DEATHBLOW, LUTHOR, BEFORE WATCHMEN: RORSCHACH and the *New York Times* best-selling JOKER, all of which were done in collaboration with writer Brian Azzarello.

Bermejo's other work for DC includes the titles GLOBAL FREQUENCY (with Warren Ellis), SUPERMAN/GEN 13 (with Adam Hughes) and HELLBLAZER (with Mike Carey), as well as several dozen painted covers. He also wrote and illustrated the best-selling graphic novels BATMAN: NOËL and SUICIDERS for Vertigo. Currently working on BATMAN: DAMNED, Bermejo lives and works in a small town in Italy.